COLLEGE
SEWELL, NEW JERSEY 08080

DANCING BEAR

An Inside Look at California Politics

by Gladwin Hill

The World Publishing Company
Cleveland and New York

Published by The World Publishing Company
2231 West 110th Street, Cleveland, Ohio 44102
Published simultaneously in Canada by
Nelson, Foster & Scott Ltd.
First Printing 1968

Library of Congress Catalog Card Number: 68-19329
Printed in the United States of America
DESIGNED BY ROBERT REED

A Note on the Title

In one of its evolutionary stages as California's insigne, the Bear was depicted not on all fours as today, but on its hind legs like the dancing bears in the circus.

This reminded me of Samuel Johnson's remark about a dog walking on its hind legs—that it might not be done well, "but you are surprised to find it done at all."

California's unique political system, by that token, seems doubly wondrous: you are surprised not only that it works at all, but that it works quite well.

That is why I called this book

"DANCING BEAR"

Acknowledgments

Anyone who delves into California politics is indebted to a fine group of scholars, official observers, and historians who have produced a gallery of basic sources on particular aspects of the subject.

These include the University of California's Dean McHenry and Winston Crouch and collaborators, with their landmark *California Government and Politics,* and Dr. Eugene C. Lee, with his reports and analyses of California voting; the University of Southern California's Dr. Totton Anderson and his lively analyses; Dean R. Cresap and his *Party Politics in the Golden State* (unfortunately outdated and out of print); George Mowry's masterwork, *The California Progressives;* San Jose State College's H. Brett Melendy and Benjamin Gilbert and their *The Governors of California;* and Carey McWilliams, the nonpareil, whose *California, the Great Exception* is a classic amalgam of history, politics, and sociology.

Special appreciation is due also to the New York *Times* for the use of excerpts from articles by James Reston, Tom Wicker, Lawrence Davies, and others; to the Los Angeles *Times* for the use of excerpts from articles by Richard Bergholz, Carl Greenberg, and others; and to California's Secretary of State, Frank M. Jordan, and his staff.

Among individuals to whom I am particularly indebted for personal wisdom, guidance, assistance, and moral support in this project are former California Attorney General Robert W. Kenny, distinguished jurist, historian, raconteur, and humanist; former Democratic National Committeeman Paul Ziffren, a zealous toiler in the political vineyard; and my fellow writers, James Bassett of the Los Angeles *Times,* Leo Katcher, novelist and biographer, Neil Morgan of the San Diego *Tribune,* and Lawrence E. Davies, San Francisco bureau chief of the New York *Times.*

(gh 12/67)

Contents

Chapter
One

Never Be Surprised

☒ ONE VISITOR SUGGESTED THAT THE HEADY perfume of orange blossoms, emanating from thousands of orchards, might in some way be responsible for California's chronic political eccentricities.

Nearly every other observer down the years has been impelled to grope for some reason—climate, geography, sunspots, public pixilation—why the state has earned such sobriquets as "The Great Exception" and "The Uncommonwealth."

A man best known for his tap-dancing was suddenly elevated by the California electorate to the United States Senate. Two years later, Californians chose as their governor another actor—a man without a day's experience in public office. Emboldened by the fact that the state survived such dalliance with conventional political mores, a large body of Californians, in quest of a United States Representative, massed palpitating behind the candidacy of a former movie child-star etched on the public memory in her rendition of a song cloyingly entitled "On the Good Ship Lollipop." Meanwhile, other professional face-makers were solemnly discussed as possible candidates for political office.

Had California gone drama-mad? Had the voters of the nation's most populous state turned suddenly into a race of pop-eyed, slack-mouthed stage-door Johnnies, confusing the delights of entertainment with the problems of public administration?

To political innocents it may have seemed that way. But to those with a longer view this was only another cycle in generations of political aberrations.

Ronald Reagan, the actor-turned-governor, and George Murphy, the tap-dancer-cum-Senator, were hardly less plausible than such figures from California's past as Governor "Sunny Jim" Rolph (1931–34), who planted floral slogans on the capitol lawn, sent a case of whiskey to a condemned man, and at the bottom of the Depression suggested that everybody just take a couple of weeks' vacation . . . or Upton Sinclair, the amiable Socialist novelist with alarmingly novel ideas about state finance, who missed becoming governor only by a relative handful of votes. Indeed, as far back as 1867 California had elected as governor a man with no experience in public office. His name was Henry Haight. He is remembered as one of the better governors—although his name, ironically, received its greatest renown on a street in San Francisco's Haight-Ashbury district when it became the capital of hippiedom.

One of the few aspects of California politics betokening a certain consistency is that, as rapidly as unexpected personalities are rocketed into prominence, others are plunged into oblivion.

One day Richard Nixon was just a newly discharged Navy officer; the next he was a candidate for Congress, starting a political career that carried him close to the White House. Then, with only a single election day intervening, he was transmogrified from a hopeful candidate for governor into a man whose future in California had evaporated. One day William F. Knowland was the distinguished recent minority leader of the United States Senate, running for governor; overnight he was relegated to the obscurity of publishing a newspaper in Oakland, with little more political influence than his one vote.

California's political deserts are white with the bones of people who have served in state and national office with distinction and then, defeated once, have never been seen again.

No one should feel inadequate about not being able to fathom such irrationalities. They have defied the experts.

"The Kennedy strategists," recalls President Kennedy's press secretary, Pierre Salinger, anent the 1960 presidential campaign, "had never fully understood California. Although it had a 3–2 edge in Democratic registration, it also had a perverse tradition of voting for the man, not the party.

"The Republican ticket had carried the state by huge majorities in 1952–56. Yet Pat Brown, a Democrat, won the governorship in 1958 by more than a million votes.

"This pattern was completely mystifying to Democratic candidates from patronage-rich eastern states who could forecast precinct results from their own bailiwick within one or two votes."

The paradoxes that puzzled the Kennedy people were only a tiny sample of the California political anomalies that, decade after decade, crop up with nerve-wracking regularity to perplex many people—including many in California.

As far back as the 1880's, the eminent political scientist

Lord Bryce wrote: "The politics of California is unique." Eighty years later, Theodore H. White, one of the keenest of contemporary political observers, said: "California is a state with the oddest political structure in the Union. . . . There is no party organization in the older American sense. . . . California politics squirm with a complexity and intrigue that defies reasonable analysis."

To the nation at large, striving to get some idea of "what's happening out there," California political campaigns seem like an irresponsible travesty of what the Founding Fathers had in mind when they blueprinted American democracy and set the stage for the two-party system.

In contrast to the systematic cultivation of political talent in other states, in California a year in advance of an election there is no certainty about who the contestants may be. Because California was one of the early states to institute primary elections in place of party nominating conventions, no aspirant for office has to declare himself until the filing deadline 74 days before the June primary election. And, as a later close look at the system will show, there is little for him to gain by doing so.

When candidates do materialize, they may have no public identification with the parties they seek to represent—and perhaps, as in the cases of Ronald Reagan, George Murphy, and Shirley Temple, little identification with politics at all.

During a campaign, the nation gets glimpses of California candidates stumping in traditional modes—hopping across country in airplanes, shaking hands at supermarkets, officiating at rodeos, dutifully munching barbecue. But what consistently emerges from all this activity is sound and fury whose meaning is difficult to glean. Party labels are submerged, and organized party activity is vague. Candidates in primary campaigns, instead of challenging the capabilities of their opponents, customarily flail away at the opposing party's anticipated nominees. In primaries and general elections alike, substantial issues are hard to discern.

Outside observers often learn with surprise that there is no such thing as a Republican mayor or a Democratic sheriff in California; all municipal and county offices are, by law, non-partisan. For other, partisan, offices there existed for nearly half a century the curious practice of "cross-filing," under which a candidate could simultaneously compete in the Republican primary as a Republican and in the Democratic primary as a Democrat, and could perhaps win both nominations. The system was abolished just about the time the public was beginning to grasp its intricacies; but its confusions linger.

Elections are further complicated by California's "initiative" device, whereby questions of public policy raised by citizen groups share ballot space, and campaign debate, with candidates. In 1966, voters were asked how they thought pornography should be suppressed. They were also asked how boxing and wrestling should be regulated, how farm land should be taxed, whether illiterates should be allowed to vote, and 13 other questions—all of them seemingly matters of the sort the voters were paying legislators to decide. In every election there are upward of a dozen such questions on the ballot. There is almost no question that might not be posed, if a small fraction of the electorate—less than 10 per cent—took it into its head to do so.

"If you give me $500,000," says one professional petition-circulator, who collects the necessary number of signatures to qualify such proposals, "I'll guarantee to get on the ballot a measure to execute the governor by Christmas."

The California campaign air reverberates with the handiwork of the professional "image-makers"—including one who contends that the most effective electoral appeal is simply endless reiteration of the slogan: "Three Cheers for Joe Smith!" Curiously enough, there is an element of validity in this seemingly whimsical theory—validity that played an important part in the election of Ronald Reagan.

Throughout the tohu-bohu of a campaign, the California electorate is customarily inscrutable. Opinion-pollers get some clues. But so historically capricious are California voters that even a huge advantage in opinion ratings seldom yields any dependable conviction about the outcome. From start to finish, a California election has the vertiginous cliff-hanging suspense of a serial whose author is only one week ahead of his audience and is improvising frantically.

A representative vignette of these perennial vagaries was California's United States Senate contest of 1964.

The seat at stake was that held by Senator Clair Engle, a Democrat. He was so popular among both Democrats and Republicans that experienced politicians on both sides hesitated to challenge him. Finally a Republican aspirant emerged: George Murphy, who had assumed an executive desk in Hollywood but whose song-and-dance performances in films showed up often on television. In his new role of candidate, no one gave him much chance.

Then suddenly it developed that Engle was so ill his ability to campaign was problematical. Attorney General Stanley Mosk, one of the Democrats' top vote-getters, loomed as the likeliest alternative. But, within a few weeks, intrigue that never was publicly explained caused his support to dissolve mysteriously, and State Controller Alan Cranston came to the fore—followed by no fewer than nine additional opportunistic aspirants.

Then, 24 hours before the primary filing deadline in March, Pierre Salinger suddenly announced his resignation as White House press secretary and descended on his native state to vie for the Engle seat.

George Murphy won the Republican nomination with a minimum of opposition. Salinger's entry, with its overtones of carpetbagging after his many years of residence in the East, split the Democrats. It was one of their most bitter schisms in years. But he won the primary and, with Democrats outnumbering Republicans by 4,000,000 to 2,900,000, most observers thought George Murphy would do a political off-to-Buffalo rather than off-to-Washington.

Then another distinctive California factor entered the affray. An initiative proposition due to appear on the November ballot posed the volatile question of the merits of California's open-housing law. Salinger campaigned militantly on the side of open housing. Murphy adroitly sidestepped the issue.

The upshot was that at the same time California voters were giving President Lyndon Johnson a resounding victory over Senator Barry Goldwater they rejected Salinger for Senator and crossed party lines to elect George Murphy

It seems doubtful that any television soap-opera audiences, over the same period, witnessed so many zigs and zags of plot.

"In California politics," remarked Assemblyman Jesse Unruh, one of the leading practitioners in the field, "I've learned never to be surprised at anything."

Until recent years, there was a tendency to dismiss California's political didoes as a side show that, while amusing or curious, had little to do with what went on in the main tent of American politics.

This feeling prevailed despite dramatic evidence to the contrary as far back as 1916. In that year, electoral acrobatics on the West Coast changed the course of national, and perhaps international, affairs. World War I was under way, and the focal question of the presidential election was whether the nation should re-elect Woodrow Wilson, whose liberal Democratic philosophy was leading the United States toward international intervention, or should elect Charles Evans Hughes, the recent Supreme Court Justice, who epitomized the nostalgia of many Americans for the old, stable days of conservative Republicanism.

On election night, with most of the vote counted, the nation went to bed assuming Hughes to be the winner. But California's tally was belated. And California, it transpired, had been the scene of critical maneuverings.

Governor Hiram Johnson, a Republican maverick, was running for the Senate. Party conservatives tried to embarrass him, when Hughes' campaign trail led to California, by arranging things so that Hughes ignored Johnson even though for some hours they were both in the same Long Beach hotel. The snub capped a long record of conservative hostility toward Johnson that proved to be a fatal strategic error.

When California's vote finally was counted, Johnson had scored a sweeping victory. But Hughes, on the same ticket, lagged far behind, and lost California by 3,806 votes. California's 13 electoral votes provided the winning margin of 277–254 that propelled Wilson into another term to "make the world safe for democracy."

Such a pivotal role for California was of course extraordinary. But down the years the state's importance has increased steadily, if for no other reason than that our political system is based on a count of noses. When Ronald Reagan swept to his spectacular gubernatorial victory in 1966, a number of national pundits proclaimed breathlessly that his coup projected him into the 1968 presidential picture. The fact was that for a matter of two decades any California governor had automatically been in the presidential picture, because of the state's voting leverage.

In 1964, California passed New York as the nation's most populous state. As this is being written in 1968, California's population is close to 20 million; every tenth resident of the United States is a Californian.

This factor of size will be even weightier after the 1970 census and the ensuing Congressional reapportionment give California representation in true proportion to its population. (It has been short-changed for the better part of a decade.) According to current projections, California's allotment of seats in the House of Representatives will jump from the present 38 to 44 (while New York drops back from 41 to 40). California's electoral vote will rise from 40 to 46, and its strength in the national political conventions will increase commensurately. Currently California holds upward of 10 per cent of the delegate votes needed for presidential nomination (the exact number of which fluctuates from convention to convention with the differing ground rules of the two parties).

In other respects—economically, technologically, scientifically, educationally, and sociologically—California has acquired influence far out of proportion to its size. Bemused laymen still choose to think of the state as an oddity. But to political professionals and people concerned with national policy, it is an entity—the most important single entity of its kind—to be reckoned with.

The reckoning requires, to begin with, an untangling of the unique web of influences that impel Californians to behave, politically, in their unique fashion.

Superficially, California's political idiosyncrasies are the result of an extraordinary spasm of reform that swept the state with the election of Hiram Johnson in 1910.

Up to that election, for more than a generation California's affairs, both political and economic, had been in the grip of one of the most pervasive and genteelly corrupt political machines ever known in the United States. The machine was that of the Southern Pacific Railroad, the state's largest landowner and the monopolistic operator of most of the state's vital transportation facilities. In an amoral preoccupation with bulwarking and enlarging its corporate empire, the Southern Pacific developed a network of corrupt political influence ranging from village constables to the United States Senate, 3,000 miles away.

California's citizenry finally mounted a bloodless revolution to eradicate this influence. With the characteristic bluntness of their frontier orientation, the people decided that since the evil was the product of a political machine the remedy was to preclude the existence of political machines.

This was accomplished by a series of laws that reduced party organizations to impotent skeletons, enshrined "nonpartisanship," and put into the hands of the people three devices—

the initiative, the referendum, and recall (discharge of public officials)—by which they could supersede any of their elected office-holders who got out of line.

These drastic innovations govern the shape of California politics to this day. But they are less than a complete explanation. Obviously there must have been preconditions that impelled Californians, in their zeal for reform, to go so much further than the citizens of any other state, before or since. And there must have been factors that caused these unorthodox mores to persist throughout the ensuing turbulent half-century, right down to the present. There had to be an unusual political climate that engendered and perpetuated California's atypical political patterns.

The chief element of this unusual climate was and is the fact that California has never been a state in the ordinary sense of a fixed community of people. Rather, the endless tide of immigration, peculiarities of geography, and the forced-draft growth of California's economy have made it a kaleidoscopic succession of states, changing from year to year, almost from day to day.

Throughout its 118 years of statehood, California has been frontier—the last stopping-place this side of the Pacific Ocean. For a century, in war and peace, in doom and depression, California's population has grown at an average rate of 3,000 souls a week. The bulk of this increase has come from immigration. In 1966, the increase was continuing at a rate of 1,290 persons a day—520 of them indigenous babies, 770 of them immigrants.

A survey in March, 1967, indicated that three out of four adults in California had come from somewhere else. In the entire population, about 60 per cent are from elsewhere. Of California's last half-dozen governors, only two—Earl Warren and Edmund Brown—were natives of California; the present governor, Ronald Reagan, was born in Illinois.

In effect, it has been a new electorate that has gone to the California polls every four years. Seventy-six thousand persons voted in California's first presidential election in 1852; 97,000 four years later; 155,000 in 1876; nearly 200,000 in 1884. The point is that the quadrennial increases were more than the margins by which most elections are won; newcomers were numerous enough each time to tilt the balance of power in a new direction. In 1966, the electorate of 8 million contained a million people who had not been qualified to vote in the preceding gubernatorial election four years before.

In the incessant infusion of somewhat atypical humankind into California's citizenry, ideas and patterns have had little chance to take root before being subjected to the challenges and mutations of other ideas and patterns.

To California's pioneers, preoccupied with carving civilization and personal fortunes out of the wilderness, government was less a fixture of social maturity than a necessary evil; the rituals of orthodox party politics were a nuisance.

A spirit of nonpartisanship burgeoned early, and gathered strength over the years. Once the Civil War was over and the national slavery issue settled, California's prime concerns were nonpartisan problems—fighting Indians, balancing the state's chronically anemic budget, establishing institutions for malefactors and unfortunates.

The generation of Southern Pacific domination, in which the apparatus of both parties was used for corrupt purposes, engendered a plague-on-both-your-houses attitude among the citizenry. When Hiram Johnson proposed the hamstringing of party activity in favor of what he chose to call nonpartisanism, people were more than ready to throw out the baby of orthodox two-party operation with the bath water of corruption.

In its place has evolved what might be called a politics of pragmatism—a milieu of opportunism and improvisation, in which party structures are weak, party loyalties are flimsy, "party responsibility" is unknown, and in which continuity, in personalities and policies, is tenuous and electoral consistency is rare.

As atypical as California's disorganized, machineless politics are, they have worked. They have maintained a surprising degree of governmental efficiency and honesty during turbulent times and decades of massive growth. Altogether, the California system, despite its confusions and shortcomings, has yielded the "better life" the pioneers sought, in such a degree that the influx of their followers continues unabated.

It is the rise of California's unique pragmatism, and its implications for both California and the nation, that the ensuing chapters will trace.

The trail is a devious one. The dean of California political reporters, Herbert Phillips, retired capital correspondent of the McClatchy newspapers, has warned: "The quest for orderliness [in California politics] has tempted many able scholars to undertake huge, solemn and painstaking chronological recitations, in the hope that political symmetry somehow would appear out of the fog. It seldom does."

But there is an alternative to the pedantic business of trying to catch history repeating its patterns. That is to think of the cavalcade of California politics as a continuing fabric, like the Bayeux Tapestry, in which the same design never recurs, but in which certain basic strands appear, become submerged, and later reappear, with varying boldness.

Accordingly, this book, although its episodes come chronologically, avoids the "painstaking chronological recitation," and focuses on illustrative highlights.

The saga is less the traditional Western of good guys versus bad guys than the interplay between two great frontier forces: the urge to experiment and the desire for security. One causes radical surges toward both left and right. The other superimposes stabilizing "moderation." It is always chancy to predict which will prevail at a given time. But if one understands that it is these forces, rather than party labels, that govern the outcome of elections, he will already have profitably unlearned one of the many misconceptions about California politics.

And, like many a good story, this one has a surprise ending. When the trends of California politics are untangled, it turns out that they are not so different from those in progress in the rest of the country. It is the *results* that up to now, in California, have been different. But it may not be very long before it transpires that in politics—as has happened in many other fields—California was not just eccentrically wayward, but was limning the shape of many people's future.

Chapter
Two

Ladders to the Sky

☒ GOVERNOR EDMUND BROWN, CHUBBY, BESPECtacled, in shirt-sleeves, paused on the way down the aisle of his official plane, The Grizzly, to hunch over and peer out the window—knocking a cup of Coca-Cola into a reporter's typewriter which has never been quite the same since.

"Gee!" he exclaimed, with the recurrent boyish innocence that was both part of his charm and one of his fallibilities, "will you look at that!" Necks craned at the landscape below.

"What is it, Pat?" several people asked.

"CALIFORNIA!" he exclaimed with a beaming gusto. "Did you ever see anything like it?"

The name California has different connotations for different people . . . sunshine . . . palm trees . . . the charms of San Francisco . . . the quite legendary "bright lights of Hollywood" . . . freeways . . . smog . . . odd politics. . . .

The images are always fragmentary. It is hard to form a total conception of California, if only because it's so big. It is bigger than Germany, Italy, or Japan. It is 800 miles long and over 250 miles wide. Its outline, superimposed on the Atlantic seaboard, would stretch from Massachusetts to South Carolina, and inland as far as Pittsburgh.

This expansive geography has had a lot to do with California's politics. And one of the few ways to get an overall impression of the state, at one point in time, is to travel with the politicians.

A favorite stunt of California gubernatorial candidates is to climax a campaign the day before election with a dawn-to-dusk "whistle-stop" plane tour, touching down at a dozen cities over the length of the state. These election trips cover a range of terrain, people, and pursuits far more diverse than in some comparable span on the East Coast.

At the southern extreme, near the Mexican border, are San Diego's aerospace manufacturing complex and naval base and the lush Imperial Valley, a vast vegetable garden for the nation, where the combination of perpetual sunshine and water diverted from the Colorado River is so potent that the land will produce a half-dozen hay crops in a single year.

(Agriculture, producing an income of some $3 billion a year, still boasts that it is California's biggest single "industry." Actually, the aerospace industry is comparable in

size, and manufacturing as a whole surged far ahead of agriculture during World War II, soaring from an annual volume of about $1 billion in 1939 to more than $5 billion in 1950. In 1965 it reached $18 billion.)

Moving northward, one comes to the Coachella Valley, whose sandy resemblance to the deserts of the Middle East is underscored by huge groves of date palms; here, again, imported water has made possible bountiful agriculture. The northern egress from the valley, near Palm Springs, is San Gorgonio Pass, whose bordering peaks, two miles high, are only a sample of mountain ranges to the north.

Then come the outskirts of Los Angeles, the nation's second largest metropolis, its 7 million people spilling over the edges of a mountain-rimmed basin of 4,000 square miles.

(California had, in 1966, nearly 20,000,000 residents. These included 1,500,000 Mexican-Americans, 1,000,000 Negroes, 160,000 Japanese-Americans, 100,000 Chinese-Americans, and 40,000 Filipinos. There were also 17,000 American Indians—whose number, oddly, has remained unchanged for a century. And 1,700,000 "senior citizens" over 65.)

North of Los Angeles is the Mojave Desert, the scene of one of the world's oldest occupations and the newest: workmen commuting to borax mines share the highways with astronauts attached to Edwards Air Force Base, the armed services' prime flight-test and aerospace-training center. Along the desert's northern edge is Highway 58, running over the low Tehachapi Mountains from Barstow to Bakersfield—the road traveled by the Okies in their great trek to California in the 1930's.

(Brown: "One thousand people enter our state every day to stay. Some bring skills but few bring jobs. They bring high hopes but no classrooms, fire departments or water. State and local government must provide those, at an average investment of $13,000 for each new family the first year.")

Now for 200 miles northward stretches California's great San Joaquin Valley, edged by the low Coast Range on the west and the majestic snow-capped Sierra Nevada on the east.

The valley is another quasi-desert transformed into the nation's most abundant agricultural area by water diverted from roaring mountain streams to the north. Here forests of oil derricks vie for space with cotton, citrus, grapes, potatoes, lettuce, carrots, and literally a hundred other crops; and the Texas and Oklahoma accents of Bakersfield mingle with the polyglot sounds of Fresno—Armenian raisin-producers, Basque sheepherders, Chinese and Japanese produce-ranchers.

(California spends nearly $2 million a day just building and maintaining highways. It spends over $2 million a day operating its state university system alone. It spends more on education than 43 other states spend on all government services. Altogether, it spends nearly $100 million a week. California gets about $1 billion a year in grants from the Federal government. But this is a pittance compared with its own resources. The income of its citizens runs more than $1 billion a week.)

Surmounting the Sierra Nevada is 14,495-foot Mount Whitney, the highest point in the continental United States; and within eyeshot of it, a few miles to the east, is the continent's lowest point, the bottom of Death Valley, 282 feet below sea level.

Suddenly the San Joaquin Valley ends, and one is over the Delta, where the merged waters of many mountain streams fan out as they approach the ocean, creating a great moist coastal plain baroquely segmented by dikes and weirs into rice paddies.

(Brown: "Our economy, if separated statistically from the rest of the United States, would rank fifth among the nations of the world.")

From not too great an altitude over the Delta it is possible to see both the unmistakable outline of San Francisco's

Golden Gate and, 75 miles inland, the city of Sacramento, where a century-old gold-domed building marks the center of California's capital.

(It is not unusual for California to place $100 million worth of bonds in the nation's financial marts in one lump. For three years, starting in 1967, California planned to issue bonds at a rate of nearly $1 million a day just for the financing of its $2 billion state water-redistribution project.)

The bird's-eye view suggests that California is not even yet an agrarian state—that it is still mainly wilderness. In spatial terms, this is true. It encompasses more than 100 million acres. Nearly half the total is still national forests, national parks, and other Federal preserves. One-third is still forested, and another 20 per cent is barren mountains and desert. Only about 15 per cent of the land is classified as arable.

(There are political implications in this. Only 10 per cent of California's people live out in these great open spaces; 90 per cent live in metropolitan areas. This means room for the state's huge prospective growth. Much of the unsettled land appears stark and inhospitable—but so did, once, parts of the state now heavily populated.)

There is still more of California to come. North of Sacramento lie 250 miles of redwood forests, gently rolling farmlands, and mountain wilderness . . . the burbling mud-pools of Mount Lassen, a quiescent volcano . . . the shrieking lumber mills of Fort Bragg and Eureka. Finally comes the invisible line where California ends and Oregon begins.

Completing the state-long plane trip one day in 1962, Governor Brown gazed at the lengthening shadows on Mount Shasta and mused: "It's almost frightening, all this vast country, all this diversity we've seen today. Just the land is awesome enough. And then when you think that there are 16 or 17 million people down there, all building their lives on this land—and the administration of all this ends up in the governor's lap. . . . It's a terrible responsibility. . . . The men who founded California had lots of imagination. But they wouldn't believe what it's come to in a hundred years. . . ."

He forgot a notable exception to that generalization—one of California's colonial governors, José Castro, who is recorded as having remarked, after contacts with the early settlers: "These Americans are so contriving that some day they will build ladders to touch the sky, and once in the heavens they will change the whole face of the universe and even the color of the stars."

Pragmatism

California's inhabitants have come from all the other states of the Union, roughly in proportion to their populations. In a sense, California is a cross-section of the United States. Despite Southern California's reputation for curiosa, Samuel Lubell, the political cardiologist, reported in 1960: "Actually Los Angeles and its environs come closer than any other part of the country to typifying the voting of the whole nation."

If this seems incredible, consider the fact that California's choice for President usually has accorded with the nation's choice. In this century there have been only two hairline exceptions, when two native sons—Governor Hiram Johnson (in 1912) and Richard Nixon (in 1960)—were on national tickets that lost.

"Look at it closely," observed *Look*'s political reporter Richard Reinhardt, "and you find that the so-called California voter is really a Southern Baptist Democrat from Oklahoma who voted for Richard M. Nixon in 1960 because he didn't want the Pope moving into the White House; or a television writer from New York who campaigned for Henry A. Wallace in 1948; or a Negro kindergarten teacher from Detroit who became a Republican this year [1966] because she felt the Democrats were taking her for granted; or a staunch Republican farmer from Indiana who gave his vote to Lyndon Johnson for fear that Goldwater would drop the atomic bomb."

But a geographical cross-section does not necessarily mean a mental and emotional cross-section. The typical Marylander, after all, is not someone who leaves Maryland to go to California. Frontiers historically attract two sorts of people: the enterprising and imaginative, and the escapists—in both cases, individualists with less than ordinary regard for conventions, established norms, and what has gone before.

There is truth in the old wheeze that California is "a state of mind." Essentially it is a huge agglomeration of people with one common desire: to live in California.

In the older eastern states, the reasons for residence may be birth, relatives, employment. The attractions of California are less prosaic. After the Gold Rush, succeeding waves of immigration sought wealth in other ways, from farming to oil extraction to real estate speculation. For a couple of generations, midwestern farmers retired to California because they heard they could live comfortably there, supplementing their nest eggs by growing oranges. Countless people came because of California's bland climate. In the last 20 years, there has been a great influx drawn by jobs in the aerospace, electronics, and computer industries.

The allures have ranged from cotton-growing to surfing. But whatever the individual case, there seemed to be a compelling objective bringing people to California and preoccupying them after they got there.

The operation of California as a state has always been more than normally subordinated to people's personal interests. Whereas Californians follow national lines in presidential elections, in state politics they treat each election as a new game, with a changed set of players and an outcome to be decided less on precedent than on the basis of what seems most feasible at the moment. Special interests tend to cut across party lines. The result is pragmatism.

Pragmatism represents a trade-off of rigidity for flexibility, and of stability for dynamism. Among its consequences have been aberrations toward both right and left, from San Francisco's Vigilantes of the 1850's to the axe-handle-brandishing Workingmen's party of the 1870's, and from Upton Sinclair's quasi-socialism of the Depression to the Birchism and Goldwaterism of the 1960's. Yet the radical thrusts in both directions have managed to offset each other, so that California, for all its vagaries, has become known as a state keyed conspicuously to moderation.

"The state has been a seedbed of extremist movements," the University of California's Paul Seabury observed recently. "Yet no extremist of either Right or Left has made a lasting imprint on the style of its government. Instead there has been a pattern of progressive 'growth legislation' in education, social welfare, labor and tax policy."

Born Full-Grown

California's birth was haphazard and to a large degree illegal—an appropriate beginning for the pragmatic extemporaneousness that has typified its behavior down to this day.

The territory belonged, of course, first to Spain and, from 1821, to Mexico. Enough intrepid pioneers had followed the trails of frontier scouts like Jedediah Smith and Kit Carson to hoist the celebrated Bear Flag at Sonoma in 1846, amid mounting friction with the Mexicans, and proclaim themselves "The Republic of California." Their quixotic gesture was engulfed, in less than a month, by the outbreak of war between Mexico and the United States, including outlying colonies like Sonoma.

Two years of far-flung, disjointed hostilities ensued. Then, in the fashion that was to become characteristic of California, there was a flurry of unpredictable events. The war ended, leaving California under United States military administration; James Marshall discovered gold at Sutter's Mill on the American River north of Sacramento; and 18 months later, with the Gold Rush in full cry, the beleaguered military governor, General Bennett Riley, without formal authorization from Washington, told California's 40,000 scrambling colonists that they should go ahead and hold a constitutional convention aimed at statehood.

The convention met at Monterey, and it produced a constitution in October, 1849. The populace ratified the constitution in November. In December, General Riley turned over the reins to the newly elected governor, Peter H. Burnett, a lawyer who had come on a wagon train from Oregon the year before, and California began operation as a state—still without sanction from Washington.

Congress was interested in the gold, in consolidating the territorial acquisition from Mexico, and in adding another free state to the alignment against the Southern slave states. It was not disposed to quibble over the facts that California was a distant, sparsely settled wilderness and that its constitution was sketchy. But nine months passed before Congress got around to voting the admission of California to statehood, on September 9, 1850. The word, traveling by ship, didn't get to California until nearly a month later. Appropriately, California's founding fathers chose for the central figure of their Great Seal a helmeted Minerva, the goddess who had sprung from Jupiter's head full-grown.

California set some sort of record by jockeying its state capital among three different places—Benicia, San Jose, and Vallejo—in its first four years, before its contentious founders finally settled on Sacramento.

The state ran through ten governors in its first 20 years. The first one, Peter Burnett, resigned in a huff after the legislature reacted churlishly to his first annual message. A successor, Milton Latham, occupied the governorship only five days before jumping to what was considered the infinitely preferable job of United States Senator. Another governor, Frederick Low, remarked disenchantedly as he hastened back to private life after completing the first four-year gubernatorial term in 1867: "There is not much chance to display one's ability in the governor's office of this state, even if you be brilliant."

Popular irreverence for elected officials, reflected in cavalier disregard for continuity of administration, didn't change much as time went on. Only rarely was a governor who had served four years even accorded his party's renomination, and up to 1914 none was ever re-elected.

It was hard work raising even nominal taxes from a scanty, scattered citizenry that, by 1860, amounted to only two persons for each square mile of California's territory. San Francisco, the state's principal population center, was an uproarious dirt-street boom town, teeming with gold-seekers and opportunists from a dozen nations. Los Angeles was still little more than a dusty Mexican pueblo. Settlers, when they weren't fortune-hunting, were busy subduing Indians and coping with the forces of nature, such as the floods that perennially left the state capital a sea of mud.

California was weeks' travel away from the main part of the United States, but it was riven by the political turmoil preluding the Civil War. Some pro-slavery Democrats denounced the state's nascent Republican party as "nigger-worshipers"; the Democrats split temporarily into pro- and anti-slavery wings. California contributed men and money to the Civil War (nearly a century later the state accepted some $8,000 in settlement of a Federal obligation for these services that had been reckoned in the millions) but geography made it a rather vicarious participant. The influx into California of Chinese by the thousands, first as gold miners, then as laborers, seemed to pose a more immediate racial problem than slavery. The resulting wave of anti-Oriental sentiment seethed as a chronic political issue for the next half-century.

Only nine years after California embarked on statehood, the problems of holding it together as a state seemed insuperable. The legislature voted to separate its northern and southern portions into two states, and the enactment was duly signed by Governor John B. Weller on April 19, 1859. Only Congress' preoccupation with the impending Civil War prevented the necessary Federal ratification. And to this day the essential existence of two Californias, northern and southern, is formally recognized in a number of state laws drawing explicit sectional distinctions.

It is recognized also in stiff-jawed tradition. The Los Angeles *Times* has long referred to an amorphous entity called "the Southland." Four hundred miles north, the Sacramento *Bee* has a department devoted to the events of "Superior California."

The worst obstacle to early unification was distances and the problem of spanning them, in an era of few roads and horse transportation.

The subject of widest popular concern was getting railroads—railroads to carry people, produce, and supplies within California, railroads to link California with the East and bring in people and capital to help tame the wilderness. It was a major development when, four years after statehood, a 22-mile line was completed linking Sacramento with the inland Sierra Nevada foothill settlement of Folsom. And jubilant community celebrations greeted the arrival from Washington during the 1850's of a flurry of gaudy but abortive schemes for transcontinental lines.

Within a few years, Californians were to get their railroad. But with it they were to get decades of political skulduggery, economic oppression, and occasional bloodshed. The consequences of all this are palpable even as Californians vote today.

Chapter Three

Corruption Incorporated

☒ A FIRE THAT SWEPT THROUGH THE LITTLE town of Port Washington, Wisconsin, on March 16, 1852, was in a curious way one determinant in the evolution of today's California.

The fire destroyed the office of a young lawyer named Amasa Leland Stanford. Flattened financially, Stanford decided to join his five brothers, from upstate New York, who had gone to get in on the California Gold Rush.

Today Stanford is remembered vaguely as a rich man whose outstanding philanthropy was the gift of $30 million to establish Leland Stanford Junior University in Palo Alto, California, in memory of a son who died in childhood. Some people may recall that Stanford's money came from railroading. Many are surprised to learn that Stanford served a two-year term as governor of California—its eighth—only 12 years after it became a state. But remembered or not, Stanford's migration to California, his governorship, and his presidency of the Southern Pacific Railroad have even today a persisting effect on the lives of millions of people.

Stanford was a founder and the front man of a corporate empire unparalleled in the nation's history in the pervasiveness of its political and economic power. For 40 years it dominated the life of California to such a degree that historians, groping for adequate descriptives, have been impelled to capsule it as "absolute dictatorship."

The corruption through which this domination was maintained was so extreme that it finally brought about its own downfall in a bloodless political revolution that was, in effect, the dawn of contemporary California politics.

Leland Stanford (he soon dropped the Amasa) was imbued with intense aspirations for money, political influence, and personal prestige—goals whose pursuit the ethos of nineteenth-century America automatically cloaked with righteousness.

Ninety days after the Wisconsin fire, Stanford joined his brothers in the operation of stores provisioning the three-year accumulation of miners in California's gold country. The following year, he was elected justice of the peace in the hamlet of Michigan Bar—the only public office he ever held before becoming governor.

In 1855, pursuing his dual objectives of money and political power, Stanford opened his own wholesale general-merchandise establishment in Sacramento, and in the fading days of the Whig party helped found California's Republican party. Three co-founders were other Sacramento merchants, Collis P. Huntington, Charles Crocker, and Mark Hopkins.

In 1856 Stanford, rapidly amassing money from his store, worked in the unsuccessful presidential campaign of California's General John C. Frémont. In 1857, he ran for the office of Sacramento alderman and lost, and was also defeated as the Republican nominee for state treasurer. By 1859, he managed to win the party's nomination for governor, but he lost the election to Milton Latham.

Then a business windfall developed to take Stanford's mind off his political frustrations. He was among a dozen Sacramento businessmen before whom Theodore P. Judah, a frontier construction engineer, outlined a plan to build a railroad from Sacramento eastward over the Sierra Nevada. Others in the group were Stanford's merchant friends Huntington, Hopkins, and Crocker. Judah, who had been back and forth to Washington on the project, pointed out that the Federal government was subsidizing railroad building, and there was a lot of money to be made.

Thanks to Huntington, one of the great connivers of all time, skulduggery enveloped the Central Pacific (the antecedent of the Southern Pacific) Railroad even as it was being born. Huntington feigned a lack of interest in Judah's prospectus, while covertly arranging a private meeting with him. This rendezvous produced, according to historian Oscar Lewis, an agreement rather extraordinary in its terms. Huntington and his three merchant friends, plus two other men (who soon disappeared from the picture), would subscribe for 800 of the 85,000 publicly offered founding shares in the venture. But, despite this very fractional interest, they would be the dominant officers of the railroad. Stanford was to be president, Huntington vice-president, Hopkins treasurer, and Crocker a director. How Judah was persuaded to accept this allocation of authority remains a mystery. Nor is the amount the four men actually invested known. The railroad's early financial records conveniently disappeared some years later when a government investigation was under way. In any case, their stake was minuscule compared to the fortunes the "Big Four" amassed in a short time.

On June 18, 1861, Stanford again won the Republican nomination for governor. Nine days later, the Central Pacific Railroad venture was incorporated. And on September 4, 1861, to round things out happily, Stanford was elected governor.

It is conceivable that, if history had been different, the other three men might have built the railroad without Stanford. But it seems improbable that they would have been able to pursue the same course, and be so phenomenally successful, without the impetus of his intense ambition and his pompous self-righteousness that gave an aura of respectability to their subsequent historic depredations.

With utterly amoral disregard for the blatant conflict of interest he was exemplifying, Governor Stanford, a big, handsome, but introvertedly dull man, said in his inaugural message to the legislature in January, 1862: "May we not, with the utmost propriety, ask the national government to donate lands and loan its credit in aid of this portion of that communication which is of the very first importance, not alone to the states and territories west of the Rocky Mountains, but to the whole nation, and is the great work of the age?"

His lofty, if convoluted, sentiment was not misplaced. Judah, back in Washington, wangled positions as consultant to both House and Senate railroad committees, and helped draft the Pacific Railroad Act, signed by President Lincoln on July 1, 1862.

This measure, and a sequel passed two years later, gave the railroad a 400-foot right-of-way through the public domain; 20 sections (one square mile each) of Federal land for each mile of the first 20 miles of line built; and construction loans, on which no principal or interest had to be paid for 30 years, at a rate of $16,000 to $48,000 a mile, depending on the difficulty of the terrain.

The Pacific Railroad Act provided the first of a long series of astonishing Federal and state subsidies that the railroad contrived to get over a number of years. It appears in retrospect that the Big Four, despite their pious lip-service to the importance of transportation, conceived of the railroad project more as the most convenient tool for gaining money and power.

Charles Crocker, a big man who likened himself to a bull, had the construction know-how. He imported Chinese by the thousands and labored mightily directing a historic engineering achievement: the clearing of a route up Sierra Nevada slopes which climbed 7,000 feet in 20 miles.

The Big Four did not wait for the railroad to approach solvency before tapping it for profits. As many as seven bills to assist the enterprise would sail through the legislature in a single session. One of the first of these was unconstitutional on its face. The 1849 constitution had set a $300,000 ceiling on state indebtedness. Yet the State Subsidy Act of 1863 authorized the state controller to issue the railroad warrants at a rate of $10,000 a mile on completion of the first 40 miles of line—a $400,000 obligation.

This was quickly followed by a law under which, in return for such token railroad services as transporting convicts to the state prison and supplying building materials for the new state capitol, the state was to take over $1,500,000 of Central Pacific bonds.

In the same way that the contemporary construction of the Union Pacific in the East had yielded scandalous profits to the Credit Mobilier, the Central Pacific entrepreneurs began siphoning money from one pocket to another.

In 1864 the legislature authorized them to issue $12 million worth of 20-year bonds, on which the state would pay the 7 per cent interest on the first $1,500,000—a gift of $2,100,000. An anual levy of 8 cents per $100 of assessed valuation was imposed on property throughout the state to meet this payment. The legislature was also induced to authorize counties to bond themselves to buy the railroad's stock. Placer county, which to this day is sparsely inhabited, subscribed $250,000; Sacramento county subscribed $350,000; and other financial assistance was contributed by San Francisco, Santa Clara, and San Joaquin counties.

The Central Pacific track was laid not by the railroad company itself but by an entity entitled the Crocker Construction Company and, later, by one called the Contract and Finance Company.

"In reality," historian Robert Glass Cleland relates, "the companies were only the Big Four and Edwin B. Crocker [Charles Crocker's brother], operating under another name; for Huntington and his associates saw the advisability from many standpoints of keeping the railroad's construction in their own hands. . . . But unlike the Credit Mobilier, [these] construction companies never revealed the details of costs and profits to inquisitive Congressional committees."

Under the "difficult terrain" provision the Big Four boosted their take by the extraordinary device of legally moving the Sierra Nevada. The higher per-mile subsidies were supposed to compensate for the difficulties of building over mountainous slopes. In the foothills just east of Sacramento, the question inevitably arose of where the coastal plain stopped and the mountains began. The Big Four managed to get this decided not on the obvious basis of topography, but on the basis of *geology;* they traced a certain underground stratum westward from the mountains to the plain, and got a ruling that the stratum's tip, 20 miles west of perceptible mountains, was where the premium payments should start.

When Hopkins died in 1878, only 27 years after the railroad started, he had in his rather secondary role as treasurer accumulated a fortune of some $40 million, then one of the largest in the country. The other three partners profited on a comparable scale. Stanford lived like a potentate, spending a million dollars on one vineyard in northern California, breeding race horses, and embarrassing the company by ostentatiously buying his wife a $100,000 piece of jewelry at a moment when the Southern Pacific was pleading to the Federal government that it was practically insolvent. Huntington, who died in 1900, left an estate of $75 million. "I'll never be remembered for the money I've given away," he once commented candidly. "You can't follow me through life by the quarters I've dropped."

The "alternate sections" grant, with public and private tracts checkerboarded, became a standard pattern as the Central (later the Southern) Pacific extended its rails up and down the state and eastward. In less than 20 years, more than 10 per cent of the state's entire 100 million acres of land was in railroad hands.

Ten per cent does not sound like a lot. But when one considers that even today a large portion of California's land is wilderness or otherwise unusable—half of it still belonging to the Federal government—it is obvious that a well-placed 10 per cent could have implications of monopoly. (As recently as 1919, long after the Southern Pacific had been transformed into a respectable corporation, it still was California's biggest landholder, with more than 2 per cent of the state's entire acreage.)

On a smaller scale, California had many other inordinate concentrations of land under single ownerships. The palpable inequity provided support for the single-tax theory ("land is the original basis of wealth") that Henry George, the California thinker, propounded in his *Progress and Poverty* (1879).

As the end of his two-year term approached in 1863, Stanford sought re-election. But the Republican nomination went instead to Frederick Low, a wealthy San Franciscan who had been in Congress. Stanford returned to private life to concentrate on the affairs of the railroad. The tortuous segment over the Sierra Nevada at Donner Pass was completed in June, 1868. In the ensuing 11 months, construction raced ahead at the rate of a mile a day to the line's historic Golden Spike junction with the Union Pacific at Promontory Point, near Ogden, Utah, on May 10, 1869.

The Soul of a Shark

The piratical manner in which the Central Pacific had been established led almost inevitably to extension of the same methods to protect and enlarge its empire.

Smaller railroads up and down the state were absorbed to produce a virtual monopoly. One of them, whose name was adopted for the whole system, was the Southern Pacific, running southward from San Francisco.

The dominance of transportation and land ownership gave rise to a fabric of influence reaching into every community of the state—the "Octopus" depicted by novelist Frank Norris. The SP's network of corruption functioned as an invisible government of California, with officials at all levels obligated in one way or another to act according to the corporation's interests.

A major device in this penetration was the party convention system that preceded the direct primary system. By starting at the local level, where bribery was inexpensive and pressures easy to exert, the railroad could manipulate local and county party conventions, and thereby virtually arrange advance control of the state conventions that selected the candidates for major office.

"In every county in California," the San Francisco *Call* recounted, "the railroad company maintained an expert political manager whose employment was to see that the right men were chosen as convention delegates, the right kind of candidates nominated and elected, and the right things done by the men in the office."

The SP also, notes Hearst's biographer, W. A. Swanberg, "controlled most of California's important newspapers by what were politely known as subsidies, and by a monopolized power over industry and advertisers that could cripple any editor so headstrong as to fight back."

The mastermind of this domination was the SP's vice-president, Collis Huntington, who did the dirty work while Stanford, living at Palo Alto, provided sanctimonious window-dressing. Huntington was described by one contemporary as having "the soul of a shark." Even Stanford once told an interviewer he would trust Huntington "only so far as I could throw Trinity Church up the side of Mount Shasta."

Huntington considered party politics no more than something that could be used for profit. "He despised all men who sought public office," commented Irving Stone, "as exhibitionists, easily and cheaply bought."

Huntington didn't care which party he was using. "There is not much that divides the parties now," he remarked cynically in the 1890's, "but seven great reasons: the five loaves and the two fishes"—meaning that it was only a question of who got the graft.

Two eyewitnesses to the creeping corruption were Thomas Storke, long-time publisher of the Santa Barbara *News-Press,* and Lincoln Steffens, the famous "muckraking" journalist.

The railroad, Storke related, "extended its evil influence to Sacramento and Los Angeles, up into Oregon, and as far East as Washington, D. C. . . . I saw the Octopus nominate and elect governors, U.S. Senators, judges, and even town constables owed their jobs to the machine. . . .

"William F. Herrin, the chief attorney for the railroad, [was] the political boss of California," Steffens wrote. "He was the prime minister of the actual sovereign. . . .

"If a man wanted political preferment," Storke added, "he had to go to William F. Herrin's headquarters at 4th and Townsend Streets in San Francisco and, hat in hand, beg permission to become a candidate."

"The bar of the Palace Hotel in San Francisco was the real state capital," recalled journalist Charles Van Devander. "Round-trip tickets from Sacramento to San Francisco were placed on each legislator's desk every weekend. Hotel bills were sent directly to the railroad company. . . ."

The extension of influence all the way to Washington was not extraordinary in that era. An issue that arose against James A. Garfield in the 1880 presidential election concerned the fact that he had been one of the members of Congress among whom the Union Pacific's Credit Mobilier had scattered handfuls of stock—$329 worth in Garfield's case—to improve the corporation's legislative prospects. Huntington was said to have chafed over the fact that California's Congressional delegation recurrently would produce an occasional "rebel" not under the railroad's sway. As late as 1906, journalists classified 75 of the United States Senate's 90 members as being at the beck of railroad, meat, sugar, oil, and steel interests. Huntington was blamed for pulling wires in Congress to delay for years Los Angeles' construction of its current capacious harbor at San Pedro, because the SP's waterfront interests were at Santa Monica, a few miles away.

The depth of SP's corruption became common knowledge. But if any proof was needed, the railroad's practices were spread on the public record, in Huntington's own words, in 1883. The widow of Huntington's aide, David Colton, sued the railroad for money she considered due her husband's estate. She brought into court bundles of letters, written by Huntington in the East to Colton in San Francisco, blueprinting the railroad's under-the-table activities. The letters listed scores of office-holders, from California to Washington, with their reliabilitity, their susceptibility, and their prices; and the letters explained the machinations necessary to get bills through Congress.

In 1879 California held its second constitutional convention. The revised constitution called for the creation of a commission to regulate the railroads.

Huntington, Steffens recounted, personally masterminded, from the legislature lobby, the railroad's fight against establishment of a regulatory commission. Defeated, Huntington said that if the railroads were going to be regulated, then the railroads would have to police those doing the regulating.

"And," Steffens said, "he went after, and he got, finally, the railroad commission." Within a short time, it was commonly accepted that two of the first three commission members were on the SP payroll. In 1885 the well-oiled Southern Pacific machine helped Stanford win election by the legislature to the U. S. Senate. He was in his second term when he died.

The Octopus

The era of Southern Pacific domination extended for 40 years, from 1870 until 1910.

Outwardly, the state flourished in that period. Its population quadrupled, from 560,000 to 2,477,000. There were ups and downs; along with the rest of the nation, California suffered in the Panic of 1873. But generally its economy boomed and diversified. Completion of the Union Pacific line to Los Angeles in 1887, ending Southern Pacific's transcontinental monopoly, touched off a price war. The fare from Kansas City dropped to a farcical $1, and southern California experienced its first land rush.

But everywhere was felt the rank incubus of political serfdom. The California legislature was characterized, writes Robert Cleland, by "dishonesty, mediocrity and confusion. . . . The concrete effects of these evils in government appeared in increased taxes, unjust assessments, poor streets, high railroad rates, water monopolies, and in a score of other abuses. . . ."

"Farmers and shippers all over the state groaned under exorbitant rates and poor service," Swanberg comments. "Nothing was done about it because the railroad made the rules by bribery so general and long-continued that it became almost respectable." It cost a San Joaquin Valley farmer more to ship barley 100 miles to the coast than to ship it from San Francisco to England. A widespread quip in the 1880's was: "Out of three drops of rain that fall in the San Joaquin Valley, two are owned by Collis P. Huntington."

The farmers' helplessness was dramatized in the 1880 battle of Mussel Slough, near Hanford in the San Joaquin Valley. Squatters on land claimed by the railroad formed the

"Settlers' Rights League" to fight the title issue in court. But one day in May three United States marshals with eviction orders, accompanied by a railroad representative, descended on a League picnic-rally. Guns blazed. Two of the officers were killed, and five farmers. Seventeen farmers were sent to prison. Public resentment ran so high that two sympathizers with the settlers went on a four-year rampage of holding up Southern Pacific trains in the valley. They were, says historian Stewart Holbrook, "cheered by virtually the whole population of the valley, and by a great majority of Californians elsewhere." There was no question in the public mind about where responsibility lay. A cartoon published in the San Francisco *Wasp* on March 12, 1881, showed Mussel Slough surmounted by a sprawling two-headed giant, the two faces being those of Stanford and Crocker.

Fifteen men held the office of governor from Stanford to James Gillett, whose administration marked the end of the SP's sway. Nine were Republicans, five were Democrats, and one was a member of the Civil War Union party. Some were subservient to the railroad, others bucked it. But none was able to really dent its golden armor.

Governor George Stoneman, the former Civil War general, for instance, complained bitterly in 1884 that the state's 1864 assumption of debt service on Southern Pacific bonds already had cost California $2,100,000, whereas the railroad's cavalier tax delinquencies were weighing heavily on the state's unbalanced budget. Before the tax issue could be ruled on by the United States Supreme Court, the state's elected attorney general agreed to an out-of-court settlement for a fraction of the total claimed.

The evil persisted partly because of public apathy and preoccupation and partly because, as with Gulliver and the Lilliputians, the railroad's myriad strands of control formed a seemingly unbreakable net.

"All is bustle, motion, and struggle. . . ." James Bryce, the great British political scientist, wrote after visiting California in the 1880's. ". . . The arrangements of his government lie in the dim background of the picture which fills the Western eye. The foreground is filled by ploughs and sawmills, ore-crushers and railway locomotives. These so absorb his thoughts as to leave little time for constitutions and legislation. . . ."

"Individualism," wrote Frederick Jackson Turner, the scholar of the frontier movement, "has allowed a laxity in government affairs which has rendered possible the spoils system and all the manifest evils that follow from the lack of a highly developed civic spirit."

"It is not surprising," adds political scientist Dean Cresap, "that when some of the managers of wealth, public officials, and party leaders, violated their trust and engaged in bribery and fraud, the great majority of the people were too busy to be concerned with the demands of civic interest."

In 1887, William Randolph Hearst took over the publishership of the San Francisco *Examiner*. He made the Southern Pacific's skulduggery the target of an editorial campaign that went on for 15 years. The *Examiner* sent Ambrose Bierce, the subsequently celebrated writer, to Washington for the special purpose of frustrating Huntington's efforts to get concessions on the railroad's debt to the Federal government.

By 1898 the original Federal subsidy loans to the SP, totaling $28 million, had grown with interest to a $59 million debt. The SP wanted to refinance the debt and get repayment stretched over another 75 years. But publicity such as Bierce gave to the railroad's lobbying helped thwart this; the SP was told to pay up. Although, Oscar Lewis notes, "railroad officials had for years proclaimed the company's inability to pay except in small amounts spread over a long period," the railroad finally agreed to liquidate the debt in ten years—and did so without difficulty.

The battle between Hearst and Huntington reached a comic-opera climax in 1899, Swanberg recounts, when the *Examiner* published Edwin Markham's famous poem, "The Man With the Hoe," which aroused international note as an eloquent plea for the common man, in implicit contrast to the contemporary "malefactors of great wealth." The ideological implications infuriated Huntington, who offered a prize for a counter-poem, while snarling publicly:

"Is America going to turn to Socialism over one poem? Markham's Hoe Man has a hoe. Let him rejoice."

The Follies of Santa Cruz

What has come down in history as the baldest example of Southern Pacific corruption was the state Republican convention of 1906, which met in the beach resort of Santa Cruz, south of San Francisco, in September, five months after the San Francisco earthquake.

The railroad had decided to replace the incumbent governor, George Pardee, with a compliant congressman, James M. Gillett, a northern California lumber dealer and lawyer. Pardee, a former mayor of Oakland, was backed by a nascent reform junta in the party.

"Never in the history of California," says historian George Mowry, "had the Southern Pacific been so brazen in dominating a state convention as it was at Santa Cruz, threatening the wavering, providing for the faithful. . . . In the drive to nominate Gillett, even the higher judicial positions were traded like commodities."

Abe Ruef, the San Francisco political boss, who collaborated with the SP machine, testified afterward that he was approached at the convention by Walter Parker, the railroad's deputy commissar, and paid $14,000 to swing his votes around to Gillett.

Afterward, Governor Pardee commented: "We have met the enemy and we were theirs on the first ballot. It is evident that the machine and Ruef didn't want me to be governor again, and . . . they were in control of the convention."

At a dinner held to celebrate the SP's victory at the convention, a photograph of some of the leading participants was taken which later became a notorious anti-railroad campaign document and an embarrassment for years afterward to some of those depicted—among them Joseph R. Knowland, the Oakland publisher, father of Senator William F. Knowland.

The 1907 legislature, which was a by-product of the Santa Cruz convention, became known as the worst in the state's history in terms of SP domination. The Fresno *Republican* reported that in that legislature there were 83 "doorkeepers" to tend three doors, stenographers on the state payroll who were illiterate, and prostitutes receiving per diem compensation as committee "clerks." A Republican state senator observed: "Scarcely a vote was cast in either house that did not show some aspect of SP ownership, petty vengeance, or legislative blackmail." Another legislator remarked: "You couldn't get the Lord's Prayer enacted in this administration without money."

But, it transpired, the Santa Cruz convention and the shabby 1907 legislature were the final fetid gasps of the SP machine. A historic era of political depravity was about to be ended by a burgeoning of the public conscience which proved even more forceful and enduring.

Chapter
Four

"The Bifurcated Volcano": Hiram Johnson

☒ THE HEADLINES THAT PROCLAIMED THE DROPping of the first atomic bomb on Hiroshima on August 6, 1945, eclipsed another significant event: the death, in the Bethesda Naval Hospital in Maryland, of California's Senator Hiram Warren Johnson, at the age of 78.

For a generation Johnson had been a pyrotechnical fixture of the national legislative scene—a dynamic, tempestuous, contentious figure, a high-collared archetype of Republican isolationism. Nationally Johnson was remembered as Theodore Roosevelt's running-mate in the unsuccessful insurgent-Republican "Bull Moose" presidential campaign in 1912, and for his part in helping scuttle United States support of the League of Nations. Noting also that he had almost been a vice-presidential candidate in the campaign of 1920—and that the man who did become Vice-President, Calvin Coolidge, succeeded to the Presidency—the New York *Times* obituary commented: "The history of the United States might have been changed if he had accepted."

Generally unappreciated at the time, and not widely understood since, is that in his day Hiram Johnson was a veritable atomic bomb in the arena of California politics, and the changes that he worked, long before he went to the United States Senate, are still shaping California's politics and thereby indeed "changing the history of the United States." To cite just one instance, if there had been no Hiram Johnson to raise the strange new banner of "nonpartisanism" over California's political battlements, there could hardly have been an Earl Warren, to progress from California's governorship to the United States Supreme Court and inspire its epochal social and juridical reforms of recent years.

Hiram Johnson was the emissary of the cataclysm that smashed California's long-entrenched political corruption and brought into being the state's unique political patterns of today.

Rebellion against established party organisms, as institutions too easily perverted to the purposes of malefactors like the Southern Pacific, had been brewing for a generation in California.

The railroad had been in existence barely a decade when some people began associating its evil with the malleable apparatus of party politics, and reasoning that the solution lay in drastic revision of party operations.

In 1873 a group, emboldened by Governor Newton Booth's

opposition to the railroad's faintly veneered larceny, organized a "People's Independent Party," and at their first convention enunciated these principles:

> One of the most serious obstacles in the way of political and governmental reform lies in the doctrine of so-called "party fealty," that tyrannical rule which degrades the citizen and sinks him to the servile partisan, rendering him the helpless tool of selfish wirepullers and caucus manipulators. . . . One of the greatest evils which earnestly demands correction is the tyranny of party discipline, which is maintained through the system of primaries and caucuses by professional politicians, aided by governmental patronage and moneyed power, and has become a despotic rule of the few over the many. . . .
>
> We hold that any citizen has the right to take part in good faith in the actions and deliberations of any political organization, caucus or convention without being bound thereby except so far as his own judgement and conscience may approve.
>
> [We oppose] the abominable and infamous practice of securing election to office by the corrupt use of money at the polls, and bribing the members of legislative bodies, which has become so prevalent. . . .
>
> We will even assert the right and authority of the people's representatives to control and regulate all such corporations as exercise any franchise or special privilege obtained by legislative enactment, and especially the incorporated common carriers of the country . . . [we are opposed to] . . . subsidies . . . to any railroad or other corporation, either by Federal, state, county or municipal governments. . . .
>
> [We support] the manly and noble stand taken by Governor Newton Booth in behalf of the popular rights and against the encroachments of unscrupulous politicians and railroad corporations on the rights of the masses.

Like other reform movements of that period, the People's Independent party did not maintain its momentum long. But it was a forerunner of modern nonpartisanism. Self-styled "nonpartisans," in fact, dominated California's second (and last) constitutional convention in 1879. There were 78 of them, compared with 11 Republicans, 10 Democrats, 2 "Independents," and 51 adherents of the short-lived San-Francisco-centered Workingmen's party.

By 1884 the Democrats at their convention were saying: "While we recognize the importance of encouraging the building and operation of railroads . . . we view with alarm the power of the railroad monopoly as manifested in its pernicious and corrupting influence in politics and in its control of officials elected by the people." And by the early 1900's, the platforms of both political parties were referring bluntly to the necessity of "emancipating California from the domination of the Southern Pacific Railroad."

A New Age

The change in California's political climate reflected a national revolution in attitudes.

As the nineteenth century neared its end, the reigning amoral political and economic mores wore thin. American public opinion swung to the outlook capsuled by the "muckraking" magazine publisher S. S. McClure: "Capitalists, workingmen, politicians, citizens—all breaking the law, or letting it be broken. Who is left to uphold it? There is none left; none but all of us."

"For ten years there has been a distinct movement among the American people," the journalist William Allen White wrote in 1910, "—a movement which indicates that in the soul of the people there is a conviction of their past unrighteousness. . . . It is called variously Reform, the Moral Awakening, the New Idea, the Square Deal, the Uplift, Insurgency. . . ."

Arthur M. Schlesinger, Sr., elaborated on this "dawn of a new age": "Farmers had been fighting a losing battle against the cities and the rising industrial magnates. Now the spirit of unrest and revolt reached the cities . . . arousing not only wage-earners, but middle-class white-collar workers and small-business men. . . . The masses in growing numbers . . . gave their support to a new group of political leaders who fought to restore government to the people."

In California there was a perceptible turning of the tide by 1900. The Southern Pacific machine had overreached itself, ironically not in the extent of its depredations but in the nature of its involvements. These became so widespread that the SP was forced to do business with local machines over whose activities it had no control. . . . When Lincoln Steffens asked William Herrin why he ever allowed all the petty grafters in San Francisco to carry on their thievery and conniving so obviously that they were sure to cause a scandal, the SP political commissar replied: "We have to let these little skates get theirs. We have to sit by and see them run riot and take risks that risk our interests too. We can't help it. The Southern Pacific Railroad and all the companies and interests associated with us are not rich enough to pay all that politics costs."

A distantly centered "Octopus" was tolerated by citizens partly because of its sheer inaccessibility, but locally based corruption was something else. In the 1880's and 1890's there had been a sprouting of "Good Government" organizations in a number of cities. Their initial success was sketchy. But there was an awakening of conscience.

By 1900, Oscar Lewis relates, "California newspapers and weeklies which for years had been accepting railroad subsidies found that their support of the corporation was costing them subscribers and prestige, whereas the anti-railroad journals reported mounting circulation and influence. As a consequence, many of the sheets cut themselves off from the Southern Pacific payroll and went over to the other side."

The year 1906 brought the great earthquake and fire that devastated much of San Francisco, and it also brought the beginning of an even more thoroughgoing demolition of California's long-standing structure of political corruption.

For five years a classically evil San Francisco municipal regime, whose gray eminence was Abraham Ruef, a lawyer, had rung all the changes on graft and extortion, from bordellos to public utility companies. A reform campaign was mounted by three men: James D. Phelan, a wealthy former mayor; Rudolph Spreckels, the financier; and Fremont Older, the militant editor of the San Francisco *Bulletin*. Through the good offices of President Theodore Roosevelt, they borrowed the services of both William J. Burns, a leading Secret Service detective, and Francis J. Heney, a San Francisco lawyer who had been handling special prosecutions for the Federal government. Working with the newly elected non-machine district attorney, William H. Langdon, the group conducted investigations that led to the initiation of a grand jury investigation in November, 1906.

Before it was over, most of the board of supervisors of San Francisco's combined city-county government had been implicated in the corruption, along with a number of prominent corporation officials. One supervisor, confessing, ticked off such bribes received as $475 to facilitate a prize-fight promotion, $750 to cooperate in rigging gas rates, $3,500 to approve a telephone company franchise, and $4,000 to support a trolley franchise.

Some 300 persons were indicted, but ultimately there were only four convictions, and three of these were reversed. Ruef alone went to prison. . . . But the housecleaning aroused reform sentiment throughout the state and was the springboard of the movement's future leader.

The most portentous product of the trials developed accidentally. On November 13, 1908, Heney, the prosecutor, was shot in the courtroom by a prospective juror infuriated at the disclosure that he had a prison record. Drafted to fill in for Heney was a rising young lawyer named Hiram Johnson. The renown Johnson received as a warrior against graft projected him into the forefront of the reform movement.

In Los Angeles, where the SP's deputy commissar, Walter Parker, was based, Dr. John R. Haynes, a scholarly philanthropist, in 1895 had started the Direct Legislation League, aimed at closing the gap between citizens and professional politics. It produced a rare thing: a new invention in government.

This was the device of recall. Using it, a small fraction of the citizens of a governmental jurisdiction could, by petition, force a vote on discharging an elected official who was considered unsatisfactory. Recall was inaugurated by Los Angeles in a new city charter in 1903. In 1908 it was adopted by Oregon as a statewide fixture.

Now, as the San Francisco reformers were mounting their attack on the Ruef machine, a "Nonpartisan Committee of 100" formed to press the cause in Los Angeles.

The sparkplug of this movement was Edward A. Dickson, editor of the Los Angeles *Express*. On July 3, 1906, an editorial in the *Express* sounded the tocsin:

> The Republican organization in Los Angeles has come to be but another name for the Southern Pacific. There is only one thing to be done, and that is to break the machine. It can be done only by refusing to vote for any machine-made candidate. No matter what else may be said of him, if he is the Southern Pacific's man, he is not to be trusted. When the people's interests and those of the Southern Pacific are in conflict, he will side with the railroad and against the people.

The Nonpartisan Committee's anti-machine slate won 17 out of 23 offices in the city election.

After the 1907 legislature had put its dirty thumbprint on history, Dickson and Chester Rowell, the prominent reform editor of the Fresno *Republican*, rallied a dozen like-minded party activists from all over the state to the formation of an insurgent "Lincoln-Roosevelt Republican League." At a convention in August in Oakland, the League issued a manifesto. The League's declared objectives were:

> —to emancipate the Republican party in California from domination by the political bureau of the Southern Pacific Railroad Company and allied interests, and the reorganization of the state committee to that end . . .
>
> —to oppose the nomination of any reactionary styled

"safe and sane" by the great corporate interests . . .

—the pledging of all delegates to conventions against the iniquitous practice of "trading" whereby political bosses effect nominations by bargain and sale, and the enactment of legislation penalizing such practices. . . .

After narrowly missing capturing control of the 1908 Republican state convention, the reformers launched an intensive missionary campaign pointed at the next gubernatorial election in 1910.

One of their leading speakers for the cause was Hiram Johnson. The Southern Pacific corruption had poignant personal implications for him. His father, Grove Johnson, a Sacramento lawyer, as a congressman and a state legislator was an unabashed cog in the SP apparatus.

Hiram Johnson was born in Sacramento three years after Leland Stanford left the governorship. He went to the state university at Berkeley for two years, then went into his father's law office, with his brother Albert. After a breach with their father over his political proclivities, the sons went into law practice in San Francisco, and Hiram joined the firm of William H. Langdon, the anti-machine district attorney who had started the prosecution of the Ruef ring.

Johnson, 44, was a leading prospect when in 1910 the Lincoln-Roosevelt League, now ascendant in the Republican party, came to select a gubernatorial candidate. For months Johnson balked at running. His wife didn't want to live in Sacramento, and he had many other reservations about taking on the assignment. But finally he agreed. His decision was as pivotal historically as Leland Stanford's decision to go to California.

Get the Railroad!

Johnson was one of the most remarkable personalities of modern American politics. Arizona's eloquent Senator Henry

Ashhurst described him as "a bifurcated, peripatetic volcano, in perpetual eruption, belching fire and smoke."

Stocky and jowly, with a made-in-America face and gimlet eyes peering intently through rimless glasses, Johnson was the choleric prototype of the early twentieth-century celluloid-collared politico who, in the days before amplifiers, would brandish an admonitory forefinger, waggle his head in ominous dismay, and thunder: "It makes . . . my blood . . . to boil! . . ."

Although in private he could be relaxed and amiable, his posture, even in personal expression, was habitually one of militance. His reaction on one occasion to a fleeting impediment in his law work was characteristic: "I can chop my way out!"

Ambitious and dauntless, he compensated for inner insecurity and chronic pessimism with vitriolic belligerence toward any opposition. A friend called him "catholic in his hatreds."

His denunciation of the Los Angeles *Times*' publisher, General Harrison Gray Otis, who at one point had the temerity to disagree with him, has become a museum piece of invective:

"The one blot on the fame of southern California, and the bar sinister on the escutcheon of Los Angeles," he roared at a rally in Los Angeles, "is Harrison Gray Otis—a creature who is vile, infamous, degraded, and putrescent. Here he sits in senile dementia, with gangrened heart and rotting brain, grimacing at every reform and chattering in impotent rage against decency and morality, while he is going down to his grave in snarling infamy."

Johnson was a man who could remain unshaken even by pleas of the President of the United States invoking the supposed national welfare. Anti-Oriental feeling, punctuating California politics since the influx of the Southern Pacific's Chinese laborers, reached a crescendo in 1913 in proposed legislation to prevent Japanese immigrants from owning land. Japan's Foreign Office protested to President Wilson, who, amid public apprehensions of possible hostilities between the two countries, took the extraordinary step of dispatching Secretary of State William Jennings Bryan to Sacramento. Bryan was accorded the unusual courtesy of being permitted to address the California legislature, to urge that the anti-Japanese strictures be tempered. But, with the legislature firmly under Johnson's sway, Bryan might as well have directed his celebrated rhetoric at a cliff in Yosemite. He returned to Washington, his mission fruitless.

Johnson's dogged determination was epitomized by his record, in later years in the United States Senate, battling for the losing cause of isolationism. He voted against United States participation in the World Court, against the London Naval Treaty, against the reciprocal trade agreements of 1937, against relaxation of the neutrality act, against peacetime selective service, against lend-lease, and against relaxation of the embargo on arms for Europe. He carried his fight against ratification of the United Nations Charter even to his deathbed, arranging, nine days before he succumbed, for his vote to be paired to cancel out a proponent.

But his intense career in California politics was overwhelmingly positive, even though, as commentator George Creel remarked, Johnson enlisted in the 1910 campaign "with an effect of peevish martyrdom." His fire and determination filled Californians' need to express their total repudiation of existing political mores, and audiences responded enthusiastically to his polemics.

The Republican reformers had adopted a massive 20-point program for governmental changes and innovations, but Johnson elected to campaign on the one most vulnerable point: "Get the Southern Pacific Railroad out of politics!" This had universal appeal: it was a goal to which both Republican and Democratic parties by then were thoroughly committed in almost identical platform terms.

Johnson campaigned tirelessly from March to the August primary. Spurning the railroad even as a personal convenience, he chugged 18,000 miles up and down the state in a red Locomobile bedecked with bells, heralded at each stop by a fife-and-drum corps whose thumping and tootling suggested "The Spirit of '76" and impending liberation from tyranny.

No less than four rivals for the gubernatorial nomination emerged from the old-guard Republican ranks, the foremost being Secretary of State Charles F. Curry. This helped Johnson, as the lone Progressive-faction entry, immensely: the anti-Johnson vote in the primary was split four ways. Even so, Johnson drew almost more votes than his opponents combined, getting 101,666 to 55,390 for second-placer Curry.

In the November election, his opponent was Theodore A. Bell, the Napa lawyer who had been the Democratic entry against the railroad's James Gillett in the preceding election. Johnson beat Bell by 177,191 votes to 154,835.

It marked the advent of a new epoch in American politics: the age of California pragmatism.

Chapter
Five

Reform: No Promise Unfulfilled

☒ IF THERE IS A STERN RECORDING ANGEL SOME-where with a book of the myriad unfulfilled promises of political campaigns, there also exists a brilliantly redeeming exception: the cataclysm of activity that burst when Hiram Johnson took the helm at Sacramento.

It was as if the whole state of California, having let its government go to pot for half a century, abruptly dropped everything else for a mass spasm of civic housecleaning and rehabilitation. What went on was of a different dimension from the familiar tortuous legislative deliberations about highway routings and fish limits.

Hiram Johnson was governor of California from January 4, 1911, to March 15, 1917. During most of that time, California was in effect conducting a marathon constitutional convention, involving everyone in the state in the most thoroughgoing remodeling of its political structure that any state had ever carried out.

Johnson and the Progressive leaders initiated the measures. A compliant Progressive-dominated legislature, swept into office with Johnson, enacted the measures. And the populace ratified the principal ones, in the form of constitutional amendments.

To a considerable degree it was a one-man show. Joseph Beek, who entered state service at that time—and was still at work as secretary of the state senate in 1967—has recalled: "Johnson expected subservience on the part of the legislature. . . . Both houses deferred to him as the acknowledged leader. This subservience . . . went so far that even the appointment of legislative committees, the awarding of important chairmanships, and the selection of legislative officers were decided in the governor's office."

Johnson's first concern, after vowing to methodically expel from state government all minions of the Southern Pacific, was to lock the door against any return of "political machines or special interests."

"When, with your assistance," he told the legislature, "California's government shall be composed only of those who recognize one sovereign and master, the people, then is presented to us the question: How best can we arm the people to protect themselves hereafter?"

His first answer was in adoption of three new governmental devices: the initiative, the referendum, and recall. Through them, citizens could enact laws themselves if the legislature was laggard or recalcitrant; citizens could reject legislation they didn't like; and citizens could oust elected officials who weren't satisfactory.

All three devices involved procuring on petitions the signatures of 5 to 12 per cent of the electorate, to qualify a proposal for the ballot. Then the proposal—to enact a new law, annul a law, or oust an official—was settled by a popular majority.

The enactment of reform measures went on for five years, through the legislatures of 1911, 1913, and 1915. But the principal measures highballed through the 1911 session. Theodore Roosevelt called these "the most comprehensive legislation ever passed at a single session of any American legislature."

At a special election held in November, 1911, the people approved 23 state constitutional amendments embodying measures Johnson had urged in his inaugural message. Among them was woman suffrage, adopted eight years before it became a national institution under the Nineteenth Amendment.

By the time the legislature adjourned, Johnson was able to say: "No pledge given to the people of the state has by this legislature been broken. Not a single promise . . . left unfulfilled."

By 1912, Johnson's accomplishments had won him national renown. He led the California delegation to the Republican National Convention in Chicago, joined in the anti-conservative, anti-Taft walkout led by Theodore Roosevelt, and was nominated as Roosevelt's running-mate on the Progressive "Bull Moose" third-party ticket. The Roosevelt-Johnson slate got only 88 electoral votes, against Democrat Woodrow Wilson's 435 votes. Thirteen of those 88 votes were California's—by a tally of 283,610 to 283,436.

In their reform measures, the Progressives ranged widely over three different fields: moral, humanitarian, and governmental.

The Progressive wave was part of the moralistic national

tide, so fervid that by 1918 it swept in the misbegotten experiment of Prohibition. The zeal for righteousness extended even to what was delicately called "red light abatement," meaning a ban on publicly sanctioned brothels. These were a long-established part of the San Francisco social structure, as well as an appurtenance of lesser communities.

Laws were passed against race-track gambling, slot machines, and dice games, and local option was instituted in the sale of liquor. As in other states, some of these strictures were later revoked, with the notable exceptions of legalized prostitution and off-track gambling.

In the humanitarian field, there were enacted the eight-hour day for women; an employer liability law in regard to occupational injuries; a ban on compulsory arbitration in strikes of public employees; and, altogether, 39 out of 41 measures recommended by organized labor.

But all these enactments were eclipsed in their impact on California by an array of basic changes in the anatomy of state government, election procedures, and party activities. These changes were the product of an oddly ambivalent design of Hiram Johnson to hamstring the familiar two-party system as a vehicle for corruption, and to superimpose on it strange procedures calculated to bolster the Progressives' reign. The magic word in this prestidigitation was "bipartisanism."

In the rousing windup of his inaugural address, Governor Johnson had thundered: "It is in no partisan spirit that I have addressed you. It is in no partisan spirit that I appeal to you for aid. Democrats and Republicans alike are citizens, and equal patriotism is in each."

Appeals to bipartisan support have resounded in the political area before and since. They are a standard gambit of the politician who senses that he cannot get by on the strength of his own party alone, and needs support from the other side. But never has the theme of bipartisanism been so portentous as when Johnson enunciated it, with the innocence of a rhetorical homily. Inconspicuously, and probably to a degree unwittingly, he was beginning the construction of a temple at which future generations of Californians, both politicians and voters, would worship.

With him, and with such successors as Earl Warren, Edmund Brown, and Ronald Reagan, bipartisanism became not just a device by which incumbents might rally support in tactical emergencies, but the springboard by which they were elected. And for California's voters, bipartisanism became not an occasional aberration but a way of life.

The reason for Johnson's innovative zeal is more obvious now than it was then. He was the product of a insurgent faction that had gained dominance, for the moment, in the mossbacky, corruption-ridden Republican party. But he was realistic enough to know that such triumphs are unstable—that the old hard-shells would not abandon the field but would soon try to resurge. To thwart that resurgence he needed strength from wherever he could get it. His own Progressive ranks needed to be fleshed out with proselytes from the Democratic party and more defectors from the old-guard Republicans. The Progressives even needed, if they could contrive it, a way of drawing attractive candidates from the ranks of their nominal foes, to carry the Progressive banner.

The steps that Johnson and the Progressives took to bring about these desired changes were imaginative, bold, complex, fascinating—and more enduring than they anticipated.

The traditional form of a state political party is pyramidal, with a base of local precinct activities narrowing to the apex of the statewide party hierarchy. Through a series of constitutional amendments and statutes, the Progressives destroyed this traditional structure.

First, nonpartisanism was imposed by law on all elective city and county offices throughout the state, including educational and judicial positions. A man no longer ran for mayor, sheriff, judge or school-board member as a Democrat, Republican, or Vegetarian; he ran only on his name.

Partisanism was maintained in higher offices—the legislature and state officials. But the base for standard machine politics was eliminated. The man elected to local or county office was not beholden to any party organization. These positions were removed from any party line of progression to higher, partisan offices—although a nonpartisan office-holder could, as a citizen, participate in partisan politics at other levels. (A recent example was Los Angeles County Sheriff Peter Pitchess, who despite the nonpartisanship of his elective office served in 1964 as a Goldwater campaign official and a Republican national convention delegate.)

Nonpartisanism in local and county offices precludes the conventional machine web of party patronage appointments; and patronage is the cement that, more than ideology, holds party organizations together. To suppress any remnants of it, any possible attempts by ambitious individuals to build nonpartisan personal machines through appointive favoritism, the Progressives took initial steps toward instituting the civil service merit system. Individuals qualified for public employment by competitive examinations; and once in jobs they could be dismissed only for cause, not simply because their party had been defeated in an election.

Then, as a knight slaying a dragon traditionally slashes it through the middle, the Progressives proceeded to divide the pyramidal structure of party organization horizontally into two permanently alienated segments.

Historically party organizations had been composed of activists selected originally at local and county conventions. Out of these would come a smaller, more elite group of delegates to a party's state convention, where nominees for major offices were chosen.

The Progressives scrapped this arrangement. Instead, party county committees were filled with persons elected in the biennial party primaries. Once elected, these county committees could hold meetings every day in the week if they wanted. It made no difference. They were dead-end debating societies. Progression from county committees to parties' state central committees was abolished, except for a handful of token functionaries.

The state committees, the Progressives ordained (with due ratification by the legislature), hereafter would be composed of the party's office-holders and election-year nominees, plus several additional persons designated by each of them—altogether, a body approaching 1,000 persons. Theoretically this was the entity that would guide the party through the forthcoming general-election campaign and the ensuing two years.

But in the short interval between primary and general elections, a new state committee could do little about party policy or campaign mechanics. All it had time to do was promulgate a party platform, too late to be of any consequence, the party's candidates already having been nominated.

Once the general election was over, a party's state central committee became essentially an honorary affair. It could not help or hinder aspirants for the *next* election: the parties' state central committees were expressly forbidden to make pre-primary endorsements or show any favoritism among candidates for nomination. All primary entrants competed on an equal basis, except for the momentum possessed by those running for re-election.

Thus the parties' high commands were effectively isolated from the grass roots, where the votes were. The operations of these curious double-ended organisms, resembling Dr. Dolittle's pushmi-pullyu, will be described in Chapter 10. For now it is sufficient to note the chief results. The arrangement served a dual purpose: it prevented outside interests from using the party's top echelon, through the old nominating-convention system, for corrupt designs, as the Southern Pacific had; and it dispersed real power among office-holders and nominees (in the main, Progressives) on an every-man-for-himself basis.

"The whole process of generating party policy and of electing party slates through a statewide party association was abolished," comments political scientist Dean Cresap. "The new legislators in effect assumed control of their parties at the state level."

Johnson and his fellow Progressives had virtually said:

"I'm aboard—pull up the rope," and had detached their portion of the erstwhile party power structure from its now impotent base. The dragon's head had been separated from its tail.

One day in 1913, in the midst of the Progressives' methodical upheaval of California's political machinery, a messenger from the state assembly toted into Governor Johnson's office an election-law revision bill that had been dutifully prepared by Speaker (later Governor) Clement C. Young, a devout Johnson collaborator.

No one knows just what discussions took place in the governor's office regarding the bill. But when it was returned to the assembly for action, it contained 38 amendments. Practically unnoticed among them was a cryptic clause reading:

> . . . Nothing in this act contained shall be construed to limit the right of any person to become the candidate of more than one political party for the same office. . . .

The provision was so obscure that, even after it sailed routinely through enactment, its import was not recognized even by the closest observer of the legislature, journalist Franklin Hichborn, who did not mention it in his exhaustive chronicle of the 1913 session.

But the provision was the seed of primary "cross-filing," the curious device that threw California party-line politics into such a turmoil for nearly half a century that even since repeal of the provision in 1959 its miasma of confusion has lingered.

"Cross-filing" meant simply that an aspirant for office could compete for nomination in the primary elections of as many parties as he wanted at the same time, as long as he complied with filing formalities. No indication of his actual party affiliation would appear on any party's ballot. Thus if John Devlin, Democrat, chose to run also in the Republican primary, and if William Robinson, Republican, sought the Democratic nomination as well as his own party's nomination, the two parties' ballots might have looked like this:

Democratic	*Republican*
John Devlin	George Adams
Frank Smith	John Devlin
William Robinson	William Robinson
Henry Wilson	Philip Young

A Democratic voter who had not studied up on the candidates had no way of knowing that Robinson was not really a Democrat; nor did a Republican voter have any help in identifying Devlin as a cross-filed Democrat.

If a candidate won the nominations of both major parties, it was usually tantamount to election, and the November general election was a formality.

The purpose of the cryptic cross-filing provision emerged after the Progressives, who had been operating as a faction within the Republican party, formally withdrew in December, 1913, and set up as a third party, the California State Progressive party.

"The Progressives," Thomas H. Reed, a Johnson aide, explained many years later, "had taken a bold step in forming a new party. Its future was uncertain. Its strength was drawn chiefly from former adherents of the Republican party. How many more of them it could get, and whether it could hold those it had attracted, were very open questions.

"The best chance of electing Progressive candidates was to have them nominated by both the Republican and Progressive parties. Hence the legislation authorizing cross-filing. It was not adopted because of any deep-seated belief that cross-filing was theoretically an ideal system. It was purely a practical political expedient."

By registering as Progressives and cross-filing into the Republican party, relates Robert W. Kenny, former state attorney general and a notable student of California politics, the Johnsonites "won most of the seats in the primary election in 1913 and 1915 from stand-pat Republicans. But wherever the Progressive lost in the primary, he was still able to run again in November against the stand-pat Republican. This device assured Governor Johnson of Progressive majorities in the legislature."

The trouble was that long after the Progressives, succumbing to the usual fate of third parties, had drifted into limbo, cross-filing continued to undermine the normal operation of the two-party system in California. By the 1950's, more than 80 per cent of all candidates were running on both Democratic and Republican tickets.

Shortly before the abolition of cross-filing in 1959, Thomas Reed indicated why its debilitating effect on conventional party politics would persist long after cross-filing expired: "Cross-filing makes impossible strong, well-organized parties and consequently any effective party responsibility. Candidates perforce fight their own battles in the primaries. More significantly, they have to finance their individual campaigns. When they succeed in getting both Republican and Democratic nominations, as the great majority do, they need not campaign to secure election. They come into office without help or hindrance from the party. Under such circumstances, the parties do not mean much."

No wonder that Hiram Johnson, while he has come down in history as a dynamic leader, has never been accused of being a political philanthropist. He was busy building a political machine—not an organization actuated by spoils and reciprocal back-scratching but an apparatus sustained by a hand-tailored, complex structure of statutes. They were laws designed, one-time state Republican chairman Caspar Weinberger commented in 1966, "to ensure that the party can never prevent the candidate with the most popular appeal—or at least the candidate who can secure the most votes—from being the party's nominee."

Johnson won re-election easily in 1914, becoming the first governor in California history to win a second four-year term. By then the spasm of reform had run its course. Johnson even learned that the innovations he had sponsored could work against him.

In 1915, he proposed that the legislature be made nonpartisan. The legislature voted in favor of the idea. But citizen opponents of the change brought the legislature's action up for public review, and in a special election in October, 1915, the legislation was nullified.

The Southern Pacific Railroad had been expelled from California politics, root and branch. The Progressives figured in California politics for some years thereafter, but they had had their big moment. Johnson, perhaps the ultimate pragmatist, wasted no time on sentimental attachments but reset his sights on Washington.

The most remarkable thing about the Progressive reforms was that none of them was unique to California, except for the bizarre restructuring of parties. Variations of cross-filing—such as the "open primary," in which a member of any party can vote for any candidate—have been used in a number of other states, notably Maine, New Hampshire, Vermont, Massachusetts, and New York. The civil service merit system has become almost universal, and nonpartisanism in local government is common. The initiative is a fixture in a number of states, although nowhere else has it become such a factor in government and elections (See Chapter 10).

In California's extraordinary political milieu the Progressive innovations had an extraordinary effect: they interacted to form a whole much larger, and more complex, than its parts.

Chapter Six

The 1920's: Eye of the Hurricane

☒ MUCH OF THE IMPACT OF JOHN STEINBECK'S classic, *The Grapes of Wrath,* comes from the fact that the vicissitudes of his beleaguered Okie families in California's San Joaquin Valley seem to take place in a nightmarish political vacuum—in a corner of the country which the wand of some perverse sorcerer has disjointed from the protective structure of public order and equity that characterizes the United States.

This was indeed the case. California was passing through the central eye of a political hurricane—a vacuous era of drift, between turbulence of the past and turbulence to come. The Okies were distinctive in their misery. But everyone, in one way or another, was disoriented.

Hiram Johnson had slain the dragon of corruption. But its corpus, the Old Politics that had sustained the evil, continued to thrash convulsively for a generation thereafter.

The half-century since Hiram Johnson has comprised two highly contrasting eras.

The first was a turgid epoch in which both parties, striving to revert to old patterns of operation, wrestled against the bonds the Progressive reforms had imposed on them. The Republicans had their try over a span of two decades. Then the Democrats, revivified by the ideological plasma of the New Deal, after 40 years on the sidelines had a fleeting four-year fling.

All the strugglings on both sides proved to be the death throes of the Old Politics. In 1942 Earl Warren, amid the dislocations of World War II and a population influx that magnified the Protean impermanence of California's body politic, commenced so vigorous a revival and elaboration of Johnsonian nonpartisanism that 20 years later its hold on the California political psyche seemed unshaken.

A politician familiar with show business looked at the retreating bulk of the Washington-bound Hiram Johnson and murmured: "An impossible act to follow—"

Johnson had made a spectacular exit. 1916 was the year the national Republican party, seeking to dislodge Woodrow Wilson, invoked the prestige of a United States Supreme Court Justice, Charles Evans Hughes, in a vain effort to turn back the clock to the comfortable days of national isolation. California's bedraggled old-guard Republicans, pushing Hughes ahead of them like a hostage, had tried to scuttle Johnson's Progressive campaign for the Senate in 1916 by slighting him.

His triumphant thwarting of their design hinged on more than the snub at the Long Beach hotel which has become a political legend (See Chapter 1). The California old guard had mishandled the Hughes campaign in other ways. One was in alienating union labor, which has claimed credit for Hughes' loss of California.

Jack Weinberger, international secretary-treasurer of the Hotel and Restaurant Employees and Bartenders Union, related 40 years later:

> Hughes' California managers misjudged the temper of San Francisco workers so far as to permit their man to cross a picket line of waiters and cooks. It was that straw that broke the elephant's back, and I was among those pickets.
>
> The summer of 1916 found San Francisco labor in ferment. . . . The dockers were out, and the culinary unions were approaching the climax of a bitter strike against the open-shop policies of restaurant employers. It became known that Hughes was to speak Oct. 16 to the Chamber of Commerce in the Commercial Club, where a large sign proclaiming "Open Shop" hung in defiance of the warring waiters.
>
> The late Hugo Ernst, then president of Waiters' Local 30, tried in vain to persuade Hughes' local backers to have their luncheon in a less controversial dining room. The Central Labor Union authorized a picket line at the club. When Hughes arrived he was confronted by a grim-faced group of waiters, cooks and dishwashers moving slowly past the door. He went through that line and made his speech.
>
> The incident so incensed San Francisco's union-minded workingmen that they toiled as never before to get out the vote that fall, urging those who responded to their call to vote for Wilson. Wilson carried California by 3,773—but San Francisco County gave him 15,132.

While Hughes was losing California by 3,773 votes, Johnson, on the same ticket, won, by nearly 300,000 votes, the Senate seat he was to occupy for the rest of his life.

The Old Guard Again

The period following Hiram Johnson's departure from the governorship has been characterized by some historians as a time when the spirit of Progressivism evaporated. It was a period of superficial reversion to old-style partisan politics. Five Republican governors in succession were elected, and they were followed by the turbulent regime of Culbert Olson, the first Democratic governor since James Budd (1895–99).

Except for the absence of Southern Pacific skulduggery, these administrations superficially resembled those of the pre-Johnson era. "In every session of the state legislature from 1916 on," says historian George Mowry, "the influence of the state's great corporations seemed to grow. . . . [In 1921] after defeating many Progressive legislators . . . their representatives descended on Sacramento in force at the opening of the legislature. One veteran reporter observed: 'It looks like the old times around the corridors and hotel lobbies. . . . The old guard has come out of its hole at last.' "

Many people, mistakenly associating the vitality of the Johnson reforms with his personal leadership, expected to see them vitiated once he had gone. Even Lincoln Steffens, the reformer-journalist, remarked pessimistically: "Hiram Johnson put the railroad out of power for a while. He gave one of the most efficient administrations any state ever had. . . . But there was no fundamental reform in the city or the state."

Time proved Steffens wrong. There never was a revival of the old corruption.

But even Johnson cooled on Progressivism as soon as he got elected to the Senate in 1916. In Congress he became known as one of its reactionary isolationist leaders. By the 1920's his regular re-elections to the Senate were being opposed by some of his old Progressive colleagues.

"Some time in the future, Johnson thought, another generation with less fear and more fervor would upset conservative control," comments Mowry. "But for his age, Johnson was sure that progressivism was through and that reform had ended."

But subsequent events imposed some qualifications on the assessment of the 1916–38 period as retrogressive. For one thing, it could not be expected that the reform crusade of the century's early years could sustain momentum indefinitely. Reform by definition is an exceptional phenomenon, and an eventual return to normalcy is implicit in it. The reformers had accomplished their major goals quickly. Their radical innovations survived unimpaired; the weapons of the initiative, referendum, and recall remained in the hands of the people, ready to be used when necessary.

The Progressive spirit endured in the legislature. Joseph Beek, the long-time state senate secretary, has observed: "Partisan affiliation played a small part in the organization and conduct of the California legislature from the session of 1913 to the session of 1935. The majority of both houses from 1913 to 1937 had been Republican or Progressive. The Progressives may be said to have been the dominating influence in the legislature from 1913 to 1931."

Johnson didn't relinquish the governorship until March, 1917, when President Wilson convoked the session of Congress that declared the United States' entry into World War I. Then he turned over the reins to Lieutenant Governor William D. Stephens, a Progressive who had been mayor of Los Angeles and had served three terms in Congress.

Amid the tensions of wartime, California experienced another crescendo of friction between organized labor and employers. The atmosphere was such that the still-mysterious bombing of San Francisco's 1916 Preparedness Day parade, with ten deaths and 40 people injured, resulted almost automatically in the historic arrest and murder conviction of two labor militants, Tom Mooney and Warren Billings—although their implication in the crime has been a matter of mounting doubt ever since.

Stephens had been in office only a few months when a bomb damaged one side of the governor's mansion. This outrage was blamed on the left-wing International Workers of the World, and 55 of its members were arrested. Nevertheless, the following year Governor Stephens granted a reprieve to Tom Mooney just before he was to be executed, and he later commuted his sentence to life imprisonment. Mooney's incarceration at San Quentin prison became a public issue that recurrently punctuated politics over the next 20 years.

"Omnipartisanism"

Primary cross-filing, which had poked its nose into the California political tent so inconspicuously in 1913, now proved to be a camel of monstrous proportions.

The Progressives had lost no time in exploiting it. In 1914, political scientist James Findley recounts, while Johnson himself ran only as a Progressive, all the other Progressive aspirants for the principal state offices competed simultaneously in the Republican primary.

This precipitated a legal showdown. Winners of dual nominations seemed entitled, under the letter of the new laws, to participate in more than one party convention. The shaken old-guard Republicans challenged the right of the interlopers to represent their party either in convention or on the November ballot. The Republican secretary of state ruled out the dual convention participation. But the state supreme court, in the big cross-filing test case, held that Ulysses S. Webb, the dual nomination winner for attorney general, was indeed the joint November candidate of both the Progressive and Republican parties.

The Sacramento *Bee* hailed this legal sanctification of nonpartisanism. It said: "Freedom from narrow, unreasoning party ties is a necessity of good government. The names of national political organizations mean nothing in state politics, nor does the election of a man tagged with such an emblem insure a good choice."

Ironically, the Republicans, the vehement defenders of partisanism at this juncture, in later years when the tables were turned exploited the obfuscations of cross-filing to maintain their sway after they had become the minority party.

Ironically also, Johnson, vainly pressing for complete state nonpartisanism, deplored the interparty rat-race that his own party-raiding device had precipitated. "The contests in this state have become not nonpartisan but omnipartisan," he complained. "Each year there is a scramble for all nominations by all candidates. We would alter this by having no scramble for any nomination, but a candidacy in the first instance before all the people."

Johnson's foes saw this as just another Johnson maneuver to cripple the old guard. "The present administration was elected on party lincs, the Progressive party," a spokesman said. "Why this sudden ambition to abandon their party fealty?"

A possible explanation lay in the fact that the Progressives had not caught on as a new national institution, as Johnson hoped when he joined Theodore Roosevelt on the "Bull Moose" Progressive ticket in 1912. By 1916, Roosevelt, as much of a pragmatist as Johnson, threw in his hand and supported Charles Evans Hughes, the old-line Republican choice for President, leaving Johnson on a Progressive limb in California—a limb fortuitously made strong by the Republicans' egregious campaign gaffes.

The election of 1916 brought an orgy of cross-filing. Five parties participated in the primary—Republican, Progressive, Democratic, Prohibition, and Socialist. The official roster of the resulting legislature lists a dozen different combinations of multinomination winners. In the following state senate membership permutations, the first party mentioned is the candidate's real affiliation:

Eight Republicans; six Democrats; four Republican-Democrats; three Republican-Progressives; three Progressive-Republicans; two Republican-Progressive-Democrats; three Progressive-Democrats; two Democrat-Socialist-Prohibitionists; two Democrat-Progressive-Socialists; one Republican-Democrat-Progressive-Prohibitionist; one Republican-Prohibitionist; one Progressive-Republican-Democrat-Prohibitionist; one Democrat-Republican-Prohibitionist; one Progressive; one Republican-Democrat-Progressive; and one Independent.

In the 1918 election, the cross-filing morris dance produced an unexpected tangle.

Stephens, running for election to a full term as governor, entered the Progressive, Republican, and Prohibition primaries. San Francisco's Mayor "Sunny Jim" Rolph, a Republican, entered the Republican, Democratic, and Prohibition primaries. The regular Democratic candidate was Francis J. Heney, the lawyer who had been shot during the San Francisco graft trials. He also entered the Prohibition party primary.

The chief feature of cross-filing that prevented it from being in effect a free-for-all open primary was the provision that if a man did not win the nomination of his own party he could not be the nominee of any other party whose primary he entered. This rule proved pivotal in 1918.

Stephens, along with sweeping the Progressive primary, beat Rolph for the Republican nomination. But Rolph beat Heney for the Democratic nomination. Rolph, however, could not legally have the Democratic nomination because he had failed to win his own party's nomination. This left the Democrats without a nominee, posing a problem that went to the state supreme court. The court ruled that the Democrats were just out of luck—that they couldn't field a candidate in the November election. All the Democrats could do was get behind the candidacy of Theodore Bell, Johnson's old opponent, who ran in November as an Independent. Stephens beat him easily.

Neanderthalism

By 1920, the organized Progressives were no longer numerous enough to qualify as a legally recognized party with their own primary ballot. After dominating three elections they had merged back as a faction of the Republican party. (They had a minor renaissance, in name but not in the same crusading spirit, from 1934 through 1942.)

It was 1922, 12 years after Hiram Johnson had made his explosive entrance into California politics, before the old-guard Republicans pulled themselves together sufficiently to recapture the governorship with one of their own kind, Friend W. Richardson. Richardson's election, according to the political analyst Richard Hyer, was engineered by Kyle Palmer, political editor of the Los Angeles *Times,* who rallied the San Francisco *Chronicle* and the Oakland *Tribune* into a journalistic triumvirate that was a big influence in Republican politics for a generation thereafter.

Newspapers in those pre-radio, pre-television days were the public's chief sources of political information. Most California newspapers were strongly oriented to the Republican establishment. With a number of them, that meant simply ignoring Democratic political activities. During a campaign, a reader might have difficulty discovering who some of the Democratic candidates were.

Richardson, on taking office in 1923, undertook to proclaim, almost formally, the demise of the Progressive movement. A dour, walrus-moustached Berkeley newspaper publisher, he had once been a Progressive, appointed by Hiram Johnson to the office of state printer. But in later years he had turned into a hard-bitten reactionary with almost a phobia about public expenditure.

In his inaugural address in 1923, he turned on the Stephens administration and declared: ". . . The people by their vote . . .

indicated that they want to stop the orgy of extravagance which has prevailed during the past few years, and that they want to put out of power the political machine which has dominated the state government." He went on, in his budget message, to assert: ". . . extravagance in educational matters has run riot during the past few years," and he urged that two state colleges, California Polytechnic and Humboldt Teachers, be closed. (They weren't closed, and they grew to become important elements of the state's education system.)

Richardson's Neanderthalism, in a conventional American two-party contest, would probably have precipitated a Democratic rebellion. But the Progressive movement had absorbed much of the electoral sentiment that normally would have been Democratic. The Progressives and the old-guard Republicans, lumped together as Republicans from 1920 on, outnumbered Democrats for a decade by as much as five to one. In 1924, at the nadir of a 40-year decline in Democratic strength, the party had only seven of the 120 seats in the legislature.

"There *were* no Democratic politics to speak of in California throughout the 1920's," recalls Robert Kenny. "Republican nomination was tantamount to election."

Governor Richardson's arch-conservatism inspired a revival of militant Progressivism in a movement called the Progressive Voters League. The old guard's hold proved impermanent.

A founder of the League was Clement Calhoun Young, the one-time San Francisco high school teacher who had prospered in real estate and insurance and had been speaker of the assembly under Johnson. In 1926, with the Progressives once again a faction within the Republican party, Young challenged Governor Richardson for the Republican nomination for the next gubernatorial term. The contest threatened to be such a close one that Senator Johnson himself interrupted a trip to Europe to come back and campaign for Young.

Many interests had become irked at Richardson, but none

more than the San-Francisco-based Bank of America, which A. P. Giannini was busy expanding into the biggest chain-banking operation in the country. Richardson's long leadership of the California Press Association, a publishers' organization, had brought him close to the business interests of California's multitude of small communities—including the many locally owned banks that didn't want the Bank of America establishing branches in competition with them. The governor accordingly had been conspicuously obstructive in regard to the Bank of America's applications to the state for new-branch permits.

The bank was too discreet to plunge into a public campaign against Richardson. Giannini, according to his biographer, Julian Dana, simply passed the word to stockholders, who "went out independently, called on the public, turned the tide."

Their missionary work may well have been decisive. Young defeated Richardson by the narrow margin of 327,000 to 311,000. He beat the Democrats' nominee, J. C. Wardell, by 814,000 to 282,451.

An interesting feature of the election, in the light of later events, was one of the also-rans—a radical novelist, not too long transplanted from the East, who got 45,972 votes for governor on the Socialist ticket. His name was Upton Sinclair.

The Crash

The years from 1916 almost to 1930 were a time of international preoccupations and domestic euphoria for the nation as a whole, and California politics ambled along in relative tranquility.

World War I was followed by the election of Warren G. Harding, one of the more two-dimensional Presidents in the nation's history; and then Calvin Coolidge, whose lack of color matched Harding's lack of depth.

The nation rode a mounting wave of postwar prosperity.

For California, this was the era of another Great Migration, from the Middle West. Between 1916 and 1930 the state's population nearly doubled, from 3,000,000 to 5,500,000. A great many of the newcomers were farmers from Iowa and environs who for years had been reading glowing accounts of California as an agricultural paradise, where you could sit in the sun, in retirement or half-retirement, counting the dollars that poured in from your automatically growing orange groves, and from rising land values. They founded dozens of southern California communities, or gravitated to ones that predecessors of their own kind had founded—on the outskirts of Los Angeles and in adjacent Orange, Riverside, and San Diego counties—tincturing the region with a strain of conservatism so iron-jawed and doctrinaire that it was still exerting a strong political influence 40 years later.

Midway through Governor Young's term, the nation's decade of postwar prosperity ended with a crash: the stock market crash of October, 1929.

The economy had been on a tremendous inflationary upswing. Everyone down to shoeshine boys had visions of getting rich by riding the soaring stock market. It turned out that the speculators had been engaged in reciprocal levitation. A sudden wave of doubts about the future of the nation's economy wiped out billions of dollars of paper profits in securities. Bankers and brokers jumped out of windows or turned to peddling apples on the sidewalk. The wheels of the nation's economy, which had been humming happily, slowed down to a dreadful groan. "Retrenchment" became the watchword. Businesses cut back activity and laid off workers; unemployment and lack of purchasing power rounded out a vicious circle.

In California, as in other parts of the country, this was regarded at first as a temporary economic setback. It was not seen as the beginning of nearly a decade of dire economic distress, which in some ways had greater impact on California than on other places.

Governor Young, a thoughtful and orderly man, saw the economic plunge as something that could be countered with a mildly augmented public works program to absorb the unemployed. Californians generally were so unconcerned that, nearly a year after the crash, they had no qualms about replacing Young with another Republican known mainly for his bonhommie, James ("Sunny Jim") Rolph, Jr.

Rolph beat the Democratic nominee, Milton K. Young, a Los Angeles lawyer, by 990,000 votes to 333,000. Upton Sinclair, again the Socialist candidate, increased his vote by nearly 10 per cent, to 50,480.

Up to then, California's post-Johnson politics had been prosaic. It was under the Rolph administration that California began projecting to the nation its image of eccentricity. Rolph had had a substantial career as a San Francisco shipping entrepreneur, banker, and mayor for the previous 19 years. It may have been the desperation of the times that impelled him, as governor, often to play the clown.

A short, rotund man, Rolph habitually affected Texas-style cowboy boots, and he was given to other sartorial vagaries, such as popping up at a winter carnival garishly garbed as "King Snow." Not too well known outside the San Francisco area when he plunged into the round of Republican musical chairs that unseated Governor Young, he made political history by campaigning over 28,000 miles in a chartered airplane, exotic transportation then. He wasn't above deliberately splitting the seat of his pants, during a hinterland milking act, to heighten the act's photographic value. "Jim knew that in small towns the local barber was often the expert on how the political winds were blowing," a friend recalled. "When he was campaigning, he'd get shaved three or four times a day."

During this period President Herbert Hoover was optimistically reassuring the country: "Prosperity is just around the corner." But nine days after Rolph took office, in January, 1931, the Richfield Oil Company, one of the state's largest, went into receivership. This was followed by a succession of collapses of investment and mortgage companies in which thousands of citizens lost millions.

Rolph was not insensitive to the public's economic straits. "The poor, the stricken, and the unfortunate shall have a first claim on the consideration of my administration," he said in his inaugural address. He established a series of labor camps for unemployed men that anticipated the Federal Civilian Conservation Corps.

But he aroused skepticism about his responsibility by performing such didoes as planting a huge floral greeting on the capitol lawn for a governors' conference; sending a case of whiskey to a condemned man in San Quentin prison; and, in August, 1931, suggesting that a good way to overcome the economic blues would be for everyone just to take a couple of weeks' vacation.

Rolph gained national notoriety for his cavalier attitude about the lynching in November, 1933, by a mob of 10,000 citizens of San Jose, of two men jailed as the accused kidnap-murderers of Brooke Hart, son of a wealthy merchant. The mob battled authorities for several hours before dragging the defendants from their cells and hanging them in a nearby park. Rolph was criticized for not sending in militia to stop the outlawry. His explanation reverberated all over the country:

"Why should I call out the troops to protect those two fellows? The people make the laws, don't they? Well, if the people have confidence that troops will not be called out to mow them down when they seek to protect themselves against kidnappers, there is liable to be swifter justice and fewer kidnappings."

This irked Californians less, however, than Rolph's growing reputation for putting friends on state payrolls and his failure to produce remedies for the state's fiscal situation, which was deteriorating rapidly in the Depression. His Republican party began losing followers at an amazing rate.

The Democrats' share of the two-party registration jumped from 21.8 per cent in 1930 to 42.6 per cent in 1932. California exceeded the nation in its enthusiasm for Franklin D. Roosevelt, giving him 58.4 per cent of its total vote, compared with the national ratio of 57.4.

When Roosevelt took office in March, 1933, and declared a two-day bank holiday to avert disastrous cash drains, Rolph extended the suspension in California for an additional nine days. The California State Grange, representing farmers hard hit by economic conditions, started a campaign to recall Rolph as incompetent, then was persuaded to drop it. But the state senate began a formal investigation of his administration.

Rolph had already had one severe illness, and in February, 1934, as he was starting a fence-mending tour aimed at the November election, he collapsed in Marysville. He was an invalid until his death from heart trouble five months later.

Rolph's administration is usually remembered, if at all, simply as a baroque interlude in California's political cavalcade. Actually, it had two major points of significance. It was trenchant evidence of the impending bankruptcy of the traditional style of complacent Republican politics in a state needing dynamic, imaginative leadership. And it set the stage for one of the wildest political campaigns that ever unfolded in the United States.

Chapter
Seven

Utopia Limited: The Sinclair Uprising

☒ "WHO ARE YOU VOTING FOR?"

"Vy, I'm foting for Seenclair."

"Why are you voting for Mr. Sinclair?"

"Vell, his system vorked vell in Russia—vy can't it vork here?"

The accented speaker was a bearded, disheveled Hollywood actor. The scene was a fictitious filmed interview as a fictitious trainload of indigents supposedly swarmed into California.

But it was presented to California voters on the screen as the real thing.

The artifices of Hollywood had been enlisted in a great statewide struggle to forfend what was considered a political fate-worse-than-death: a vote in November in favor of the utopian conceits of a benign little vegetarian novelist. This was California politics' most frenetic hour.

Shallow-rooted politics are susceptible to extremes. An unusual problem arises, and people's instinct, instead of turning to established structures for a solution, is to unfurl a new, special-purpose banner. In other words, pragmatism.

A full year before "Sunny Jim" Rolph died in June, 1934, California had begun to feel the full impact of the Depression. This was before the welfare state; the grim "poorhouse" was a national fixture. But there weren't enough poorhouses for one per cent of the people in distress. Tens of thousands were on relief, and the welfare rolls were mounting steadily. A major element of the state's economy was agricultural shipments to the East, which now lacked the money to buy. So did the people in California. Crops rotted in fields for lack of a market.

The spectacle of want in the midst of plenty struck a particularly responsive chord with Upton Sinclair, the idealistic novelist who had moved to California from the East in 1915.

The name Upton Sinclair sounds almost ominously imposing, and Sinclair has sometimes been represented as an ogre, bent on bomb-tossing. Actually he was a slight, bespectacled, wispy man of exceptional gentleness and good will—a man who, but for an extraordinarily active mind and a gift for commercially lucrative writing, might have been just another of the obscure people who frequent health-food stores. But Sinclair, then in his early fifties, already enjoyed international renown as a social reformer and author, through his books—such as *The Jungle* (1906), *King Coal* (1917), and *The Brass Check* (1919)—pillorying corruption in fields ranging from meat-packing to journalism. He was a Socialist who had been crusading against the inequitable distribution of the earth's goods even during good times. For years, like Norman Thomas, he had gone through the motions of running for office, as a gesture to keep the flag of Socialist thought flying.

The course of events seemed now to present a laboratory case for application of Socialist preachments. "The proprietor of a small hotel down at the beach," Sinclair related, "asked me to come and meet some of his friends, and I went. His proposal was that I should resign from the Socialist party and join the Democratic party, and let them put me up as a candidate for governor. I didn't think I could possibly win."

"I felt utterly unqualified to be governor," Sinclair told the present writer in 1964. "I didn't go into the campaign to win. My main purpose was education and propaganda." Win or lose, Sinclair felt, if he drew a big vote it would "force the Roosevelt administration to take relief measures, and we would have made all America familiar with the idea of production for use."

On September 1, 1933, Sinclair went from his comfortable Beverly Hills bungalow down to the city hall and changed his party registration. Early in 1934, he announced his candidacy for the Democratic nomination for governor, and detailed his "End Poverty In California" plan in a tract, "I, Governor of California, And How I Ended Poverty."

Sinclair's program first amused, then terrified, those who felt that California could and should ride out the Depression without impairment of the free-enterprise system. His theme was "Production for Use," as opposed to production for profit. He envisioned impoverished masses from the cities being resettled in rural "land colonies," where they would live communally and raise a plentitude of food for everybody. Other unemployed would be put to work manning Depression-idled factories and new factories to be set up by the state, producing goods for the entire population. Workers not in communal colonies would be paid in scrip exchangeable for goods and services. There would also be a barter system. Homes and farms that had been lost through foreclosures would be restored to their original owners through state aid. Sinclair promised "plenty and comfort" for everybody. The program called for state support of all those unable to work. The aged, widows, and the physically incapacitated would get pensions of $50 a month (later developments showed this feature of the plan to be modern in concept).

The incalculable costs of this transformation would be paid by the state, through radical changes in the tax structure. The sales tax would be abolished, a state income tax introduced, and inheritance taxes greatly increased. Unused land would be taxed at the inordinate rate of 10 per cent. Under an adaptation of Henry George's single-tax theory (aimed at land), new taxes would be imposed on "all sources of natural wealth."

Any fiscal deficiency from all these sources, Sinclair projected optimistically, could be met by state sale of bonds, both in California and to helpful souls elsewhere.

There was no way, of course, that anyone could estimate how much Sinclair's plan would cost. It called for an economic revolution.

As economically radical as the program was, it did not ring as so alien to a populace which, in its economic plight, was spontaneously organizing hundreds of "self-help" cooperatives for the cashless exchange of necessities. People's desperation was such that, among a flurry of other economic nostrums, a weird movement called the Utopian Society quickly attracted 500,000 followers. It lacked any well-defined economic philosophy, but it had a spectacular chain-letter recruiting system and diverting mystic rituals. Its first public meeting, at the Hollywood Bowl in June, 1934, drew 25,000 people.

Sinclair began an energetic campaign, stumping the state in a rickety automobile, organizing Sinclair clubs—eventually there were 800 of them—and selling copies of his pamphlet by the thousands.

"I was astonished by the tidal wave that came roaring in and gathered me up," he said later.

"So swiftly had the Depression engulfed thousands upon thousands of middle-class elements in California," comments historian Carey McWilliams, "that people thought nothing of enlisting in the campaign of an internationally famous Socialist, selling his pamphlets and books, and preaching the doctrines of 'production for use.' "

The curious attachment of a pension plan to a utopian program that was supposed to solve all of society's economic difficulties—including, presumably, the need for pensions— had particular significance. Several hundred thousand Californians were retired people with "fixed" incomes from investments that now had no prospect of yielding income. Some long-range remedy besides welfare was wanted, and talk of respectable public "pensions" was in the air.

It was right at this time that a retired physician from South Dakota, Dr. Francis Townsend, coached by a Long Beach real estate promoter named Earl Clements, was dressing up someone else's printing-press-money idea as Old Age Revolving Pensions, Limited. The plan called for a Federal sales tax of 2 per cent on all business, which would finance $200-a-month pensions to all persons over 60. It would be paid in scrip which had to be spent within a month—thereby, it was hoped, boosting business volume to offset the tax. It had a certain plausibility, and the transcendent virtue that, pending trial, its infeasibility couldn't be demonstrated. The Townsend plan never was adopted. But what the lanky, solemn doctor had started would reverberate through California politics for decades afterward.

"Hail to Thee, Our Soviet"

The public response to Sinclair's campaign panicked California's economic "establishment." From bankers to movie producers, businessmen were appalled at the economic implications of the EPIC program.

"His election would mean a threat to private industry, small or large—a menace to every investor, be his investment only a few cents on an insurance policy. It means chaos to California," intoned one of the energetic Republican campaigners against Sinclair—the district attorney of Alameda county, Earl Warren.

In a conventional political context, such a radical movement might have gotten nowhere, even with wide popular support, because it would have conflicted with the vested interests of the established party organization. But Johnsonian "nonpartisanism" had left party structures too uncoordinated to cope effectively with such an incursion.

The consternation resulted partly from the shaky position of the Republicans. In the wake of California's 1932 vote for Roosevelt, the Democrats were about to become the majority party in registration. The understudy who had taken over on Rolph's death in June, 1934, Lieutenant Governor Frank Merriam, was a lackluster old-guard Republican. He had angered organized labor and liberals by calling out the militia to quell a San Francisco general strike involving more than 100,000 workers, after two months of disorders. The Republicans were thrown into disarray by the Progressive candidacy of Raymond L. Haight, grandson of California's tenth governor.

Organization Democrats were likewise distressed about Sinclair erupting in their midst. At that point one thing Roosevelt's New Deal didn't need was additional identification with radicalism. Regular Democrats got behind journalist George Creel, who had been Wilson's World War I propaganda chief and had become Roosevelt's pipeline for Federal patronage in California.

The Democratic primary vote was split among no fewer than nine gubernatorial aspirants. Sinclair came out on top. He got 436,000 votes to the 288,000 of the runner-up, George Creel. Many other EPIC candidates won nomination as well: Sheridan Downey, Sacramento lawyer and candidate for lieutenant governor; 39 candidates for the 80-member state assembly; three candidates for the 40-member state senate.

Governor Merriam won the Republican nomination, but, cross-filed in the Democratic primary, ended up with a two-party vote that was an alarming 90,000 less than Sinclair's.

The Sinclairites seized control of the party machinery at the state convention a month later. The Democratic platform emerged as an only slightly watered-down version of the EPIC program. The state chairmanship went to the nominee for Los Angeles county's state senate seat, a Los Angeles lawyer named Culbert L. Olson.

Sinclair traveled to both Hyde Park, New York, and Washington, D.C., to enlist the support of President Roosevelt and other high administration officials, but he got only hollow encouragement.

The Democratic National Committee, bewildered for neither the first nor the last time by California politics, urged Californians to vote for Senator Hiram Johnson—the unopposed nominee of all three parties—"and the entire Democratic ticket."

Raymond Haight, the Progressive aspirant, tried to make a deal with the EPIC movement to carry its banner if Sinclair would withdraw as "unelectable." EPIC strategists declined, feeling Haight would help their cause more by attacking Merriam. If they had accepted, history might have been a lot different, for Haight might have won.

Haight meanwhile had shaken up the Republicans with a charge that Merriam had been given as much as $250,000 to suppress the San Francisco strike dramatically with troops, and he named an oil company and a bank as sources of a $30,000 deposit to Merriam's bank account. He also said he had been offered $100,000 and a sure U.S. Senate seat if he would withdraw.

Undoubtedly, memories of the "Johnson revolution" contributed to fears of what Sinclair might be able to do if he became governor. The beleaguered conservative establishment mounted one of the most vitriolic and massive campaigns in the nation's political history.

The motion picture industry was reported to have pressured its higher-salaried employees into contributing a day's pay to an anti-Sinclair fund that totaled $500,000. But the studios' most spectacular contribution was the production, and exhibition to captive theater audiences, of a series of purported "newsreels" of trainloads of advancing indigents and Bolsheviks.

The newspapers played up adverse news from Russia; one "exposé" reported that starving Russians had resorted to cannibalism. A fiction serial entitled *Thunder Over California* limned a picture of oppression under a Sinclair administration in terms similar to those used later about the Nazis. One installment included a photograph of a tramp-laden boxcar, labeled California Special, with the verse:

> California, here we come!
> Every beggar, every bum
> We'll soon be with you, you can bet
> When your Sinclair plan is set.
> Hail to thee, our Soviet!
> California, here we come!

The Sinclair opposition, recounted Charles Van Devander, "plastered every billboard in the state with anti-EPIC posters and slogans. They used payroll slips, form letters, and paid as well for plenty of newspaper space to convince employes that quick and inevitable personal and individual disaster would follow if Sinclair were elected. Industries, singly and in groups, threatened to close up or move out of the state. Teachers and other public employes were warned of payless pay days under government by the impractical Sinclair and his horde of crackpot supporters."

An eleventh-hour maneuver of the anti-Sinclair forces was to try to disqualify 24,000 Democratic voters through a farfetched civil court action in which the voters' names were published in a legal newspaper of less than 2,000 circulation, along with an allegation of invalid registration. The state supreme court summarily quashed this as a "sham proceeding and a perversion of court process."

In an ultimate measure of desperation, Governor Merriam

endorsed the Townsend Plan, a move that under ordinary circumstances would have been grounds for excommunication from his own Republican party.

Estimates of the amount spent to defeat Sinclair ran as high as $10 million—about twice as much as has been spent on any other California gubernatorial campaign, to this day.

"On election day," Van Devander said, "the banks, insurance companies and other public institutions closed their doors and sent their frightened employes out to vote against Sinclair."

Sinclair was beaten—but not by much. He got 879,537 votes, to Merriam's 1,138,620. Haight, the Progressive, got 302,519 votes. The election figures showed that Haight's votes came largely from the Democrats: ironically, the name Progressive had served to defeat California's most "progressive" gubernatorial candidate.

With Sinclair's defeat, the EPIC movement—even though he boasted, "We are the Democratic Party of California and we are going to stay that"—disintegrated almost as rapidly as it had formed.

But the Sinclair effort was far from fruitless. The Democrats moved close to a majority in the state assembly, increasing their representation in the 80-seat chamber from 25 to 37; their minuscule share of the 40-seat senate rose from 5 to 8. By election day, the Democrats had achieved the registration advantage they have held ever since, shading the Republicans by 1,555,705 to 1,430,198. Sheridan Downey, Sinclair's running mate, even in defeat gained the impetus to beat Senator William Gibbs McAdoo, chieftain of the "regular" Democrats, four years later. And the campaign made Culbert Olson, the Sinclair-faction party chairman, gubernatorial timber.

Perhaps most important of all, the Sinclair defeat dramatized to the Alameda county district attorney, Earl Warren, the effectiveness of a bipartisan vote.

Frank Merriam has been described as "the last of the

nineteenth-century governors." He had been Iowa's state auditor before coming to California and serving in the legislature. Despite his extensive political experience, however, he now began his gubernatorial term with the stigma of having been to many voters the lesser of two evils. Depression problems piled up during his regime, and whereas he was attentive to many phases of state government he failed conspicuously to manifest the dramatic leadership the times called for.

He vexed conservatives by his endorsement of the Townsend Plan, liberals by his opposition to a public-power-distribution plan, and citizens in general by an array of new taxes he initiated to try to balance the state's Depression-drained budget.

This was the era of the "Grapes of Wrath." In 1936 alone, nearly 100,000 Dust Bowl Okies streamed into California, aggravating poverty in the distressed farming areas. When some 3,000 lettuce pickers staged a strike at Salinas, Merriam sent in 150 officers of the state highway patrol with clubs and tear gas to break up their demonstrations. Newspapers were full of grim stories of "Cossack" police methods employed against the strike, and the governor was charged with illegal use of the highway patrol.

Merriam's ultimate strategic error was in fostering an investigation of legislative lobbying. This caused the leading lobbyist, Arthur Samish (later publicized as "the secret boss of California"), when the 1938 election approached, to throw his substantial weight against Merriam's bid for renomination, and support George Hatfield.

The Republicans split, seemingly unaware that in their new status of a minority party this was a luxury that could no longer be indulged. It was the first instance in recent times of what has become an axiom of California politics: the party with a primary fight is almost certain to lose the general election.

For six years, since the 1932 election of Franklin Roosevelt, California had been outside the national mainstream in its internal Republican orientation. Now the time for a change had come.

1/12 Dozen Governors

Although Upton Sinclair had long since gone back to his books, the winds of economic radicalism were still buffeting the California landscape.

Dr. Townsend's pension movement had reached its peak in 1936, when it was reported to have taken in nearly $1 million in dues and contributions, in addition to $2,000 a week reportedly yielded by the *Townsend Weekly,* which had a circulation of 150,000. But as the movement lost ground, a tub-thumping Los Angeles radio commentator, Robert Noble, began talking up a new "$25 every Monday" pension plan. Two Hollywood advertising men, Lawrence and Willis Allen, moved in on Noble's scheme, changed the war cry to the more euphonious "Thirty Dollars Every Thursday," and gave the program the catchy all-American name of "Ham and Eggs."

California was now spending about $5 million a month on pensions of $35 a month to the needy over 65. The Ham and Eggs promoters proposed to extend the beneficence to all unemployed persons over 50. To finance such an outlay—which, it was estimated, would cost $30 million a week—they concocted an economist's nightmare. It involved $1 "warrant certificates" on which a 2-cent tax stamp had to be affixed every week; a $20 million bond issue to establish a state "warrant bank"; the issuance of $52 million in stock to be sold to the public; and a 3 per cent income tax.

By the eve of the 1938 election, Carey McWilliams recounts, the Ham and Eggs movement had 200,000 enrolled followers yielding $2,000 a day in contributions. Momentum was sustained by a corps of 100,000 volunteers, tightly organized into precinct captains, telephone canvassers, petitions circulators, and other functionaries.

"So effectively had the Allens attended to the organizational details," writes McWilliams, "that by simply sending out a call for letters, they could inundate any state official with from 25,000 to 30,000 letters in 48 hours."

When the Allens circulated initiative petitions to get the Ham and Eggs proposal on the 1938 election ballot, their forces quickly corralled 789,000 signatures—25 per cent of the electorate.

"As soon as the politicians were informed of the number of signatures," McWilliams says, "they all began to shout 'Ham and Eggs' in a deafening chorus."

As the 1938 campaign commenced, the Democrats seemed to have everything in their favor. After 40 years' exclusion from the state administration, except for a minority of legislative seats (the last Democratic governor had been James Budd, 1895–99), the Democrats had a rapidly mounting electoral majority. In only six years, between 1930 and 1936, the Democrats had increased their numbers fourfold, from 456,000 to 1,882,000, and their share of the two-party vote from one out of five voters to three out of five. By 1938 the Democratic proportion was 62.4 per cent and it seemed high time that the national wave of sentiment for Roosevelt's New Deal caught up with California, or vice versa.

In contrast to Merriam's doleful personification of obsolete Republicanism, the Democrats had a fine figure of a gubernatorial candidate. Olson was tall and distinguished-looking, with an air of forthright, understanding diligence. "If you'd called Central Casting for one-twelfth dozen governors," a Hollywood friend remarked later, "Culbert Olson is what they'd have sent you."

Olson had some 30 years' experience in politics: in the legislature of Utah, his birthplace; as an anti-Merriam leader in the California legislature; as an adversary of the powerful oil companies; and, finally, as party chairman in the Sinclair crusade.

He won handily over Merriam, after the Merriam-Hatfield primary fight. The legislature remained split, with a Democratic majority, achieved two years before, in the state assembly, but with Republicans in command of the senate. The only major Republican winner in the election was the candidate for attorney general: Earl Warren.

The 1938 voting indicated the impact of constant immigration on politics. Merriam got a bigger vote in losing to Olson than he received in 1934 in defeating Sinclair. His total in 1934 was 1,138,620; in 1938 it was 1,171,019.

Olson was scornful of Hiram Johnson as a bogus progressive. He said Johnson "hadn't a progressive hair on his head." Olson aspired to surpass him with a latter-day reform program. He wanted to attack the lobbies, promote public power, curb the exploitation of oil resources, institute compulsory health insurance, establish a unicameral legislature.

But this was a different era from Johnson's. Olson lacked the impetus of nationwide and statewide pressures for reform, and a resultingly compliant legislature. He was a victim, says Robert Kenny, of "the belief that he, like Roosevelt, had a mandate to create a millennium in the biennium."

Lacking Hiram Johnson's instinctual understanding of California dynamics, he was unaware that the Progressive revolution had invalidated conventional party operation.

"He looked upon himself as the leader of a great Democratic party of the state, and upon the more than two million registered Democrats as his followers," writes Dr. Robert Burke, in one of the best studies that has ever been made of any California gubernatorial regime. "He considered his administration as a phase of Franklin D. Roosevelt's New Deal, and as such, virtually invincible."

One of Olson's first official acts was to free Tom Mooney, San Francisco's alleged Preparedness-Day-parade bomber, thereby ending a generation of agitation over Mooney's presumed innocence. This was one of Olson's few clear-cut, unobstructed accomplishments. After that, his administration became a doleful chronicle of frustrations and mistakes.

At the outset he was assailed by the Ham and Eggs people. Their initiative had been voted down, narrowly, in the election.

They wanted another shot. Olson was pressured into calling a special election for November, 1939. This time the goofy proposal was rejected decisively, by 1,933,557 to 993,204, not carrying a single county. Nevertheless, Olson's yielding to the Ham and Eggs fanatics irritated many people.

Olson tried to manage the legislature as Johnson had. He even had a "hot line" telephone to the assembly speaker's rostrum. But one after another of his proposals aroused legislative hostility. Finally there was a rebellion. A new speaker was installed—and the telephone was ceremonially yanked out.

By the 1940 election, California's Democrats were so riven that Roosevelt sent out Interior Secretary Harold Ickes to mediate. His failure was reflected in the appearance of no less than four competing Democratic slates in the Presidential primary.

Olson refused to face the fact that wholesale patronage was a thing of the past; he aroused widespread criticism by trying to load the payroll of the state relief administration. This agency was already in disfavor because it was overstaffed, was costing nearly a million dollars a day, and was being influenced by an avowed Communist. Finally the legislature simply balked at appropriating money for the agency; relief was left to the counties.

The approach of World War II brought the culmination of Olson's troubles. By then, everything he did automatically engendered obstructive controversy. Three recall movements were mounted. In the clamor there emerged one figure whose words resounded with dispassionate, persuasive leadership: Attorney General Earl Warren.

Chapter Eight

Warren: "A Democrat and Doesn't Know It...."

☒ EARL WARREN WILL GO DOWN IN HISTORY AS the Chief Justice of the United States who steered the Supreme Court onto an epochal course of liberalism in respect to racial equality, legislative apportionment, and the rights of accused persons.

But if the passage of years brings one of its frequent adjustments of historical perspective Warren will be noted also as the man who did perhaps as much as any other to shape the politics of California, in ways whose national impact may have yet to be fully felt.

Hiram Johnson, the vehement reformer, first raised aloft the banner of nonpartisanism as an answer to California's political waywardness. It remained for Warren, a generation later, to demonstrate the extent to which the preachment of nonpartisanism could be put into practice. In exploiting and cultivating California's tendencies toward "independent" voting, he gave nonpartisanism a new dimension, and he set a pattern to which succeeding eras of both politicians and voters were impelled to pay tacit if not explicit homage.

If the abandonment of partisan rigidity in voting habits eventually gains the national prevalence that recent trends presage, it will be another change in mores which to some extent can be appended to the roster of events that have already acquired the name of "the Warren revolution."

Earl Warren was governor of California longer than any other man in its history—ten years and eight months, starting in 1943—some four years longer than Hiram Johnson, the only other governor to win a second four-year term. Warren was the only governor ever elected to a third term. He was the only governor to be elected as the candidate of both major parties—a feat it has been impossible to duplicate since the abolition of primary cross-filing in 1959.

In other ways as well, Warren was a phenomenon. It was typical of the remarkable contradictions of his personality that, to begin with, he seemed the unlikeliest person to have anything to do with revolutionary works.

In the vernacular, Warren was square—a monolithic six-foot, 215-pound slice of wholesome-looking apple-pie Americanism right out of an idealized Norman Rockwell grocery-store-calendar painting. A friend once remarked that when Warren raised his hand to take the oath of allegiance, "you expected to see the little finger bend down under the thumb in the Boy Scout salute."

Warren revered Hiram Johnson; at one time, Johnson's portrait was the only picture on the wall of his Sacramento office. But where Johnson was a choleric, tub-thumping political evangelist, Warren resembled more the earnest, white-smocked automotive doctor the General Motors ads assure you will see that your carburetor is adjusted right.

There are indications that Warren not only read the Horatio Alger stories but took them as a sort of personal gospel. One of the reasons why he remained, for all his plainness and forthrightness, such an inscrutable and unpredictable figure is that down the years he fended off analysis by fostering a Horatio Alger biographical picture of himself so firmly stereotyped that journalists were lulled into not going behind it.

The Warren Legend includes a humble birth as the son of a struggling Los Angeles railroad mechanic; a boyhood of bicycle newspaper-delivering in Bakersfield (with wistful eyes on the county courthouse, the seat of Law); the rising young lawyer in Oakland, espying in a community swimming pool a young lady whose eyes alone (no crass anatomical allusions) projected the magnetic allure that could mean only matrimony; the crusading district attorney, curbing the misdeeds of a procession of thugs and ruffians right out of the Rover Boys; a respectful wait of years, until the state's patriarchal attorney general headed voluntarily for pasture, before stepping into his shoes; and, finally, the altruistic public servant thrust into the governorship, almost against his will, by the pressures of the age, and then perpetuated in office by an appreciative citizenry.

All this is substantially true, or it would not have stood up under the endless reworkings of a generation of chroniclers. Warren would have recoiled from sponsoring anything mendacious, even as he was impelled after many years to correct the myth that, as a prosecutor, every conviction of a wretched defendant nauseated him; that was only true, he said, in capital cases.

It is just that this Warren Legend omits so much of the whole truth. It reveals little about his aspirations, his maneuvering to realize them, and the recurrent frustrations; it skips over significant dilemmas, changes of outlook, affinities, and animosities; and in particular it stops short of his total impact on the politics of California—namely, the blow he dealt to the stubborn patterns of old-time partisanism.

Honest Guile

Warren operated under quite different circumstances from Hiram Johnson. He did not ride into office on a wave of reform. His problem was not to extirpate corruption, using a new political party and a rubber-stamp legislature; it was to stabilize a monstrously growing state while revivifying a last-gasping political party and redirecting it on modern progressive lines, superimposing a new format on the gangrenous, rejected Old Politics. And all this had to be done while keeping an eye on national politics and their opportunities for a man from California.

Although Warren started his career as virtually a protégé of the Republican old-guard wing headed by Oakland publisher Joseph Knowland (a detail customarily omitted from the Warren Legend), he early learned the advantages of nonpartisanism. For 13 years, starting in 1925, he was district attorney of Alameda county, across the bay from San Francisco. Under the old party politics, his vigorous enforcing of the law might have cost him his job after one term. But under the Johnsonian reforms, district attorneyships had become nonpartisan offices. Warren was re-elected in 1930 and again in 1934; that same year, riding the dual horses of nonpartisanism and partisanism together, he was elected Republican state chairman.

That was the year when, in the midst of the wild Sinclair campaign, Democratic registrations surged ahead of the Republican enrollment for the first time in living memory. A generation later, there still were innumerable Republicans who had not yet grasped the implications of their status as a minority party, and continued to regard Democrats as only something to be sneered at. But Earl Warren got the message as soon as the scales tipped. Amid the settling dust of Frank Merriam's defeat of Sinclair, Warren hastened to proclaim to Californians that the outcome was "a great nonpartisan victory against radicalism."

In 1936 Warren headed California's delegation to the Republican national convention that nominated Kansas' Governor Alfred M. Landon in opposition to Franklin D. Roosevelt's bid for a second term. Then, as in other presidential years, Warren had occasion to be very critical of Roosevelt's policies.

But Warren was not opposed to guile, as long as he deemed it honest guile. Two years later, amid the propaganda maelstrom of the California election, there emanated from his campaign headquarters a leaflet whose principal message was a quotation from Mr. Roosevelt:

> Under a perfect party system of government, a bid for political favor should rest solely upon political principle and good administration. We should seek through every possible means to move toward that objective. In these days the voters—especially the younger voters—are bringing us closer to that ideal. They are less and less concerned with mere party emblems; they are saying more and more: "I belong to this or that party but actually I always split my ticket." That is a happy sign for the future of America.

The borrowed sentiments sanctioning ticket-splitting accompanied a statement that Earl Warren, district attorney of Alameda county, was "a candidate for the Republican, Democratic and Progressive nominations for Attorney General."

Warren had been waiting deferentially for years for Ulysses S. Webb, the nine-term incumbent, to retire, and he had been cultivating the support of such leading Democrats as Los Angeles' Superior Judge Robert Kenny. He got only token opposition in the Republican and Progressive primaries. The Democratic primary vote was split among seven entries, and Warren, a cross-filed candidate, ended up 28,000 votes ahead of the top real-Democratic contender. Thus, while the great Democratic comeback of 1938 was still inchoate, and Culbert Olson's defeat of the politically bedraggled Frank Merriam was still months away, Warren had clinched the attorney generalship.

Warren demonstrated quickly that his nonpartisanism was not just campaign talk. His first official act in 1939—growing out of a telephoned tip he found on walking into his office—was to lower the boom on Frank Merriam's executive secretary, whom the outgoing governor had appointed to a judgeship but who, Warren quickly established, had been selling pardons to state prison inmates. Warren set in motion the machinery that sent the man to prison.

Then he engaged as his chief assistant William Sweigert, a prominent lawyer and a Democrat—the first of countless appointments he was to make over the next 14 years which were based on capabilities rather than party affiliation.

On May 11, 1941, when Governor Culbert Olson's term had some 18 months to go, the Los Angeles *Times* published a significant item under the by-line of Kyle Palmer. Palmer was not only the *Times'* political editor. He was probably the top strategist of California's Republican party, and he was the *Times'* grand vizier in a political axis comprising the *Times,* the Oakland *Tribune,* and the San Francisco *Chronicle,* whose collective staunch Republicanism had been a party bulwark during an uncomfortable decade of fading registrations.

The report, under the coy headline, GUBERNATORIAL WHISPERS FILL THE AIR, said:

> . . . Should Attorney General Earl Warren set aside his personal preferences, which would lead him to ask the voters to retain him in the office he now holds, and respond to statewide pleas that he become a candidate for the Republican nomination for governor, State Senator Robert W. Kenny could be expected to file for Attorney General. As the Republican nominee for governor, Warren would be one of the strongest challengers the Republicans could put up against any Democrat. . . .

What these purported "whispers" really meant was: "We have decided that Earl Warren is the man the Republicans should run against Olson. If Senator Kenny will go along with this, and settle for a shot at the attorney generalship, even though he's a Democrat, we won't be inclined to give him too much trouble."

The "whispers," another Republican strategist, Murray Chotiner, divulged later, were an operation of the Republican establishment, quarterbacked by Joseph Knowland's son, the subsequently noted William F. Knowland.

Nothing resulted immediately. Palmer, a genial and puckish native Tennessean who looked like a reincarnation of Henry Clay, was practiced in lining up his ducks well in advance.

But seven months later the outbreak of World War II, with its attendant complications for California's defense, touched off a vendetta between Warren and Governor Olson, whose deteriorating administration was lurching from one inadequacy to another. One of the few things the two men did not have a blunt disagreement about was the summary incarceration, under Federal orders, of California's 110,000 Japanese-Americans—70,000 of them United States citizens—in concentration camps for the duration. Warren's collaboration in this Draconian action has stood out ever since in anomalous and inexplicable contrast to his later ardor for civil rights.

Announcing his candidacy for governor on April 9, 1942, Warren detailed his philosophy on nonpartisanism:

> My experience has been in the field of nonpartisan government. I have served in the Army, in the government of my city and county, and was nominated to my present office of Attorney General by the voters of the Republican, Democratic and Progressive parties. And I have sought to discharge my responsibilities without regard to partisan considerations.
>
> I believe in the party system, and have been identified with the Republican party in matters of party concern, but I have never found that the broad questions of national party policy have application to the problems of state and local government in California. For over 30 years, all county and city officers, as well as those of the judiciary and the school system, have been nonpartisan by statute. During the same period, the legislature and most of the

> constitutional officers have become so by practice.
>
> These officers deal with such problems as the security of the people in their homes, the administration of our schools, business methods in government to prevent overtaxation, civil service to prevent the spoils system, conservation of our resources, both human and natural, to prevent exploitation, the social services to raise living standards, cooperation with the agencies of the Federal government to carry out national policies, and now civilian protection to further the war effort.
>
> None of these problems permits a solution through partisanship. They cut entirely across party lines. This is particularly true of civilian protection, which at the moment I consider to be the most vital problem either presently with us or on our immediate horizon.

Six months later Warren wound up his campaign with a statewide radio broadcast that was a far cry from what California had known since the days of Hiram Johnson, nearly 30 years before.

"No partisanship of any kind," he said, "should be permitted to interfere with the maintenance of a good understanding between the state's highest administrative officer and the state's legislative body. None will interfere if I am elected."

Professing, somewhat cryptically, ". . . nonpartisanship with me is not a political creed, nor is it a catchall for political favor," he went on: "My conception of nonpartisanship in the state of California foresees and embraces a condition that brings to the public service men and women of all political faiths, of all creeds and races and colors, without partiality or preferment—the sole consideration being the ability, the integrity, the capacity of each to perform the service that he or she is assigned."

To what extent this philosophy was simply a self-serving acknowledgement that it was no longer possible to get elected in California with Republican votes alone has long been a matter of argument among Warren-watchers. But those who contended that it was only a fleeting campaign expedient found themselves disproven.

Olson, a party man to the end, disdained to cross-file, and Warren, who did cross-file, came close to beating him in the Democratic primary, getting 404,000 votes to the hapless governor's 514,000.

"Olson's general election campaign never really got going," relates his biographer, Robert E. Burke. In a foretaste of the factionalism that would still beset the Democrats a quarter of a century later, "a bitter contest developed at the Democratic state convention over who should be vice-chairman of the state central committee," Burke said. The contest resulted in the virtual defection of the party's San Francisco contingent. The November vote was Warren, 1,275,287; Olson, 932,995.

The Old Politics were dead.

"Driving to Sacramento for the inauguration on January 3, 1942," Attorney General-elect Robert Kenny—the only major Democratic winner—recalled, "Warren told me that none of the old Merriam officeholders could expect to make a comeback in his administration. They never did. Warren's appointments were uniformly excellent, without any traceable adhesions to the stand-pat regime that had gone out when the Democrats took over in 1939."

The 6,000-Mile Appointment

Moving quickly to clean the dead wood of the Olson regime out of state government, Warren began with a dozen major appointments. Seven were Republicans, five were Democrats, and two were of indefinite persuasion—a pattern he followed throughout his administration.

Nor did he act like the Republican governors of yore. Quickly establishing close collaboration with the legislature—now Republican-dominated—which Olson had kept at telephone's-length, he launched an eye-opening program that included lowered taxes, increased old-age pensions, and broadened unemployment insurance.

The death of Senator Hiram Johnson in 1945 occasioned what many people construed as a memorable suspension of Warren's habitual objectivity in appointments. To fill the vacancy, he reached out 6,000 miles to Europe to designate a man still on duty with the Army, a prewar state legislator from Alameda county who happened to be the son of Warren's original booster. The Senator-designate was William F. Knowland.

Warren's vigor quickly projected him into the speculation about 1944 presidential contenders. But he renounced any interest—some said because he foresaw the resounding defeat that befell New York's Governor Thomas E. Dewey under the Roosevelt fourth-term juggernaut. Instead, Warren settled for the role of keynoter at the Republican national convention.

California went thoroughly Democratic in the election, giving Roosevelt a 500,000-vote margin, re-electing Senator Sheridan Downey, and increasing the Democratic majority in the state's congressional delegation from 13 to 16 of the 25 House seats. The Republicans lost three state assembly seats, while retaining a majority of 41 to 37; they increased their state senate majority by three seats, to 26–14.

Problems of the war and of prospective sweeping postwar readjustments were in the forefront, and in 1945 Warren uncorked what some observers appraised as the most ramified program of social legislation since Hiram Johnson. It included further old-age-pension increases, more tax reductions, an elaborate mental health program—and measures, ranging from housing to education, anticipating an influx of 850,000 ex-servicemen. What really stamped Warren as a heretic by Republican standards, and caused reverberations throughout the country, was his proposal of one of the first "medicare" plans, to be financed by joint employer-employee contributions. His plan became one target in the nationwide campaign against "socialized medicine," but Warren kept pressing the proposal at one legislative session after another.

"He's a Democrat—" Harry Truman opined cordially, "and doesn't know it."

By 1946, Warren was in a strong position to renew his appeal for bipartisan voter support. Announcing his candidacy for re-election April 14, 1946, he said:

> I am a Republican, but in keeping with the practice of those who have sought state office in California since our direct primary was established 30 years ago, I shall seek the support of voters of both parties.
>
> I can do this honorably because I am independent and therefore in a position to serve the people fairly regardless of their party or mine. My approach to state government demonstrates that I believe in and practice the principle of independent administration in state affairs without blind partisanship or political manipulation. I am not interested in machine politics. I have not tried to build a political machine. No man should be permitted to be both governor and a political boss. I am not running because of the insistence of any group. I will need the support of every independent Californian.

His opponent was his old Democratic friend Attorney General Kenny. Kenny taxed Warren with conducting a "do-nothing" administration but did not have any really heavy ammunition to lob at him. The Democrats' main hope was to achieve party unity; if they could do that, they would automatically snow the Republicans under. But a deep party split developed over the rival senatorial ambitions of Ellis Patterson, who had been lieutenant governor under Olson, and Representative Will Rogers, Jr. (son of the humorist), who won the nomination.

"All my efforts for four years to bring about a coalition of all wings of the party were destroyed," Kenny said later.

Warren didn't even have to oppose Kenny in the November election. In the June primary, Warren cross-filed and captured the Democratic nomination as well as the Republican, beating Kenny in 56 of the state's 58 counties. It was the only time in California's history that a governor had won through bipartisan nomination.

1946 marked the apogee of bipartisanism in statewide contests. Along with Warren, dual nominations were won in the primary by the perennial state treasurer and secretary of state, C. G. Johnson and Frank M. Jordan, and also by a man Warren had appointed to the vacant state controllership, Thomas Kuchel. Will Rogers, Jr., lost in November to Senator Knowland to round out the Democratic rout.

Roman Riding

Now came the time for Warren to demonstrate that a man could bring off the Roman-riding feat of decrying partisanship in California while earnestly embracing it in the national political arena.

With President-by-succession Harry Truman running for his first full term, 1948 looked to national Republican leaders like a year when they might finally dislodge the New Deal. California's 25 electoral votes were an important bloc, and Earl Warren had dramatically demonstrated his ability to corral the California vote.

"Like the moist 'fogs' that drift in from some mysterious bourne to harass California chambers of commerce," a New York *Times* correspondent wrote nearly a year in advance of the 1948 election, "an aura persistently taking the shape of the word 'President' has been gathering with increasing density above the broad shoulders of Governor Earl Warren. . . ."

By December, 1947, new sounds were coming from the resonant Warren throat: "I believe our party, the Republican party, is the one great political organization in the United States today to which people can turn for competent leadership."

One of the artifices that made Warren politically human—while contributing to the Legend's claim that he was a slightly unearthly superman—was his habitual pose of modestly holding higher office at arm's length. He had courted his original appointment to the Alameda district attorney's office by professing horror at the employment of political influence. He had demurred at running for attorney general—while instigating, in the interim, a doubling of the position's salary to a viable $10,000 a year. And he had taken to the field against Culbert Olson ostensibly only after the governor's provocations allowed no alternative.

Now, perhaps by coincidence, the outlines of a similar strategy appeared again. As governor, Warren automatically headed a national convention delegation nominally pledged to his own "favorite son" candidacy. But he said, "I have made a distinction between being willing to serve if called upon to serve, and the position of being an active candidate, which would take me away from my job as governor, and require me to solicit campaign funds."

"Aside from agreeing that the California delegation should put him in nomination," writes Irving Stone, his campaign biographer, "he made no organized effort to secure the nomination, nor would he allow anyone to solicit the support of delegates in other states."

It was notable, however, that at the Chicago convention, where the California delegation's legal "pledge" did not extend beyond one ballot, not until after the second ballot—when Thomas E. Dewey needed only 33 more votes—did Warren formally release his delegates from their pledge and urge them to vote for Dewey. Warren ended up as the vice-presidential candidate, on a major-party ticket—which was slightly more than Hiram Johnson had achieved as "Bull Moose" nominee. But, along with Dewey, Warren got no closer to the White House than the erroneously anticipatory "Republican victory" headlines in some copies of the Chicago *Tribune,* which had to be frantically recalled from newsstands.

Growth

Warren's speeches were consistently heavy quilts of homilies, and they seldom contained any theme more exciting than the news that California was "growing." Yet, aside from his concept of nonpartisan (actually bipartisan) government, Warren's great gift to California was his unswerving insistence that this fact of growth was paramount.

During his tenure, California acquired over 3 million more inhabitants—an increase of nearly 50 per cent. As a concomitant of World War II and the beginning of a new era, this growth called for a "quantum jump" in the facilities and concepts that had served the old horse-and-buggy California. Warren's administration as a whole was devoted to discerning, projecting, and meeting these needs. Highways, water resources, housing, education, prisons, mental health facilities, recreation, and the various aspects of social security all had to be amplified on a multi-billion-dollar scale, with commensurate financing.

The greatest testimonial to his efficacy was that there was little subsequent regimes could point to that he had not done or tried to do. Inevitably, he ran into opposition from the less imaginative. His "medicare" plan was repeatedly blocked. The petroleum industry bucked, unsuccessfully, his program of gasoline taxes to build highways. His billion-dollar project for moving water from north to south was stymied by sectional jealousy. The recurrent need to increase pension, welfare, and unemployment benefits simply to keep abreast of rising living costs and standards riled foes of "welfare statism."

But the reverses were a small part of the picture. In 1950, Warren's second four years in office ended. This time the Democratic effort to dislodge him was spearheaded by James Roosevelt, eldest son of Franklin D. Roosevelt. A Los Angeles insurance broker and California's Democratic national committeeman, the 42-year-old Roosevelt had not gotten the message about bipartisanism; like Olson, he mounted a party-line program, on the theme of "bringing the Fair Deal to California." The Korean War erupted, and Warren was able to make the same appeal for bipartisan unity that he had made after Pearl Harbor. Winning his unprecedented third term, he defeated Roosevelt by nearly 2 to 1.

The Supreme Court

Republican old-guard outrage at the course on which Warren was leading the party had welled up as far back as 1946, when factional spokesmen called his policies "tragically akin to those of the Congress of Industrial Organization's Political Action Committee and all the radical riffraff elements of California." By 1949, the eve of Warren's third-term campaign, his ambitious lieutenant governor, former Superior Judge Goodwin Knight, muttered about "creeping socialism" and got ready to challenge Warren; but he was dissuaded by party leaders.

When Warren once more prepared to lead a "favorite son" delegation to the 1952 national convention, the old-guard opposition crystallized in a rival slate of delegates headed by Representative Thomas Werdel of Bakersfield, who was close to oil interests Warren had antagonized. The Werdel slate, publicly committed to supporting "anyone except Warren" at the convention, was defeated in the Republican primary by more than 2 to 1.

National attention was centered on the struggle between the forces of General Eisenhower and Ohio's Senator Robert Taft to win the Republican presidential nomination. Warren was the leading prospect in the event of a deadlock between them, and he left no doubts that this time his "favorite son" candidacy was more than a token affair. The deadlock was averted—in consummate irony, through the action of Warren himself. In the pre-convention fight over delegate seating which really finished Taft, Warren swung the California delegation to the Eisenhower side. "If anyone ever clinched the nomination for me," Eisenhower was quoted later as saying, "it was Earl Warren." Any chance that Warren had after that, it has been alleged, was scuttled by backstage machinations of California's junior Senator, Richard Nixon, on behalf of Eisenhower's nomination and his own ensuing selection as vice-presidential nominee. (This will be considered later.)

In any case, Warren returned from Chicago empty-handed.

But even before the November election, according to Warren's biographer, John D. Weaver, Eisenhower mentioned to Warren the possibility of an appointment to the United States Supreme Court. In the summer of 1953, just before starting on a European vacation trip, Warren lunched with the President and Attorney General Herbert Brownell, Jr. The meeting is presumed to have produced an understanding that Warren would be offered the next Court vacancy. On September 3, shortly after returning from Europe, Warren made a laconic announcement that he would not run for a fourth term. Five days later, Chief Justice Fred M. Vinson died suddenly. It was three weeks after that before Warren's appointment as Chief Justice was announced. In the interval, according to Weaver, there were discussions between Warren and the administration about whether Warren should get just a seat on the Court or the specific Chief Justice chair that had become vacant—with Warren characteristically insisting on precisely what had been promised.

On October 4, 1953, Warren turned the administration of California over to Lieutenant Governor Knight and headed for Washington.

Warren left a state vastly different from the one he had taken over a decade before—greatly changed in externals, but also reoriented in its politics for generations to come. An analysis that Raymond Moley wrote after Warren's 1946 victory seems equally applicable as an epilogue to the Warren regime:

> It was not a victory for orthodox Republicanism. It was an exceedingly generous vote of confidence for an unusually independent politician. Orthodox Republicanism enjoys only a minority position in the Golden State. Registered Democrats outnumber Republicans 2 to 1. Roosevelt's majorities in California in four elections averaged 600,000. But neither of these circumstances resulted from devotion to

the Democratic party. For the Roosevelt vote, like that for Hiram Johnson in 1934 and 1940, and for Warren in 1942 and now, was composed of a great number of assorted groups, beliefs, movements and preferences that had little to do with the issues between the national parties.

The political philosophy, as well as the machinery, of California is nonpartisan. Cross-filing in the primaries, nonpartisan local and judicial elections, and the liberal use of the initiative and the referendum—all are part of the old "progressive" revolt against party machines and bosses. Hiram Johnson . . . was the perfect flower of this California temper. Earl Warren has shrewdly grasped this fact and owes much of his strength to his refusal to follow a party line.

[Elmo] Roper's surveys show that most American voters now consider themselves to be Democrats. . . . This would indicate a less stable party vote, a vote favorable to a candidate who appears to be free from party orthodoxy. Such voters are not basically independent, but they are less bound by party tradition. That is what California voters are like.

Chapter
Nine

Report from Glocca Morra: The Parties

☒ EVERY TWO YEARS, EARLY IN AUGUST, WORD goes out to the world that California's two major parties are about to hold their conventions in Sacramento.

To many people, this news may conjure up pictures of bedizened auditoriums, rousing band music, oratory, confetti, demonstrations, frenzied electioneering.

On the contrary, the California conventions are sedate

gatherings in the chamber of the state assembly which last only one day and do only one thing: they go through the formality of adopting a so-called party platform—which practically no one looks at thereafter. A veteran legislator, Assemblyman Charles Chapel, once remarked, "I have never known a candidate who either stood or ran on the platform of his political party."

This sterile ritual in a sense is a wake—a memorial to the political forms that existed before Hiram Johnson. But there is no gloom, because in another sense these gatherings are implicit celebrations of the purified, watered-down, corruptionless—if hollow—party politics that the Progressive reforms brought about, and that California's churning populace has tacitly endorsed ever since.

So a contented, buoyant atmosphere pervades the lobbies of the Senator and El Mirador hotels overlooking the capitol during these convocations. It is "homecoming" time for party activists from El Cajon and Buttonwillow, from Oceanside and Downieville, from Napa, Sonoma, and Mendocino counties—people who don't see each other from one year to the next, and have little contact even by official correspondence. Like a state fair, it's a nice pretext for getting together, under the sanction of statutory necessity. The rationale, or irrationale, behind this empty pageantry is the key to contemporary California politics.

By the end of Earl Warren's regime, California party politics and California government had firmed into the shape they have today. To understand what is going on, one needs a close look at both these institutions—party politics and government. In a survey of them, the spicier aspects of life, such as sex, appear only by implication. But the technics constitute the political mating-dance now indulged in, directly or indirectly, by one-tenth of the citizens of the United States.

A group of Californians who want to become a recognized political party, with the dignity of a primary ballot and a slate of candidates, has several avenues open to it. First, it can qualify if any candidate bearing the group's label (such as Prohibitionist or Vegetarian) drew at least 2 per cent of the total state vote in the preceding gubernatorial election. Failing this, the group can attain formal recognition if it enrolls members equal in number to 1 per cent of the preceding state vote. (This was the course chosen by boosters of Alabama's George Wallace and his American Independent party in 1967.) Or, if enrolling members is too hard for it, the nascent party can qualify by petition, if it gets signatures numerically equal to 10 per cent of the preceding election vote.

In the years since the Progressive revolution of 1910, seven other minor parties have enjoyed legal status for various periods—the Socialist, Prohibition, Liberty, Commonwealth, Communist, Townsend, and Independent Progressive parties. The longest-lived of these was the Prohibition party, whose following did not dwindle enough to disqualify it until after 1962. In 1968, the American Independent and Peace and Freedom "third" parties qualified.

One sometimes is given to wonder whether the effort of qualifying a party is worth it. Out of the maelstrom of Progressive election-law reforms came this murky definition of the functions of a state party organization: ". . . [to] appoint committees and appoint and employ campaign directors and perfect whatever campaign organizations it deems suitable or desirable. . . ."

No one has ever figured out exactly what this was intended to mean—if indeed it was not deliberately meant to say nothing. Under the law, a party organization acquired flesh and blood only in the course of the primary election. The inference was that it had no role at all to play in the all-important business of sifting nominees.

The primary election produces nominees. They, together with holders of state office who belong to their party, become the official delegates to the party's biennial state convention. These delegates appoint three to five persons each to join them in forming the party's state central committee. Then this committee, at a meeting following the state convention, elects officers. The officers are the state party hierarchy for the next two years. With a few "Return to Go" cards, the whole thing would resemble the game of Monopoly.

Convention delegates, as it turns out, number 170: The nominees for, or incumbents of, ten state offices, from governor on down; the 38 House of Representative seats and the two United States Senate seats; and the 40 state senate and 80 state assembly seats.

A party state central committee, ballooned out from this nucleus of 170 by appointees and various ex officio members, comprises between 700 and 1,000 persons. The committee's principal link with the rank-and-file party membership is its inclusion of the chairmen of the party's 58 county committees, whose members are elected in the primaries. The Progressives' purpose in thus divorcing the rank-and-file from the party hierarchy, it will be recalled, was to keep the party reins in the hands of office-holders and nominees.

A state central committee of 1,000 members, so scattered that some are nearly 1,000 miles apart, obviously is too unwieldy to guide party affairs from week to week or even month to month. The sketchy party leadership, therefore, devolves on the handful of top officials, principally the party chairman. The chairmanship, the law specifies, must alternate between a northern Californian and a southern Californian, the dividing line being the Tehachapi Mountains that cross the state near Bakersfield.

A party organization in California hence really consists of a letterhead, offices in San Francisco and Los Angeles with skeletal staffs, and a dispersion of unpaid, spare-time officers who have no way of mobilizing efforts on behalf of the party except through unpredictable tides of sentiment. In the virtual absence of patronage, they can offer no rewards; nor can they impose penalties for noncompliance with their exhortations.

Two of California's foremost political scientists, Dean McHenry and Winston Crouch, have said:

> Political parties in California fail to perform adequately the services which justify their existence. . . . Party has been relegated to a meager and nominal role—impotent, starved and ill-organized . . . a structure resembling a pyramid in shape, and just as lifeless.

This impotence is the reason why a political aspirant in California is pretty much on his own, and the reason why personality, rather than party or policies, has come to be so important in elections.

Herein also is the root of the quadrennial difficulty, such as beset President Johnson's forces in 1967–68, in trying to mesh California into national campaigns. An intermediary from Washington is confronted with an array of factions, most of them not speaking to each other.

"It's like a banana republic where they have a revolution every month," one despairing national official moaned. "You never know who to deal with."

The titular state party chairman may represent no more than a clique within the state committee. The party's national committeeman and committeewoman from California have no necessary relationship with the rest of the organization; they are the choices of the state's last national convention delegation in each party.

A convention delegation is simply a panel of partisans named by a presidential aspirant—who perhaps comes from some other state—to carry his name in California's presidential preference primary. There may be several such panels. If a candidate wins the California primary but fails to get the national nomination, the delegation that represented him, along with the national committee members the delegation has elected, become lame ducks. Thus, in 1952 Senator Estes Kefauver of Tennessee won California's Democratic presidential primary, but after the nomination went to Adlai Stevenson the Kefauverites were quickly eclipsed in California party affairs.

Charades and Remnants

The average Californian, apart from the fact that he can vote and then is governed by the majority's choice of candidates, has little more involvement in the party politics of California than he would have if he lived in some other state.

He is bombarded with partisan oratory, and he hears remotely of workings of party mechanics. But to him, as to people outside California, it all has a dreamlike unreality.

The reformers, from Hiram Johnson on, wittingly or unwittingly shaped things that way. While solemnly preserving conventional political nomenclature, they left little in substance that a voter could attach himself to.

California has a state election every two years, when it chooses its entire 80-member assembly and half of its 40-member state senate, which has a four-year term. It elects a governor every four years, midway between presidential elections.

A year or more before a California election, a citizen begins hearing speculative reports of possible candidacies. The reports usually have some partisan coloration, but they seem random, unorganized, and impromptu in origin. That is exactly what they are. Such a report signifies no more than that someone has decided he may, given sufficient support, run for office.

The reports, no matter how prominent the aspirant, conspicuously lack the imprimatur of an official party organization or its officers. Political parties are expressly forbidden by law, right down to the county level, to give pre-primary endorsements to any candidates. The theory has always been, since the Progressive days, that a primary should be an equal free-for-all—aside from the built-in advantage held by the people already in office.

Several months before an election, tables appear near the

entrances of stores, banks, and other public places, manned by polite and patient ladies; they are deputy registrars of voters. Any citizen over 21 who has lived in the state for a year, in a county for three months, and in an election precinct for 54 days, can step up and register to vote. He can enroll as a Republican, as a Democrat, as a member of any other party, as a nonpartisan, or simply as someone who "declines to state" his partisan affinity. Normally, when only the two major parties have legal recognition, only registered Republicans and Democrats are handed party ballots in the primary election; other voters get a truncated ballot covering only nonpartisan contests, such as those for city and county offices and judgeships. A voter's registration lapses if he misses an election. He can change his party affiliation any time by re-registering.

Election frauds, such as "tombstone" voting in the names of nonexistent people, familiar in the old Eastern politics, are unknown in California. Probably this is not because the people are essentially more honest but simply because there is nobody to organize such skulduggery.

Registered voters get campaign literature in the mail, perhaps from both sides; they may be solicited over the telephone; and, just before an election, they receive an official sample ballot listing candidates. Along with this come the texts of any initiative "propositions," with officially sanctioned summaries of arguments for and against the proposals.

Beyond these formalities, the average citizen's involvement consists mainly of being the target for confusing barrages of propaganda via radio, television, billboards, and personally stumping candidates. The main sources of all this solicitation are the individual candidates' headquarters, bearing such names as the "Snively For Governor Committee." "Committee" is more than a euphemism here. It represents the candidate's financing sources and his campaign apparatus. For neither of these essentials can he rely much on the regular organization of his party, even if he wins its nomination.

The candidates' appeals involve much double-talk. It is

standard for them to extoll—as Messrs. Knowland and Nixon were fond of doing—the "free and open primary," and to enthuse about the vitality that such competition brings to a party. Candidates, however, usually mean just the opposite. Orthodox primary competition would involve their criticizing each other. But in California it has become axiomatic that the candidate who has a hot primary fight is likely to lose the general election. Voters are so loosely oriented to party lines that they recoil from a nominee who has been involved in a blood bath, and in November they will vote for a less disheveled nominee. Party labels mean that little.

The simplest way to avoid such hazardous intraparty hostilities is for a candidate to ignore his primary opponents and concentrate his rhetorical fire on the man he thinks will be his opponent in the general election.

This routine is a hangover from the 45 years of cross-filing, when candidates competing in two or more party primaries were in no position to take a militant party line. If one was seeking the Democratic nomination as well as the Republican, one obviously could not afford to draw invidious ideological comparisons.

With city and county politics kept rigorously nonpartisan by law, the California scene is bereft of many traditional American political appurtenances. Voting precincts exist only on election day; ward bosses and ward heelers are unknown. Such organization as exists is based on state assembly districts, and most citizens would have trouble naming their assemblyman, let alone his local proconsuls.

If a politically conscious citizen seeks to join some local party unit, he may be able to locate a Democratic or Republican club. But the chances are slim. Throughout the state, the aggregate membership of such units in either party has never amounted to much more than 50,000 persons—less than 2 per cent of the electorate.

On the primary ballot, a citizen can vote for members of the county central committee of his party; in Los Angeles, the largest county, there are seven members for each of 31 assembly districts. These committees meet monthly, and anyone can attend. But, it will be recalled, these bodies organically are dead-end streets. The 58 county-committee chairmen are a tiny honorary minority in the 1,000-member state committee.

Sessions of county central committees are as parochial and specialized as gatherings of coin collectors. A good deal of the activity is factional maneuvering among *aficionados* of politics who are seeking toeholds to advance themselves or friends. The deliberations are so remote from the mainstream of state politics that they seldom receive much attention from the news media, and a citizen is hard put to find out even what went on.

"County committees," Robert Kenny has remarked, "are a vestigial remnant of the convention system—a debating society."

The only substantial change in the curious matrix imposed on California party politics by the reforms of the Hiram Johnson era was abolition of cross-filing in 1959.

From the inauguration of cross-filing, in the 1914 election, until 1952 the number of candidates for the state legislature and for Congress who won automatic election by capturing the nominations of both parties ran as high as 90 per cent, and never was less than 18 per cent.

From 1934 on, cross-filing served primarily the minority Republicans. In party-line votes, they would have been swamped; by competing in Democratic primaries, and capturing Democratic nominations along with their own party's, they were able to avoid party-line showdowns in the November elections.

For years the Democrats chafed at this legalized larceny, and sought vainly to get cross-filing eliminated. Finally, in 1952, John B. Elliott, a wealthy Los Angeles oilman and Democratic party patriarch, organized an initiative campaign to abolish cross-filing. To thwart this, the Republicans were forced to offer a compromise; they put on the ballot a competitive initiative proposal that called for retaining cross-filing but required that a candidate's true party affiliation be stated on the ballot. Both proposals were approved by the voters. But the Republican compromise got more votes.

As a result, the party primary ballot that previously had looked like this:

Democratic
Fred Brown
Henry Smith
Arthur Stone
Irving White

. . . now looked like this:

Democratic
Fred Brown, Dem.
Henry Smith, Rep.
Arthur Stone, Dem.
Irving White, Rep.

Thus there was no longer any reason for a voter to be hazy about party affiliations. Voting now tended more to follow party lines.

The extent to which cross-filing's "masquerade" had been propping up the Republican party in office was suggested by the quick decline in Republican strength after the adoption of the party-label requirement in 1952. From then on—until 1959, when cross-filing was at last abolished—no Republican candidate for any statewide office was able to capture a Democratic nomination.

In the three elections after 1952, Republican strength in the 80-member state assembly dropped from 54 to 33; and in the 40-member state senate it dropped from 29 to 12.

From 1952 on, the labeling so effectively nullified cross-filing that by 1959, after the Democrats had swept a state election, people were ready to scrap the device entirely. A repeal of cross-filing sailed through the legislature.

But a bipartisan outlook on elections had become such a fixed trait of the California psyche that orthodox interparty competition never fully revived. Candidates still go on paying lip service to "free and open primaries," but they continue to make ambivalent appeals to voters of both parties.

Rise of the Volunteers

Politics abhors a vacuum as much as nature does. With the official party organizations inhibited in so many ways from meaningful activities, it was inevitable that pressures would develop to circumvent this. Consequently, in both the Democratic and Republican parties, "unofficial" organizations formed to carry on conventional party functions.

The first of these was the California Republican Assembly. It was started in 1934, when the Republicans lapsed into minority-party status, as a central organization to knit together fragmented local Republican clubs throughout the state; the CRA became their representative, coordinating body. To reduce the debilitating dispersion of Republican votes among competing primary candidates, the CRA established a system of local and statewide "fact-finding committees" to screen primary entries and select one on whom the party could unite. This process lessened intraparty competition and helped focus the party vote in the confusions of the cross-filing system. It was a major factor in the Republicans' continuing to win elections long after they were outnumbered. Theoretically, the CRA was a "mass membership" organization; any Republican could join one of its local units. In fact, it never claimed a membership of more than 25,000. It became an elite party organ, overshadowing the "official" party structure.

The successful Republican CRA served as a model for the long-eclipsed Democrats. After the 1952 national election, seeking to harness the partisan enthusiasm aroused by the candidacy of Adlai Stevenson, they formed the California

Democratic Council, a federation of Democratic clubs throughout the state.

The CDC went further than just pre-primary endorsement of candidates. As the purported voice of the party rank and file, it also undertook to formulate party policy. Because it was helping candidates get elected, the CDC felt it had a legitimate interest in what they did after election. Although it never claimed a following of more than 50,000 dues-paying members, it became the closest thing to an organization in which the party "grass roots" could participate and be heard.

Thus, for more than a decade in the case of the CDC and for three decades in the case of the CRA, these organizations served as the voices of their respective parties. When "California Democrats" or "California Republicans" were reported to have taken one action or another, it was usually these unofficial rank-and-file volunteer organizations that had done it, rather than the impotent official party organisms.

The unofficial groups' conventions at San Francisco or Bakersfield, Fresno or San Diego, became the settings for the traditional irrepressible phenomena of American politics—the swarming and back-slapping, the impassioned oratory and heated debate, the earnest resolutions on far-flung subjects, the wire-pulling and wheeling and dealing.

Unfortunately, perhaps, these organizations had inherent weaknesses, which in recent years have caused them both to wither on the vine—a decline that will be viewed more closely in later chapters. Essentially their trouble was that they lacked real mass support, because of Californians' ingrained disaffinity for conventionally regularized politics.

With California's Rube-Goldberg party structures, and the sway of bipartisan "nonpartisanism," it has been difficult for either party to consolidate dependable voting blocs. The state's approximately 1,000,000 Negroes vote about 90 per cent Democratic, and other minority groups lean toward the Democrats. But a significant number of the approximately 1,500,000 Mexican-Americans may swing either way. Organized labor, particularly since the Warren era, officially has collaborated with whichever party is in power at Sacramento. The rank-and-file, to all appearances, likewise has remained bipartisan.

Northern California is more Democratic than Southern California, where so much of the settlement has been from the Republican Midwest. The rule of thumb is that in an election a Democratic candidate should amass a margin of a couple of hundred thousand votes in the north to offset the deficit he is likely to incur in the San Diego-Riverside area and in Orange county, which is the celebrated stronghold of reaction in California.

The precise causes of Orange county's ultraconservatism are still unclear. On the periphery of Los Angeles, it has a population of 1,000,000, and to some degree it has become a "bedroom" exurb. But until recent years it was distant enough to be quite self-centered in its century-old agricultural economy. Many of its families go back for generations and are so addicted to the mental patterns of the 1920's or earlier that they have, for instance, given solid support to the Santa Ana *Register*. The publisher of that newspaper, Cyrus Raymond Hoiles, was such a devotee of laissez faire that he came close to being a pacific philosophical anarchist—opposed in principle to government-operated postal service and dubious about the validity of public libraries, public schools, and even barriers at railroad grade crossings "to protect people from their own stupidity."

Orange county is virtually the only populous county among California's 58 that can be depended on to vote Republican come hell or high water. In 1964 it was the only large county that voted for Goldwater over President Johnson by a sizable margin (224,000 to 176,000). The only other populous county that went for Goldwater—San Diego—did so by just 214,000 to 211,000.

The rest of California reserves the right to be capricious. Whether this is the effect of weak party organizations, or is the cause of them, or is both, remains a hen-or-egg enigma. Essentially the reason is simply that California is peopled with Californians.

"If they aren't that way when they come here," an old-timer remarked, managing to be at once both cryptic and lucid, "they soon get that way."

Chapter
Ten

The House That Nonpartisanism Built

☒ POLITICS' ONLY PURPOSE IS TO PRODUCE GOVERNMENT.

What kind of government has resulted from California's unusual politics? The answer is: a governmental mechanism that has proved remarkably effective, albeit involving many peculiarities hidden under a deceptive veneer of conventionality.

A visitor to Sacramento, 75 miles inland from San Francisco and hard by the gold-laden foothills so much involved in the state's emergence, at first sees nothing unusual. Sacramento has the picture-postcard serenity of most state capitals: lush shade trees and sleek green lawns, manicured at the taxpayers' expense; a sprawling complex of stark, boxlike modern buildings housing acres of computers and card-files and an army of civil servants; and an ever-moving pattern of officially purposeful activity. The terminology is all there—"legislative," "executive," "judicial"—and so are a governor, a legislature, courts, and a labyrinth of departments, agencies, boards, and commissions numerous enough to fill an inch-thick manual.

But one quickly senses an antiseptic aura about Sacramento. It is devoid of the pungent aroma of gut politics that permeates most state capitals.

The uniformed guard at the entrance of the capitol building (the familiar scaled-down architectural derivative of the Capitol at Washington) doesn't look like somebody's parasitic brother-in-law, smug in a sinecure; he looks like a career civil servant. The oil portraits of past governors that line the marble-floored lobby have a stagelike, neutral quality. The large piece of statuary that dominates the capitol rotunda is a remarkable study in neutrality as well; a rather banal tableau of Columbus confronting Queen Isabella, it has no discernible connection with California, except that it was presented to the state by a wealthy latter-day pioneer, Darius Ogden Mills.

Legislators, ambling or scurrying past this cryptic display, seem less like hardened politicos than like the well-groomed sliderule-wielders of an aerospace firm. Even the seasoned corps of lobbyists have a sort of musical-comedy artificiality; their elite have a luncheon club that meets weekly at Posey's restaurant, where they are impelled to identify themselves by self-consciously wearing cartoonlike derby hats, otherwise unknown in California.

These intimations of unreality hint subtly that this is no ordinary state capital actuated by the traditional forces of American party politics.

This is the house that nonpartisanism built.

To put Sacramento's activities into perspective, it should be noted that the Gold Rush-era squabbling about where the state capital should be has led to a compromise, in deference to the complexities of administering a state that stretches over mountain, desert, and forest for 800 miles, and half of whose population is clustered some 400 miles from the capital.

When anything extraordinary happens in California, the first problem is to locate the governor. He may be at, or en route to, any of three places where he maintains official headquarters: Sacramento, San Francisco, and Los Angeles. Particularly in election years, governors find it advisable to establish a secondary residence at Los Angeles. The dead center of the state's population is on its outskirts, and within the Los Angeles metropolitan area is some 40 per cent of the state's vote.

California's attorney general conducts a similar three-base operation. The University of California's board of regents, rotating its monthly meetings among the huge institution's nine campuses, plies a circuit spanning 600 miles. The state supreme court, nominally based in Sacramento, divides most of its sittings between San Francisco and Los Angeles. (An old constitutional provision said the justices had to reside at Sacramento; a few years back they conveniently ruled the provision unconstitutional.)

California's wide-screen geography may not be a decisive factor in the state's individualistic political mores—but it helps. It accentuates sectionalism and the citizens' sense of detachment from politics, particularly from the sort of coordinated statewide partisan politics in which Sacramento is singularly lacking.

This difference is perhaps most evident in that poignant area of government known as patronage. "The governor gets $44,000 a year—and that's about all he gets," a recent occupant of the office remarked in wry allusion to this subject. In some states, the patronage positions at the governor's disposal are counted in the thousands. In California, the choice appointive positions number fewer than 100; 98 per cent of the 167,000 persons on the state payroll are under civil service or its equivalent in the state university system.

An incoming governor has some 30 key department and agency directorships, paying up to $30,000 a year, and an equal number of assistant directorships, where he can replace incumbents with his own appointees. But even these positions cannot, at least in the California tradition, be passed out purely as partisan plums. They call for special kinds of competence, which often must be sought without respect to party.

There are nearly a thousand judgeships, from the municipal level to the supreme court. During a four-year term, a governor will have several hundred judicial appointments to make. But again, the special abilities involved—plus laws imposing professional screening on many positions—tend to remove these appointments from the realm of self-serving politics. Once appointed, judges at all levels are subject to periodic endorsement by the voters in elections.

The biggest slice of out-and-out patronage, California's single anomalous counterpart of the Tammany Hall type of political spoils, ironically falls not under the governor but under the elected state controller. This patronage is the appointment of some 150 inheritance-tax appraisers, who earn an average of about $25,000 a year for the simple part-time work of evaluating estates. In return for such appointments, campaign contributions to the controller are not considered amiss. The positions, paradoxically, were established during the Hiram Johnson regime, presumably to exclude temptations to favoritism or kickbacks in the judicial system. Efforts to end the appraiser-appointment system and make the work a civil service function have repeatedly been rejected by the legislature, whose members presumably have had friends interested in the art of inheritance appraisals. In 1967, the newly elected Republican state controller, Houston Flournoy, announced that if he could not get the system abolished he was going to institute qualifying examinations to deodorize it somewhat.

Like other states, California has large chunks of Federal patronage—postmasterships, Federal judgeships, Washington appointments, and other positions, by the dozen. But these jobs are parceled out mainly through such channels as the state's congressional delegation and party national committee members, rather than through state officials.

So, altogether, a California governor does not have enough patronage to begin to build a machine to perpetuate his career or give continuing impetus to his party. Every campaign brings forth fervid allegations of "machine politics," but the terminology is ludicrous applied to California, in comparison with what goes on in other states.

"Impressive Persons"

California treats its 80 assemblymen and 40 senators better than any other state does its legislators. They are paid $16,000 a year (plus a per diem expense allowance of $25). Only New York and Michigan, with salaries of $15,000, come close to that; half the states, as of 1966, paid under $3,000. Whatever visions the nation may have of its legislators working in luxury, the fact is that only six states provide their legislators with private offices; and California is one of them.

California used to follow the common biennial system in which legislators trekked to the capital every two years for most of the lawmaking, with alternate years devoted to abbreviated budget sessions. In 1967, legislating was made virtually a full-time job, with annual sessions scheduled to run from January to July; a series of urgencies protracted the 1967 session through most of the year.

The caliber of California's legislators is high. A visiting British student of government, Hugh S. Thomas, rated the 1966 state assembly "a very impressive collection of persons—at least as well educated as Britain's House of Commons." Eighty per cent of the assemblymen had college degrees, and more than half had postgraduate degrees. By occupation the largest portion, nearly one-third, were lawyers; another third were businessmen; 9 per cent were ranchers or farmers; and 7 per cent were teachers. About 7 per cent listed their legislative service as their only occupation. Less than half the members were native Californians.

Assemblymen, who have two-year terms, are elected on the basis of population, with districts re-bounded periodically to equalize representation. The state senate—half of it elected every two years, for four-year terms—has been another story. Up to 1966, senators were elected by counties, without regard to population. Sparsely inhabited "cow counties" dominated the senate, and thereby had an inordinate influence over the work of the legislature as a whole. "Remember, son," a grizzled senator once told a new member of the chamber, "your job here is to protect the people of California from the acts of the assembly."

Measures were often obstructed for legislative blackmail or just sectional spite. The most aggravated instance was a decade's delay in activating the current $2 billion state water redistribution project. Initiated in the Warren administration, it angered the northern "cow counties" because it involved diversion of some of their surplus water to the arid south. It took years of horse-trading in projects tailored for the north to resolve the impasse.

The California senate figured prominently in the national move to rectify urban-rural imbalance in state legislatures. The chamber had one of the worst cases of disproportionate representation anywhere. Los Angeles county, with more than 6 million residents, had no more representation—one senator—than one mountain constituency with only 15,000 inhabitants.

This ended in 1966, under reapportionment ordered by the United States Supreme Court. Los Angeles received 15 senate seats instead of one. Now the three metropolitan areas of Los Angeles, San Francisco, and San Diego can, for better or worse, dominate the legislature.

In California's legislature, partisanism is a very dilute and diaphanous entity.

Back in 1915, Californians voted down Hiram Johnson's proposal that the legislature be made formally nonpartisan. (Nebraska and Minnesota are the only states with nonpartisan legislatures today.) But the forces that the Progressive reforms set in motion in California politics produced substantially the same result. Under cross-filing, a majority of legislators were elected not as the nominees of just one party, but after winning nomination by both major parties. This brought about what political scientist Francis Carney has called "a virtual hiatus in party direction of state government."

Candidates who achieved election thought of themselves as legislators first and party members only incidentally. As legislators, they joined in a sort of mutual protective association. To this day, their protracted haggling over redistricting, after each decennial Federal census, arises only in part from the dominant party's urge to gerrymander. Much of the dickering is to avoid displacing incumbents, regardless of party.

"Over the years," observed Robert Blanchard, a Los Angeles *Times* capital correspondent, "incumbent legislators built up their own little armies of followers and campaign workers, and became entrenched in their own little empires much like the feudal baronies of old. This independence allowed them to pay lip-service to party leadership when it suited their fancy, and to ignore it when they so desired."

The speaker of the assembly—generally considered the state's most powerful politico after the governor—names the chamber's committees, naturally giving his own party the lion's share of appointments. This gives him putative stop-and-go control over the parliamentary progress of bills. But the rest of the lawmaking process has tended toward a distinctly nonpartisan coloration.

On the basis of nearly half a century's first-hand observation, Joseph Beek, the senate secretary, commented in 1960:

> Roll calls in the two houses of the legislature follow different alignments on nearly every issue, with Democratic and Republican votes on each side.
>
> On rare occasions, some question arises which calls for a vote on party lines. But, running over the records, very few roll calls have been discovered wherein all the Republicans voted on one side and all the Democrats on the other.
>
> Differences on matters of party affiliation, when they arise, are taken as a matter of course and seldom provoke heated debate or cause ill will among the members. . . . The words Democrat and Republican are not often heard on the floor of the houses, and when they are heard, it is frequently in some friendly or humorous connection.

Since the abolition of cross-filing in 1959, legislators have been able to win the nomination of only one party, and they therefore have more explicit party ties. Partisan lines have become somewhat more conspicuous in the legislature. But because the legislators' constituents tend to be ambivalent in respect to party, and because the skeletal party structures provide little basis for party discipline, the legislature is still a long way from the partisanism of other states.

The "Third House"

A cliché of American politics is the allegation that California's free-form politics have all but turned state government over to lobbyists. Because of lack of party discipline, party regularity, and "party responsibility," the argument goes, manipulators for special interests have virtually a free hand. Even locally, the "legislative advocates" are often referred to with a knowing leer as the "Third House" of the legislature. It is often cited that there are "four lobbyists for every legislator." Eyes roll when mention is made of Arthur Samish, the corpulent representative of liquor and other commercial interests, who received notoriety during the Warren administration as "the secret governor of California." Governor Brown once remarked, when lobbyists' expenditures at a legislative session were reported as exceeding a million dollars, that although lobbyists had a legitimate role "blandishments on that scale need looking into."

All such talk contributes to a colorful legendry. But it remains to be demonstrated that lobbying at Sacramento is significantly more extensive or more venal than elsewhere, or that such conditions are a distinctive concomitant of California's unconventional politics. In theory it could be argued just as well that lack of partisan cohesion makes it that much more difficult for lobbyists to align support.

The very fact that Samish is the one California lobbyist in decades to have become notorious suggests that he was exceptional. He did not in fact go to prison for legislative corruption but for income-tax evasion. Although he was known as a font of largesse for legislators—primarily in the legal form of campaign contributions—bribery, direct or indirect, was not the real basis of his influence. It was the clever manipulation of coalitions of disparate interests.

"Samish invented the invisible lobby in California," remarked former California Attorney General Robert Kenny. "If a legislator tried to move against the banks, then the oil companies, insurance companies, trucking concerns and railroads all would join in helping out the banks. It was a system of mutual aid."

Lobbying, of course, is recognized as an integral part of American democratic government—the means by which special interests, be they profit-making oil companies or altruistic conservationists, can express their desires in the process of lawmaking. It is when advocacy moves beyond verbal suasion to bribery that lobbying becomes bad. No law can be designed that will preclude occasional bribery. The best safeguard against improper lobbying is for lobbyists' activities to be spread on the public record. In this regard, California is far ahead of most other states, and ahead of the Federal government's regulation of lobbying in Washington.

The Federal government's major regulatory move was a 1946 law requiring Washington lobbyists to register if their "principal purpose" on behalf of clients was influencing legislation. This provided an escape hatch: for instance, a lawyer who spent the majority of his time in legal work for a client, as opposed to part-time contacting of legislators, could claim exemption from registering.

Registrations under the law have ranged from as few as 204 in a year to as many as 942. Senator Mike Monroney estimated in 1967 that the latest total of 384 registrations represented only about 10 per cent of the actual lobbyists.

California, by contrast, requires all paid legislative advocates operating at the capitol to register and list their clients; to file sworn monthly reports of what legislation they were concerned with, their salaries, and how much they spent; and to record such public activities as advertising and propaganda campaigns.

Sacramento's annual roster of "legislative representatives" runs to about 500. But many of these are individuals registered for one-time appearances; it is doubtful that more than 200 are full-time operatives.

In recent years one of the most active lobbyists has been James D. Garibaldi, a Los Angeles lawyer and former judge. He has represented, simultaneously, both the Hollywood Park and Del Mar race tracks, the California Beverage Distributors Association, the Signal Oil Company, the Blue Chip Stamp Company, and several other organizations. In a typical month's activity, he reported spending $4,485.

The lobby that is often considered the most influential in

Sacramento is not, as might be expected, some big corporate interest but the California Teachers Association, represented in 1967 by William H. Barton. The association comprises 145,000 of the 170,000 full-time teachers in California, whose "industry," education, gets more than 40 per cent of the state budget.

Lately, the reported expenditures of Sacramento lobbyists have aggregated about $600,000 during a six-month legislative session, and up to $1,300,000 for a calendar year. If one assumed that 200 full-time lobbyists spent $1 million over a six-month period, it would average out to less than $30 a day apiece, a scale of expenditure hardly likely to corrupt anyone.

Most of the lobbyists' expenditures go for maintaining personal contacts in such ways as picking up restaurant checks, maintaining "hospitality rooms," giving parties, and taking legislators on fishing trips. A great hullabaloo arose after the 1963 session over reports that a few lobbyists had imported a half-dozen call girls from San Francisco to influence legislators. A three-month investigation by the state attorney general's office produced only the anticlimactic report that "at least two assemblymen patronized call girls."

Princeton University's Dr. Duane Lockard, after a study of California lobbying, concluded:

> Interest groups did purchase legislation through [campaign] contributions in the most successful days of Artie Samish. But this is not the customary practice . . . in California today. Although special interests contribute to legislators who they believe share their viewpoint, or who they hope will do so, they carefully refrain from demanding a specific quid pro quo.

Apart from their officially scrutinized capitol activities, lobbyists are recognized as a considerable source of campaign contributions to legislators, and one would be naive to assume that no skulduggery goes on here. But in general a lobbyist has so many legislators to get along with that his campaign largesse has to be spread thin. A survey made a few years ago of legislators' campaign funds indicated that contributions from lobbyists were too nominal and too diversified in source, and amounted to too small a portion of overall campaign costs, to bulk as a corruptive influence. A typical assemblyman got $200 from an oil lobbyist, $200 from a medical lobbyist, $200 from a beer lobbyist, and $100 from a pharmaceutical trade association. But the aggregate from the lobbyists was eclipsed by a $1,250 contribution from a group of labor unions. The total contrasted sharply with 1964 campaign expenditures ranging up to $42,000 for an assemblyman and $64,000 for a state senator, with the average for 100 legislative candidates coming to $17,000.

Seemingly of far more significance than lobbyists' bounty as an improper influence on legislators is the matter of personal conflicts of interest. This is in no way unique to California; but, again, California has been exceptionally progressive in dealing with the problem.

A Los Angeles *Times* investigation of legislators' finances in 1965 concluded:

> Many legislators are involved in a variety of financial interests which offer the potential at least of conflicting with their responsibilities as representatives of the people; a surprising number of them have obtained stock in savings and loan associations and banks chartered by the state, some having decidedly political overtones; forty-seven of 119 interviewed are attorneys whose representation of certain clients, particularly in matters before state regulatory agencies, also creates a conflict-of-interest problem.

In 1966 the legislature passed what sponsors described as the "toughest" conflict-of-interest law in the country. Carrying a misdemeanor penalty for violation, the law states:

> The Legislature . . . recognizes that members and legislative employees may need to engage in employment, pro-

> fessional or business activities other than legislative activities, in order to maintain a continuity of professional or business activity, or may need to maintain investments, which activities or investments do not conflict with the specific provisions [of this law]. . . .
>
> However, in construing and administering [the law] weight should be given to any coincidence of income, employment, investment or other profit from sources which may be identified with the interests represented by those sources which are seeking action of any character on matters then pending before the Legislature.
>
> No member of the Legislature, state elective officer, or appointee of any such officer, or judge or justice shall, while serving as such, have any interest, financial or otherwise, direct or indirect, or engage in any business or transaction or professional activity, or incur any obligation of any nature, which is in substantial conflict with the proper discharge of his duties in the public interest and of his responsibilities as prescribed in the laws of this state.

Dr. Alexander Heard, political scientist at Nashville's Vanderbilt University, commented recently: "The California legislature has perhaps done more to improve its capacity to meet the extraordinary problems it faces than has any other."

"Proposition X"

A tour of California government would be quite incomplete without a glimpse at the activities of one very specialized and energetic bloc of lawmakers: the citizens themselves.

Governor Hiram Johnson, it will be recalled, in his fear of any resurgence of legislative corruption, sought to "arm the people to protect themselves." The weapons adopted were: the initiative, a form of do-it-yourself citizen legislation; the referendum, by which citizens could nullify legislators' enactments; and recall, which is the dismissal, by popular vote, of unsatisfactory office-holders.

The tradition of "direct legislation" is still vital. Other

states have instituted the initiative, the referendum, and recall. But nowhere do these devices figure so actively in government and politics from year to year as in California.

In the state election on November 8, 1966, voters had about three times as many decisions to make about state laws as about selecting officials; there were only six statewide offices at stake, but there were 17 numbered "propositions" on the ballot. One involved a routine bond issue. Fourteen were proposed constitutional amendments, referred to the voters at the instance of the legislature, on matters ranging from benefits for the blind to taxation of insurance companies. Another proposition, placed on the ballot through a citizens' initiative petition, outlined a law to suppress "obscenity." Finally, there was a proposal from the legislature to amend a prize-fighting law; this could be done only with citizen approval because the law had originated in a citizen-initiative proposition in an election years before.

This spate of propositions in 1966 was not extraordinary. Each election brings up from one to two dozen. One reason for so much of this activity is that California's monstrous 60,000-word constitution of 1879 has become a catch-all for enactments that should really be ordinary statutes; but, being constitutional provisions, they can be altered only by popular vote. Moves for a complete overhaul of the unwieldly constitution have repeatedly come to naught. The people apparently prefer to keep renovating it piecemeal in elections.

Hence, since 1912, some 473 constitutional changes have been submitted to voters—an average of more than 17 at each biennial election. In 391 cases, the proposals went on the ballot formally by vote of the legislature, responding to public pressures. In 82 cases, public petitions put the proposed amendments on the ballot. Over the same period, 59 proposals for new statutes, as differentiated from constitutional amendments, originated in public initiative petitions.

The device of the referendum, which Governor Johnson felt important for citizens to have as a club over the legislature, has been used less often. Voters have invoked it only 35 times since 1912; in 22 cases, enactments of the legislature were nullified.

The last of the three Johnson weapons, the recall of unsatisfactory officials, is used constantly in local government. "The smaller the community, the more often it comes up," one observer remarks. But it has rarely been invoked at the state level. No governor has ever been recalled, although there have been some uncompleted gubernatorial recall movements, notably against Governors Rolph and Olson.

As this is being written there are, as usual, more initiative campaigns being mounted. To get an initiative proposition on the ballot, a group of citizens first take their proposal to the secretary of state, who gives it a title, a brief description to head each petition sheet, and a number. The number is important, because that is how the proposal becomes identified in the ensuing campaigning: "Vote YES on 16" . . . "NO on 9!" Sponsors strive to get low numbers, which will appear high up on the ballot. Measures particularly distasteful to the incumbent administration have been known to end up with number 13.

Sponsors of a proposal then have 130 days to collect the required number of signatures by registered voters. The number is 5 per cent of the vote in the preceding election.

In Hiram Johnson's day, it took only about 30,000 signatures to qualify a proposal for the ballot. Now it takes about 500,000 signatures. This has given rise to the specialized business of signature collecting, which several firms now do for fees that may run to more than 25 cents a signature. This means that initiative campaigns, with the necessary publicity, cost hundreds of thousands of dollars, and have moved a long way from the theory of a simple citizen effort. Sponsors of 1964's subsequently invalidated Proposition 17 to outlaw pay television—notably theater-owners—reported spending $1,900,000.

The principle of "direct legislation" has remained controversial down the years. The chief allegations against it are that it has become a "rich man's" device; that it is only an inefficient way of doing what the legislature is elected and trained to do; and that it is too easily perverted by unscrupulous people promoting unworthy causes. But the public seems unswayed by these alarums. An opinion survey in 1965 indicated that while 5 per cent of voters thought the initiative should be abolished, 31 per cent wanted only changes in the process, and 47 per cent favored keeping it just as it was.

"Willingness to Grapple . . ."

The government that has evolved, either in spite of or because of California's atypical politics, has been receiving more and more favorable recognition.

Trevor Armbrister, who made an in-depth survey of state governments across the country in 1966 for the *Saturday Evening Post,* reported: "California is not the sole repository of political virtue in the United States, nor is its virtue uniform. . . . Yet in its demonstrated willingness to grapple with gut issues, the state can serve as a qualified example to its 49 sisters."

There are, of course, no precise criteria for such a comparison. The main test of government is whether it works. And California's not only has worked in the ordinary sense but has produced some remarkable accomplishments in the face of more formidable problems than those of perhaps any other state.

California, despite its reputation as a demiparadise, was less than perfectly endowed by nature to accommodate the 17 million people who swelled its population in the half century after Hiram Johnson. Much of the state to this day is wilderness and desert. Nearly half the total is under Federal jurisdiction yielding little or no tax revenue. Most rainfall is concentrated in a minor fraction of the state, leaving the rest arid. California's thousand-mile coastline is singularly lacking in natural harbors. The body of the state is inconveniently segmented laterally and longitudinally by a half-dozen mountain ranges. Except for evanescent gold and oil deposits, there is little natural basis for industry.

Yet California's government proved equal to the myriad problems of assimilating 17 million people. It used epochal engineering to rationalize the water supply; it knit the state together by a matchless network of highways; it shepherded the state through successive economic transitions from mining to agriculture, conventional industry, and finally aerospace and esoteric electronic technology; it built the largest state-sponsored university and college system in the world; and it pioneered in developing solutions to such nationwide problems as urban-traffic management and air pollution.

All this is taken largely for granted now, amidst preoccupation with problems still unsolved. What often is overlooked is that all that has been done could have been botched, or not done at all, leaving a California developed to only a fraction of what it is today.

That things evolved as they did is undoubtedly due in large measure to the phenomenal collective imagination and initiative of California's citizens. But their efforts would have been anarchic and unfruitful without the stabilization, coordination, and leadership of an exceptional instrument of government.

Chapter Eleven

Musical Chairs: Nixon, Knowland, and Knight

☒ ONLY IN CALIFORNIA COULD A POLITICAL party have a million more members than its opposition and still be out of power.

Yet that was the situation in the fall of 1953. For 20 years the Democrats' share of registered voters had been mounting steadily, until they now outnumbered Republicans by 3 million to 2 million. But the stratagems begun in the Hiram Johnson era to strengthen an incumbent minority—notably, hamstrung party structures and the obfuscations of cross-filing—had perpetuated Democratic impotence.

The end of this anomaly began on a sun-drenched November weekend in Fresno, the "raisin capital," in the heart of the San Joaquin Valley. It began so inconspicuously as to escape immediate notice by the three men whose careers, years later, would be most poignantly affected by the development.

Governor Goodwin Knight was preoccupied in Sacramento, fingering the reins he had taken over from Earl Warren only two months before. William F. Knowland was in Washington, luxuriating in the Senate seat to which he had been returned virtually unopposed the year before. Richard M. Nixon, rounding out his first year as Vice-President of the United States, was 12,000 miles away on a global tour, making a speech in Ceylon, tossing rhetorical barbs at the Communists.

Ironically, at that very moment, the most imminent Communist ploy was right back in Nixon's home state of California. Local Marxists, alert to organizational stirrings among the Democrats, were plotting to infiltrate. Five hundred Democratic activists from all over the state had converged on Fresno that weekend. Among them were members of the Fifth Column.

The dim-lit meeting room in the Fresno Hotel was steamy with bodies jammed elbow-to-elbow on folding chairs. In the center of the throng, a tall, muscular, shirt-sleeved young man had taken the floor to say a few words on behalf of Democratic unity. He was John Despol, state secretary of the Congress of Industrial Organizations.

"We've got to do this, and we've got to do it right!" he exhorted. "We've had only one Democratic governor in this century, and that was over ten years ago. We just lost a presidential election. Yet we have a million more members than they do. I say it's time to do something about it. Let's *get together!*"

For the first time in living memory, California's Democrats seemed on the verge of forming an effective organization —an "unofficial" association, to circumvent the legally ordained impotence of the official party organization. But Despol, a veteran of the industrial unionizing wars, was known to be militantly anti-Communist. For four, five, six, or eight shadowy figures scattered strategically through the room, he was the enemy. His voice should not be allowed to keynote the new movement.

Out of the shadows the voices came. Carefully spotted. No two together. One on his right. One just in front of him, on the left. Two behind on one side. Three on the other. The voices cut in like whipcracks.

"Point of order!"

"Siddown, ya bum!"

"He's a Fascist!"

"He shouldn't be speaking for this organization!"

"Mr. Chairman! . . ."

"Point of order!" . . . "Mr. Chairman, I'd like to express the true feelings of this group." . . . "Let's hear from a *real* Democrat. . . ."

Despol, perspiring, glanced around him. Most people would have been cowed. The heckling was vicious, relentless. But he recognized the hecklers. He'd seen them operate before. He waited them out, measuring his breathing, like a fighter. Waited till their canned static was spent. Then he went on. . . .

That afternoon, the Communist boarding-party repelled, the California Democratic Council came into being—a federation of the hundreds of Democratic clubs up and down the state, now bent on exerting the power of superior numbers that had been dissipated for 20 years in disorganization and factionalism. Alan Cranston, a writer, real estate developer and, subsequently, state controller, was chosen as the Council's first president. Other prime movers were State Senator George Miller, Jr., and Paul Ziffren.

A few days later in Los Angeles, Ziffren, a tall, hawk-faced lawyer who was an alumnus of the Jacob Arvey school of practical politics in Illinois and later California's Democratic national committeeman, talked about the Council's future: "Patronage is the glue that ordinarily holds a political organization together. Here in California, we haven't got the patronage. If you don't have patronage, you've only got one thing to go on: ideological affinity. We never had that before. But Adlai Stevenson's campaign gave it to us, even though he didn't win. California Democrats are excited. If we can harness that excitement, we'll come out on top. It's going to take a lot of work. It won't happen tomorrow. . . ."

His eyes, behind professorial horn-rimmed spectacles, narrowed. "I'd say if things go right, you'll see results by . . . maybe 1958. . . ."

Audition for Disaster

Ziffren's target date of 1958 proved remarkably prescient. That was the juncture when some Republicans, discontented, turned to the unlikely remedy of party hari-kari. Governor Goodwin Knight, the gregarious, back-slapping ex-judge, had been a bitter disappointment to California's conservative Republicans.

On taking office October 5, 1953, he had hinted that he might be less liberal than Earl Warren. While disparaging "the rigor mortis of reactionary policies," he added reassuringly: "I shall reject all the St. Vitus dance theories of radicalism. . . ."

But Knight, a Harding-handsome type whose shrewdness in gold-mining and commodity-market speculation had gained him a nice nest-egg, had his sights set on nothing less than the White House. To offset his conservative ties, he had romanced organized labor.

"No California governor in the last 20 years has assumed office with such strongly avowed labor support," wrote Herbert Phillips, the capitol correspondent.

Knight sponsored three increases in unemployment insurance, raising it from $25 to $40 a week. Disability insurance, workmen's compensation, and widows' benefits were also increased. Legislation was adopted to protect workers' pension and welfare funds.

"Never in my years in Sacramento," state AFL leader Cornelius Haggerty told friends, "have I had a governor, Republican or Democrat, call me into his office as Governor Knight has, and say: 'Neil—this is your bill. You write it. Tell me what you want in it, and I'll see that you get it.' "

The conservatives considered themselves betrayed. They wanted a real conservative at Sacramento. They wanted labor put in its place. They thought they knew the man for the job.

Late in the afternoon of January 7, 1957, there occurred in Washington one of the more unexpected events in many years, which proved to be another turning point in the California saga.

After a courtesy call at the White House, the Senate minority leader, William F. Knowland, called a press conference to announce that, when his term ended nearly a year thence, he would not be a candidate for re-election. He was cryptic about his reasons, intoning in his ponderous bass that he hoped to "return to California" to spend more time "in closer proximity" to his family.

But there could be only one reason for this curious renunciation. "Big Bill" Knowland, a personification of the Republican elephant, was, in a characteristically cumbersome way, serving notice that he was going to run for governor of California in 1958.

Knowland had spent half his 49 years in public and party office, as a state assemblyman and state senator, as a Republican national committeeman, and as a United States Senator for 11 years since his original interim appointment by Earl Warren. In 1952 he had won dual nomination, drawing more votes as an interloper in the Democratic primary than the party's own entry, Representative Clinton McKinnon.

The disclosure of Knowland's gubernatorial aspirations pleased the Knight-haters. But among California's more realistic Republicans his announcement caused astonishment and consternation.

In his cubicle at the Los Angeles *Times,* the usually ruddy Kyle Palmer, party strategist, turned white. Typically, in California's loose-jointed party system, Senator Knowland had not mentioned his scheme to those who would have to bear the brunt of the battle.

His strategy was apparent. To get the governorship, he would have to bulldoze his fellow Republican, Governor Knight, out of the way. But Knight would be a good foil in a primary mock-battle, which Knowland felt he could win.

It was a gamble. But the stakes were maximal. Once in the governorship, with his Senate background, Knowland would be set for a pass at the Presidency of the United States.

But more objective Republican strategists assessed his scheme differently. They saw in it the schismatic makings of a party disaster.

One man whose outlook was a little different was Vice-President Richard Nixon. Nixon, Knowland, and Knight were the "Big Three" in California Republicanism—men whose ambitions had long been on collision courses.

Knight had quite candidly been nursing dreams of a presidential try ever since rumors started circulating in 1955 that Ike might decline to run again.

"I would certainly like to be President," he told a reporter in May, 1955. "Any politician who is forthright, honest and candid must confess that it is the greatest honor that can come to a citizen. I'm not going to lie to the people, and I'm not going to be coy."

The Big Three's competition had been dramatized at the stage-play Republican National Convention in San Francisco in 1956 that went through the motions of renominating Eisenhower and Nixon. Because of the intense Nixon-Knowland-

Knight rivalry, California's delegation had had to be split three ways with mathematical precision—23 delegates to each man, with the 70th seat assigned to a "neutral," Senator Thomas Kuchel.

There was little question that California would support Nixon for renomination, despite a national "dump Nixon" movement some party mavericks had mounted. Knowland automatically swung his faction to support the Nixon bloc. But cagey Goodwin Knight, playing his hand down to the last deuce, held out over the whole pre-convention weekend on the off chance that something would happen to Nixon and he could lunge for the opening. It didn't work. By the time Chairman Leonard Hall opened the great convention with his euphoric: "Is everybody happy?" Knight had nothing to do but support Nixon too—for the time being. But with the leverage of the California governor's chair, Knight had remained a vague threat, a small cloud over Nixon's future.

A less astute political operator than Nixon might, after Knowland's amazing announcement of January, 1957, have seen in the prospective Knowland-Knight primary battle the setting for his rivals to kill each other off. But that would have meant the certain shattering of the California Republican party, which was Nixon's only real base. There was an alternative: shunt Knight from a primary collision with Knowland into the contest for Knowland's vacant seat, thereby perhaps ameliorating the party split; and let Knowland fight it out with whomever the Democrats put up in November.

The plan was not immediately imparted to Knowland.

Potomac Myopia

Although the campaign was more than a year away, Knowland lost no time in drawing the battle line with Knight: the issue was to be labor. At a Los Angeles dinner in April, 1957, Knowland went out of his way to assert that "the right to earn a living as an employee or proprietor of a small business is a civil right of the first magnitude." This was a tacit endorsement of the contentious "right to work" (open shop) principle, rejected by California voters in 1942, which Knight had promised labor would come into California only over his dead body. A new drive for the open-shop law was afoot all across the country. Eighteen states already had the law. It was a 1958 election issue in five states besides California.

In mid-August, snorting defiance of Knowland's still-undeclared candidacy, Knight announced he was running for governor again. On October 3, Knowland declared his candidacy, offering elaborate, if specious, rationalization for the primary battle he was precipitating.

Asked in effect what reason there was for elbowing Knight out of the governorship, Knowland responded with the cliché: "The voters are entitled to a choice." He went on to indicate that the "choice" he had in mind was a choice between Knight's alliance with organized labor and his own predilection for the open shop.

Moments after Knowland read his announcement to newsmen in a second-floor parlor of Sacramento's Senator Hotel, Governor Knight counter-volleyed from his office across the street, denouncing Knowland's course as "a hydra-headed bid for the Presidency" that the California electorate would "view with serious reservations." To this Knowland was naive enough to respond with the comment that became a doleful litany throughout his campaign: "Well, no one has a crystal ball. . . ."

Knowland was a conspicuous victim of an affliction known in California as "Potomac myopia"—the notion that years of prestigious activity in Washington can be translated into voting strength back in California. It is a delusion that has often misled Washington commentators in their assessments of California political situations, and it has been beguiling enough to betray even such a political sophisticate as Richard Nixon.

Knowland also exemplified another handicap that has shown itself to be a very important factor in California politics: the stigma of carpetbagging—making an abrupt descent on the political scene from outside the state.

Time and again California voters have shown that they resent anyone's assumption that he can convert alien stature into political legal tender in California. They like to think of their arena as select, so that an aspirant for public support must prove himself on the scene. And they resent any implication that California office is merely being used as a stepping-stone to a better position elsewhere.

This attitude may be provincial. But it prevails, and it does not seem any more provincial than an outsider's presumption that the California electorate can be easily taken by storm.

Several politicians have come to grief by relying on two fallacious notions to overcome this electoral prejudice. One is the idea that being a native son of California takes the curse off carpetbagging.

Nativity means nothing if the person concerned has been out of the state for a period of years; he is automatically identified with his other milieu. Knowland suffered from this. Both Richard Nixon and Pierre Salinger were subsequent casualties.

The other fallacy, which repeatedly has been naively voiced by newcomers to the political scene, is the notion: "Most Californians come from somewhere else, so this is an attribute I share with them."

This idea is invalidated by a fundamental quirk of human psychology. Most Californians have come from somewhere else. But there's no zealot like a recent convert, be it to a religious faith, or the water wagon—or residence in California. The latter-day pioneers who arrived ten years ago look down on the ones who arrived only five years ago, and the psychological pecking order runs right down the line. And at the end of the line is the politician who hove into sight just in time for the current campaign.

Musical Chairs

It took only a few weeks of pressures from Nixon intermediaries and party leaders in California to maneuver Knight out of the gubernatorial race. On November 5, he emerged from ceremonial calls on President Eisenhower and Vice-President Nixon in Washington to announce:

"I have reached the conclusion that my best and most constructive course would be to run for the United States Senate next year . . . a Knight-Knowland struggle would split the party so badly it would in all probability lead to the loss of the state to the Democratic party. . . ."

"I had no other choice," Knight lamented later. "I was like a man in the middle of the ocean, standing on the deck of a burning ship."

Almost simultaneously with Knight's *démarche* came the announcement of Knowland's campaign organization. Observers were not surprised to find the list peppered with Nixon people—obviously as a result of some backstage collaboration. The ostensible alliance is catalogued as a choice example of Nixon's political address.

"Nixon killed two birds, or two potential rivals, with one stroke, by helping maneuver Knight out of the gubernatorial race, in the name of party harmony," commented Stewart Alsop in the *Saturday Evening Post*. "Knowland's primary punching-bag was gone; and Knight's future was made to hinge on the outcome of a very formidable contest for the Senate."

Knowland later tacitly corroborated this. "Neither I nor anyone authorized to represent me," he declared, "had anything to do with the governor's change of decision."

The "Big Switch," in moderating a big collision, set up a smaller one. San Francisco's Mayor George Christopher had already announced his candidacy for the Knowland Senate seat.

So there was more elbowing aside to be done, in the face of the formidable Democratic opposition of Representative Clair Engle, who had repeatedly proved himself a strong bipartisan vote-drawer.

Once upon a time, such an intraparty conflict would have been subject to resolution by the party's "unofficial" screening arm, the California Republican Assembly. But now, when the chips were down and a critical choice was to be made, the organization revealed its inherent weakness. It didn't have the rank-and-file following to support a decision one way or the other. So it didn't make any decision.

"Nixon, Knowland, and Knight played a game of musical chairs," the whimsical Robert Kenny remarked later. "And when the music finally stopped, it appeared that Mr. Nixon was occupying all three chairs."

Chapter
Twelve

1958: Nonpartisanism Rides Again

☒ IT SEEMINGLY TOOK SENATOR KNOWLAND much longer than most Californians to realize that he had jumped into political quicksand. In Biblical times, the handwriting might have appeared on the wall. In this instance, the portents were conveyed electronically.

Onto the television screen, one autumn night in 1958, came a view of a street corner in Boyle Heights, a Mexican-

American district of Los Angeles. A chubby, bespectacled man in a neat business suit was happily pumping the hands of passers-by. Behind him, on a parked bus, a banner with two-foot letters proclaimed BROWN FOR GOVERNOR.

"You're Manny Gonzales?" the hand-pumper exclaimed. "Don't you have a brother in the attorney general's office in Sacramento? . . . I thought so—he's one of our best people!"

Quickly the television picture shifted. Los Angeles' Grand Central Market. Senator Knowland, handsome, earnest, was singling out an elderly lady.

"You've lived in California 30 years? Well—hah—as we say in the Senate, that gives you *seniority*—hah!"

Station KNXT continued its television report on the split-level day the rival candidates had spent working the state's biggest city. Now the camera cut to Chinatown. In front of an ersatz pagoda, a cluster of grinning Asiatic faces greeted Brown. . . . "You know, I'm the fellow that has to enforce the laws in this state. Have we been doing all right for you on civil rights? . . . You're going to vote for me, aren't you?" A cheer went up.

A shopping center. Knowland talking to a young mother pushing a baby carriage: "Born right here in Los Angeles, was he? Well, not too many of us were born in California. As we say in the Senate, that gives him *seniority*. Hah!"

The Democrats had steadily gathered strength since that steamy Fresno afternoon in 1953 when the California Democratic Council was born.

The "unofficial" Council had frankly modeled itself after the "unofficial" California Republican Assembly, which for more than two decades had been instrumental in keeping its party in power despite a minority following. Like the CRA, the CDC's chief function was the pre-primary endorsement of selected candidates, to focus the party vote and minimize primary attrition.

Unlike the CRA, whose endorsements came out of small

"fact-finding" committees, the CDC made its endorsements by mass action at rollicking and often stormy conventions. As the number of local Democratic clubs throughout the state mounted from little over 100 to 200, 300, and finally 500, with a claimed aggregate membership of 50,000 partisan zealots, the representative CDC conventions became the biggest Democratic assemblages in the nation in terms of delegates, replete with bunting, emotional oratory, and back-room maneuvering.

Some 1,400 delegates swarmed back to Fresno on February 6, 1954, to sift candidates for that year's election.

The gubernatorial campaign was already too close on for effective action. The CDC endorsee, and subsequent party nominee, was Richard P. Graves, one of California's top professionals in public administration and the head of the League of California Cities. But Governor Knight, who had inherited Earl Warren's impetus, was not to be that easily dislodged.

There were compensations, however. With 30 Congressional seats at stake, not one Republican captured a Democratic nomination. Among 140 contests for Congress, the legislature, and statewide constitutional offices, there were only 30 bipartisan nominations. For the first time since the introduction of cross-filing 40 years before, the party was able to place a full slate of Democratic candidates for statewide offices on the November election ballot. John Despol, the recently beleaguered orator, observed that the primary outcome marked "the end of one-party domination of the primary election."

In 1956 California, while voting along with the rest of the country for President Eisenhower, gave Adlai Stevenson his only improved showing in any state, cutting Eisenhower's 1952 lead by about 100,000 votes. The Democrats ran in a dead heat—20-20—with the Republicans for the state senate, coming within an ace of controlling that chamber for the first time since 1890. The Republicans' state assembly majority was whittled from 45–35 to 42–38. Democratic candidates for the legislature won seven dual nominations, the Republicans only two.

Between 1952 and 1958, two out of every three new voters joined the Democratic party. The Democrats' registration margin rose from 957,000 to 1,199,000, as party membership increased to 3,996,000.

By the time Knowland made his fateful announcement, Republicans were candidly acknowledging their opponents' momentum. Under the scare headline, REPUBLICAN PARTY LOSING STATE LEGISLATURE!, a Republican membership bulletin said: "The Democrats of California have made tremendous progress and assisted their statewide candidates greatly through the use of the council of Democratic clubs. . . ."

The Lone Moose

Nevertheless, when it came to the 1958 campaign the Democrats still had only one of their number in statewide office: Attorney General Edmund Gerald (Pat) Brown. As district attorney of San Francisco, he had been the only major Democratic winner in 1950. While Earl Warren was winning his third term, the Republicans split over their nominee for attorney general.

Brown was not only a native Californian; his roots went back to the Gold Rush. His German-born grandfather on his mother's side, August Shuckman, had driven a stagecoach between Sacramento and the celebrated mining center Hangtown, now Placerville. His Irish paternal forebears had come by ship around the Horn in 1859. Brown was born in 1905 in San Francisco, where his father operated a theater and a cigar store. He acquired the nickname Pat as a schoolboy orator, given to quoting Patrick Henry.

Brown could claim bipartisan background. His first stab at politics, as a neophyte lawyer in San Francisco, was an unsuccessful race for the state assembly as a Republican. He switched to the Democratic party early in the New Deal; after one unsuccessful try for the district attorneyship of San Francisco (which has a combined city-county government), he won the office in 1943.

Brown was pudgy, friendly, buoyant; well read but with no intellectual pretensions; and utterly honest. His instinct for practical politics, however, was impaired by an excessive dislike of offending people. This led to recurrent spells of indecisiveness that produced the epithet "a tower of jelly." But he did not lack moral courage; once in San Francisco, in the face of public wrath, he asked a judge to dismiss a case he had prosecuted to sure conviction, because he ascertained that a key witness had lied.

Some three weeks after Knowland announced his candidacy for governor, Brown announced his, with a blast at the Republicans for presenting voters with a choice between "a wavering incumbent, deserted by his own party [*Knight*], and a reactionary who views the state's highest office only as a pawn in presidential power politics."

Brown, like other aspirants before and since, invoked the hallowed shibboleth:

". . . I believe the governor must call on the most able and experienced men and women of our state, without regard to partisanship," he said. "I intend to guide our state government in the great tradition of Earl Warren and Hiram Johnson!"

Nonpartisanism was on the march again.

It was one of those perverse ironies of politics that the year the Democrats achieved their greatest strength was the year they needed it least. Big Bill Knowland, described in the New York *Times* as "the Lone Moose," was intently committing political suicide in a manner that pained even his opponents.

In a bipartisan milieu, he had a figurative placard around his neck that said "Mr. Republican." His very presence in California, after his prominence in Washington, led to inferences of carpetbagging. In response to taunts about presidential ambitions, he never produced anything more serviceable than his equivocal, "No one has a crystal ball—"

His "Potomac myopia" kept showing. He was wont to wind up speeches with a heart-rending vignette of the Hungarian freedom fighters (which seemed singularly irrelevant to the problems of San Luis Obispo and Buttonwillow) and top that off with a ringing quotation from Thomas Jefferson about being determined to fight "tyranny in any form"—which, if it was meant as an allusion to labor unionism and "right to work," did little to illuminate the issue.

Knowland had hoped, with "right to work," to split the labor vote and project an issue that would cut across party lines. Opinion polls a year in advance of the election had produced a majority in favor of a "right to work" law. But soundings so far ahead are notoriously unreliable. The issue boomeranged in two ways.

On January 11, 1958, an employers' group calling itself the Citizens Committee for Democracy in Labor Unions took out papers for an initiative petition campaign to put the open-shop question on the ballot—"Proposition 18." Some 322,000 signatures were required but, with the sponsors' resources, collection of these by a commercial organization was no problem.

Knowland sedulously associated his campaign with Proposition 18. That was a mistake, a trap that others fell into before and after Knowland. The proposal would succeed or fail irrespective of whether Knowland was elected. By identifying himself with it, he ran more risk of losing votes from opponents of the measure than of gaining votes from people who happened to agree with him.

Secondly, the issue didn't split organized labor. It united labor, provoking the most massive opposition campaign organized labor had ever mounted—one that cost ultimately about $2 million. The opposition strategy was so thorough that labor even whipped up a sly diversionary action. A big campaign was staged on behalf of Proposition 17, a measure purporting to cut consumer sales taxes and shift the burden to income and corporate taxes. This was calculated to terrify employers and make them expend effort opposing it, distracting them from pushing "right to work." It did.

Brown, meanwhile, in a succession of succinct, warm speeches, was outlining a program of "responsible liberalism" for California—and shaking hands and crystallizing votes—while Knowland was wearing thin his feeble sally, ". . . that gives you seniority."

Both candidates coasted through the primaries without significant opposition, except from each other. More than one out of five Republicans voted for Brown as a cross-filed entry; only one out of seven Democrats voted for Knowland.

Out of a total primary vote of 3,954,000, Brown got 1,890,000 Democratic votes and 374,000 Republican votes. Knowland got 1,290,000 Republican votes and 313,000 Democratic votes. The aggregate margin for Brown was 662,000.

In the senatorial primaries, the Republican vote went 49.2 per cent to Knight, 34.7 per cent to Christopher, and 10.8 per cent to Engle, cross-filed; the Democratic vote went 72 per cent to Engle, 17.8 to Knight, and 10.2 per cent to Christopher.

Campaign of Curiosa

The campaign that followed, comments Dr. Totton Anderson, University of Southern California political scientist, "was one of the strangest collections of curiosa in the state's rather unique political history. The first paradox was the abandonment by the Republican party of a time-tested formula: a candidate who blurred party lines, preempted the middle of the road, and forced the Democratic aspirant into a posture allegedly left of center. The bemused electorate was offered instead a choice between a wealthy, arch-conservative, militantly partisan, austere, Protestant Republican, and a self-made, middle-of-the-road, relatively unpartisan, friendly Catholic Democrat."

Knowland fell victim to one of the most potent weapons an adversary can ply in California politics: the "nice guy" role.

The "nice guy" gambit involves more than just personal demeanor. It means pre-empting the *defensive* position, contrary to the classic rules of warfare, which put the premium on offense. The "nice guy" candidate takes the high road, and he deals in constructive-sounding truisms at which few voters can take offense. He identifies himself implicitly with all that's solid and worth while, maneuvering his opponent into the offensive role of fault-finding, criticizing, carping, and throwing brickbats. Soon the opponent starts looking like a disruptive boat-rocker, a negative figure. Then he is finished. California's populace, rootless by definition to begin with, and now wedded to a veritable state of flux, dislikes any injection of further instabilities. What the people really want is reassurance. The "nice guy" candidate offers this.

The strategy has been used to advantage time and again. It was one of Earl Warren's assets—you could disagree violently with his position, but you couldn't fault him on sincerity, good intentions, and positivism. His protégé, Senator Thomas Kuchel, became a skilled exponent of the "nice guy" posture, and twice shellacked State Senator Richard Richards—whose personality was essentially warmer than Kuchel's—by maneuvering him into a negative position. Brown worked it to good effect against Knowland.

From his unpromising position in the June primary Knowland's campaign went steadily downhill. Later analysis indicated that his campaigning simply lost him votes at a rate of 2,000 a day. His troubles were augmented by two curious gaffes ascribed to his wife. She sent a caustic seven-page letter to 200 Republican leaders throughout the state, blasting Knight as having a "macaroni spine," asserting—quite implausibly—that "Big Labor" had given Knight "the old heave-ho" out of the primary because it feared his defeat, and declaring: "California may be the last hope of saving our country from the piggy-back labor-socialist monster which has latched onto the Democratic party." Senator Knowland acknowledged that he had known of the letter, but said he did not interfere because his wife had "a right to express her own views."

Less than a month before the election it was disclosed that Mrs. Knowland also had distributed 500 copies of a pamphlet attacking labor leader Walter P. Reuther. Called "Meet the Man Who Plans to Rule America," it was written by Joseph P. Kamp, a right-wing propagandist of scant prestige.

Knowland ended his campaign with wild-swinging charges against Brown, attempting to blacken him with guilt by association three degrees removed, through alleged long-past underworld connections of Democrats unconnected with Brown's administration.

An unintentionally wry commentary on the orientation of the Knowland campaign emerged from Knowland headquarters just before the debacle of November 4. It was an announcement headed:

KNOWLAND INDORSED
BY HERBERT HOOVER

When the votes were counted, the Republican party in California was out of business—and would stay out for eight years. It was a Democratic sweep.

Brown won by more than a million votes—3,140,000 to 2,110,000—and the entire Democratic slate swept in, with the exception of the candidate for secretary of state, Henry Lopez, who was edged out by the virtually immovable incumbent, Frank M. Jordan. Others elected were Lieutenant Governor Glenn Anderson, Attorney General Stanley Mosk (who had entered politics as secretary to Governor Olson), Controller Alan Cranston, and Treasurer Bert Betts.

Governor Goodwin Knight was beaten for the Senate seat by Representative Engle, 2,927,000 to 2,204,000.

The Republicans lost seven of their 20 seats in the 40-member state senate, giving the Democrats a numerical majority (as distinct from a working majority) for the first time since

1890. The Democrats won 10 more seats in the 80-member state assembly for a total of 47—their first majority there since 1942. They also shifted the balance in the U.S. House of Representatives, from a 17–13 Republican advantage to a 16–14 Democratic majority.

The "right to work" initiative was defeated by a 3–2 margin—3,070,000 votes to 2,079,000. The diversionary Proposition 17 was defeated by better than 4 to 1.

More than $2,500,000 was reported spent to defeat the "right to work" proposition. Most of the money came from organized labor—some $828,000 from the State Federation of Labor and $587,000 from a Los Angeles county labor committee. The total was more than double the $954,000 reported spent on behalf of the measure.

The San Francisco *Chronicle* wrote this epitaph over the Republican downfall:

"An extreme group in the California Republican party decided . . . to take California back into the 19th century, away from the 'modern Republicanism' that the members of the group so heartily loathe; away from the Progressive tradition . . . of the great Republican governorships of Hiram Johnson . . . and Earl Warren; away from Goodwin Knight, whom they hold in contempt for the odd notion that the way for Republican candidates to win is to try to gain support from all elements of the public, including labor."

The Plunge Toward Oblivion

The 1958 campaign was the classic laboratory example of the dynamics of California politics.

It was the last year of that curious institution, cross-filing. Even with its obfuscations lessened by candidate-labeling, cross-filing was a factor in 1958; Knowland's weak two-party showing in the June primary contributed to the steep downhill slide of his general-election campaign.

The campaign illustrated trenchantly some of the recurrent pivotal factors in California elections: the theme of nonpartisanism; the handicap of the party label; the hazards of the "carpetbagging" and "stepping-stones" motifs; the dangers of party splits; the risk of associating candidacies with "propositions"; and the serviceability of the "nice guy" stratagem.

The campaign also was a milestone in the fortunes of the "unofficial" party organizations. The California Republican Assembly had shown itself impotent when it came to resolving a first-magnitude example of the candidate-conflicts the organization had been created to deal with. By passively sanctioning Knowland's misbegotten effort, the CRA marked itself as an agency not of Republicans but of the atrophied Republican old guard. After 1958, the organization became more and more a right-wing splinter.

The CDC also went downhill from 1958, toward comparable ignominy. In part this was attributable to the demise of cross-filing, which meant that the function of pre-primary endorsements was less crucial than it had been.

But the CDC was up against two more fundamental problems. It had become a rallying point for intellectuals and ideological liberals, who were far less interested in the nuts and bolts of politicking, the "doorbell-ringing and envelope-stuffing," than in debating cosmic problems. A statewide "issues conference" in February, 1960, sounded more like the United Nations than a California party organization. It adopted declarations concerning "human rights," "underdeveloped nations," "military and diplomatic policy," and inflation, with little attention to the immediate problems of Californians. This divisive digression into what one CDC founder called "globaloney" compounded the CDC's basic problem: its relationship, as an organization of volunteer "amateurs," to the party's office-holding "professionals."

As the purported voice of the party rank-and-file, serving as a power base for office-seekers and office-holders, the CDC claimed the right to a major role in formulating party policy.

This pretension quickly became a bugbear, both to the party's "legal" hierarchy, concerned with unifying a membership that extended far beyond the 50,000 CDC activists, and to the office-holders. For an office-holder, CDC pronouncements tended to commit him to controversial positions and reduce his most valuable asset as a politician—the flexibility to maneuver.

This abrasive amateur-professional relationship paralleled one that developed nationally in the 1950's. A group of liberal Democratic leaders ventured to set up the so-called Democratic Advisory Committee, whose purpose was to exert guidance if not pressure on the party's incumbents in Congress. The latter—including their leader, Senator Lyndon Johnson—were infuriated at what they regarded as a presumptuous intrusion on their traditional prerogatives. And the Advisory Committee was nullified by being ignored.

Lyndon Johnson's counterpart in legislative leadership in California was Assembly Speaker Jesse Unruh. Unruh, elected to the state assembly in 1954 from the Los Angeles suburb of Inglewood, was trying to counter the Hiram Johnson heritage in his own way. He was trying to build his own machine, through years of adroit wheeling and dealing as legislative quarterback and in his reputed role as prime disburser of lobbyists' campaign contributions.

Unruh, as a practitioner of stark power-politics, viewed the CDC's congeries of unpredictable and unmanageable zealots as nothing less than a blight, habitually referring to them as "woolies" and "wingies," and doing everything he could to neutralize them. As it turned out, his exertions were hardly necessary. Within a few years, the CDC's propensity for "globaloney" itself neutralized the organization.

Most significantly of all, perhaps, the 1958 campaign dramatized harshly the transience of political existence in a state bound to electoral pragmatism and bereft of the conventional, firmly implanted institutions of politics.

As of 1956, Knowland, Knight, and Nixon each had some

potentiality for national office. They had put in a sizable part of a lifetime in politics, with some degree of distinction, however controversial.

But in the California political context, their careers were sustained by personal momentum. As soon as they lost momentum, like airplanes they began plunging toward oblivion.

When the dust of the 1958 Republican calamity settled, William F. Knowland represented, in California's anarchic milieu, scarcely more than the single vote possessed by every citizen. Although obtuse about some things, he seemed aware of this. He announced he would not run for office again and withdrew to manage the family newspaper in Oakland. He emerged from obscurity as nominal state chairman of the 1964 Goldwater campaign, but his role was rather symbolic.

Goodwin Knight essayed a comeback in the 1962 gubernatorial contest, but illness aborted that.

Nixon, only a vicarious party to the 1958 shambles, remained standing after the hurricane. But he had not been running for office; his survival did not invalidate the rule. His Waterloo was yet to come.

Chapter
Thirteen

"Easy Come, Easy Go": Nixon

☒ THE SMALL BALLROOM OF THE BEVERLY HILton Hotel on the edge of Los Angeles had a bleak morning-after look. A stepped platform along one side, left over from some previous event, bore several rows of chairs. Fifty bleary news people, weary from a 13-month campaign topped off by an 18-hour day, straggled in and sat down. They faced an improvised stage—a wooden platform backed by a velvet curtain of depressing mouse color. Otherwise the room was stark, bare, overlighted.

No one was laboring under the impact of any surprise. It was November 7, 1962. Nixon had just been shellacked by Governor Pat Brown, as expected by most people, with the apparent notable exception of Nixon himself. He had not conceded until dawn, when he awakened from a fitful sleep in his suite upstairs to check with hovering campaign aides. Not until 10 A.M., when the reporters were assembling below, had he dictated a perfunctory telegram of congratulation to Brown, and a message to campaign workers.

At 10:10 A.M. Nixon's press secretary, Herbert Klein, stepped onto the platform. "I have the text of two messages I'll read to you," he said. "The boss won't be down. . . . He plans to go home and be with his family. . . ."

What Klein didn't say was that Nixon, upstairs, was in such a distraught state—from fatigue, disappointment and, according to reports, the perversely stimulating effects of tranquilizing pills on top of some drinks—that his aides had been struggling to prevent him from coming down.

But 12 minutes later, as Klein was pursuing a rambling colloquy with the reporters, there was a sudden buffeting of the velvet drapes behind him. Klein turned and his jaw dropped. Nixon, neatly dressed in a blue suit, blue shirt, and blue tie that emphasized his blue-jowled haggardness, stepped out and made his way to the cluster of microphones.

"Good morning, gentlemen," he began. "Now that Mr. Klein has made his statement, and now that all the members of the press are so delighted that I have lost . . ."

There is a story about a small-time prize fighter whose arduous years in the ring had tended to dull his wits. One night after a murderous bout, he got dressed and tottered out of the building, with $50 in his pocket for the battering he had taken. A short distance down the street he walked past an alley and was jumped by two thugs. He came to, some time later, to find his earnings gone. "Well," he mumbled philosophically, "easy come, easy go."

The story has a certain grim parallel in the workings of California politics.

In most other states, there is an established apparatus within which a person of political bent has a chance to pursue a career: serving an apprenticeship; producing for his party; and—with moderate luck—making his way up the ladder of public office, with the expectation that reasonable fidelity and acumen will keep him in employment as long as he can stand the gaff.

No such apparatus exists in California. Party organizations, as we have observed, are hollow shells. There is no orderly mechanism for discovering, recruiting, and cultivating political talent. Nature abhors a vacuum, and the arena of politics inevitably attracts a steady procession of volunteers. But they are obliged largely to operate as free lances, unduly dependent on uncontrollable events and on whims of the electorate in its inclination to deal in personalities rather than issues. Today's hero is tomorrow's reject—tomorrow coming perhaps after a single campaign, or after a year's service, or, with equal abruptness, after many years. California politics, like a roulette wheel, has no memory; after each spin the chances of red or black, odd or even, tend to revert to 50–50. The man who entered the game without much difficulty can be squeezed out of it just as unceremoniously.

Of this phenomenon there is hardly any more dramatic, and in some ways tragic, example than Richard Milhous Nixon.

Pink Sheets

There is a myth that Richard Nixon got his start in politics by answering an advertisement for a candidate for Congress. It wasn't quite that pat. He had grown up in Whittier, a post-card-bucolic community in the citrus belt south of Los Angeles;

had gone through Duke University law school; and had set up practice back in Whittier when World War II intervened. After Navy duty in the Pacific, he was serving out his discharge assignment in Baltimore when a Whittier friend telephoned him one day.

Somebody had put his name on a list of "possibles" being considered by the California Republican Assembly's local screening committee for the 12th Congressional District. They were looking for a candidate to unseat Representative Jeremiah Voorhis, an able young New Deal Democrat whose "socialistic" tendencies—such as countenancing cooperatives—had disturbed the conservative burghers around Whittier. The candidacy proposal piqued Nixon's interest enough for him to make a trip back to Whittier and discuss it. He decided to run. The local political activists didn't have too much to offer in assistance. But they did arrange to provide him with the part-time services of Murray Chotiner, a Los Angeles lawyer and long-time Republican strategist, who had worked in Warren and Knowland campaigns. The rest is history.

The most important detail of the 1946 campaign was that Voorhis' vulnerable point appeared to be his left-of-center leanings. Chotiner and Nixon bore down on that, with a barrage of spoken and printed references to "lip-service Americans," and officials "who front for un-American elements," and for "the Communist-dominated PAC (Political Action Committee of the Congress of Industrial Organizations)" and candidates who "consistently vote the Moscow-PAC-Henry Wallace line."

This tactic helped bring Nixon victory, and started him on the road to being an international political figure, who came within 113,000 votes of being President of the United States. But it was almost as if the fates, gracing him with a blessing, at the same time ironically inflicted on him a curse. The device of anti-Comunism, wielded a thousand times in countless variations, helped carry Nixon higher and higher in politics. But simultaneously, like a drug, it contributed toward his eventual frustration.

Although Nixon never sincerely became as obsessed about the Red Menace as did the John Birch Society (which could see even in the *absence* of Communists another proof of Communist deviousness), the anti-Communist thrust as a demagogic device became a conditioned reflex with him that sometimes made him absurd. Thus when the left-wing W. E. B. DuBois (pronounced "du-boyce") Clubs were labeled by the United States Attorney General in 1966 as a Communist-front organization, Nixon, noting the similarity in sound to the Boys' Clubs of America, of which he was a nominal official, solemnly intoned that the leftists "are not unaware of the confusion they are causing among our supporters and among many other good citizens—an almost classic example of Communist deception and duplicity."

In Congress, Nixon achieved remarkable impetus at the outset, and easy re-election to a second term, through his part in the unmasking of Alger Hiss, the strange Moscow-oriented Ivy Leaguer in the State Department.

1950, being an even-numbered non-presidential year, brought another California state election. It was the one in which Governor Earl Warren, running for a third term, trounced James Roosevelt. More important for Richard Nixon, it was the year that Sheridan Downey, the Sinclair era's emissary to the United States Senate, decided to retire.

Typically, the vacancy found neither party with a candidate who had been groomed for this inevitable senatorial opening. On the Democratic side, attention swung to Helen Gahagan Douglas, a Congresswoman who had the advantage of recognition in the Los Angeles area, where about 40 per cent of the state's vote was concentrated. She was an actress—the wife of actor Melvyn Douglas—who had been drawn into politics by the New Deal (and she thus stands as an early and often-overlooked example of theatrical fame being parlayed into public office in California). One of her leading supporters was a Democratic fellow thespian named Ronald Reagan.

Typically also, Mrs. Douglas' liberalism irked the large

number of conservative Democrats. From their ranks emerged Manchester Boddy, politically inexperienced but with a name and some influence as the publisher of the Los Angeles *Daily News*.

The Republican candidacy fell to Richard Nixon. Murray Chotiner again was the impresario of the effort.

Nixon started off his campaign a full year before the election with the serviceable "Red" issue, asserting that the contest was "simply the choice between freedom and state socialism."

He charged that the California Democratic party, like the national party, "has been captured and is completely controlled by a group of ruthless, cynical seekers after power—committed to policies and principles completely foreign to those of its founders.

"Call it planned economy, the Fair Deal, or social welfare," he said, "but it is still like the same old socialist baloney, any way you slice it."

Biographer Earl Mazo says that Nixon carefully studied the tactics of Florida's Representative George Smathers in successfully pinning the label "Red Pepper" on liberal Senator Claude Pepper, and that Nixon paraphrased this tag into "Pink Lady" as a campaign barb.

The oversimplified legend is that Nixon beat Mrs. Douglas by "anti-Communist" smear tactics. Certainly he used these. The prime example was a scurrilous "pink sheet," falsely likening Mrs. Douglas' voting record to that of New York City's Communist-line Representative Vito Marcantonio.

Primarily, though, the contest demonstrated that classic pitfall of California politics, the lethal primary fight. Chotiner has emphasized, correctly, that—the "pink sheet" aside—the principal ammunition Nixon used against Mrs. Douglas was what Manchester Boddy had brought forth vainly in the primary. Mrs. Douglas ended up in the large gallery of California candidates who have survived primaries only to emerge so battered as to be unpalatable to an electorate favoring unmussed nominees.

Anyone for Rug-Pulling?

Nixon's senatorial victory proved to be only a stepping stone. 1952 brought the presidential election in which Governor Earl Warren's chances depended on an Eisenhower-Taft stalemate. Nixon, as a Senator, was automatically a member of the Warren delegation to the national convention. The law required that the delegates sign a pledge stating: "I personally prefer Earl Warren as nominee [and] . . . shall, to the best of my judgement and ability, support Earl Warren. . . ." The accepted meaning of this was that a delegate would stick until explicitly released by the candidate.

There had been no great cordiality between Warren and Nixon ever since 1946, when Warren had seemed to favor Jerry Voorhis. A word that has always been high in Warren's lexicon is "fairness," and it seems likely that he was not pleased by the slashing, free-form Nixon-Chotiner tactics.

The general impression, supported by circumstantial evidence, is that Nixon worked against Warren, covertly throwing his support to Eisenhower before the convention even opened, in return for the prospect of getting the second spot on the ticket. He could not have got it with Warren as the nominee because of the constitutional obstacle to the President and Vice President coming from the same state.

Among those who expressed this view of Nixon's actions was Senator Knowland, the delegation chairman, who, whatever his shortcomings, was given neither to falsehood nor to gratuitous aspersion of fellow Republicans.

Just before the convention, Nixon took it upon himself to conduct a mail-questionnaire opinion sampling of 23,000 Californians, asking who their choice for the Republican presidential nomination would be. This had the earmarks of a Chotiner stratagem. Such a survey was unprecedented, and its inevitable effect, regardless of the findings, was to diminish the stature of Warren's "favorite son" candidacy. The results were a consensus, probably expected, for Eisenhower.

Nixon went to Chicago on July 1, six days before the convention started, as a member of the platform committee. He flew back to join the California delegation train at Denver on July 4—spreading the word that it looked as if Eisenhower could win on the first ballot.

"Nixon's efforts to undercut Warren were obvious," recalled one delegate, Mrs. Patricia Crawford, a long-time party official. "On the train back to Chicago, his operatives were doing their best to round up support for General Eisenhower as early as the second ballot." Nixon got off the train outside Chicago, so that he was conspicuously absent from the "Warren delegation" arriving for the convention.

Nixon has insisted that he stuck with Warren "until the finish." But the point, Warren adherents emphasize, is that "the finish" was foreordained before the convention opened, when Eisenhower supporters prevailed in excluding a critical bloc of contested Taft delegates. This gave Eisenhower the nomination on the first ballot. Warren himself, while he never made a public declaration on the question, by oblique indications in later years left no doubt that he thought Nixon had engaged in double-dealing.

Nixon's questioned activity had three important repercussions.

First, it moved irate Warren supporters to disclose the existence of the $18,000 "Nixon fund" (contributed by well-wishers to supplement his senatorial emolument), which became a dramatic issue of the 1952 presidential campaign.

Second, it accentuated the deleterious Nixon-Knowland-Knight cleavage among California Republicans.

Third, it was one of a number of quasi-skeletons pulled out of the closet to help defeat Nixon in his disastrous 1962 bid for the California governorship.

Causes célèbres were becoming a motif of Nixon campaigns, and another developed in the spring of 1956. The Senate's Subcommittee on Investigations aired allegations that Murray Chotiner had been using his intimacy with Nixon as a "back door" to get special treatment for a number of law clients who had problems with government agencies. Chotiner denied any improprieties, and the committee, chaired by Senator John L. McClellan of Arkansas, with Robert F. Kennedy as its counsel, never lodged any formal charges. But the publicity was adverse enough to necessitate Chotiner's being sidelined as a Nixon strategist, and it stimulated the transitory "Dump Nixon" movement.

The Democrats' statewide landslide in 1958 left a feeling that California's 32 electoral votes—a block exceeded only by New York's 45—were, come the 1960 presidential contest, within Senator John F. Kennedy's reach.

By tradition, California's governor would head a delegation nominally dedicated to his own "favorite son" candidacy, but actually the delegation would be uncommitted and flexible. Senator Kennedy made a confidential agreement with Governor Brown not to muddy the California waters by entering a rival slate in the Democratic presidential primary. In return, the governor agreed to shelve any vice-presidential aspirations he might have; he was a Catholic, and two Catholics on the ticket would have aggravated the religious issue.

That was about the last conspicuous help Kennedy got from that quarter. At the Democratic national convention in Los Angeles, wrote Theodore H. White in his superb *The Making of the President, 1960,* "the control of Governor Brown over his delegation had collapsed. On Tuesday evening, July 12, California split wide open—30½ for Kennedy, 31½ for Adlai Stevenson, and the rest scattered."

White erred a bit on the side of flattery; Brown had never had "control" of the delegation, even though he was instrumental in composing it. To survive with his fractionated fellow Democrats after the convention, come what might, Brown had had to make the delegation a potpourri. Its division reflected the old cleavage between rank-and-file party "amateurs," nurturing dreams of Stevenson even as he was counting himself out, and the "professionals," realistically leaning to the man who had lined up the delegate votes.

The presidential rivals stumped the state, with not even Nixon, the "native son," rousing the California electorate out of impassivity. It amounted to a small bombshell in the campaign when the Democratic maverick, ex-Congressman Samuel Yorty, from his temporary position as a private citizen, jumped the party traces and came out for Nixon, promulgating an unusual manifesto, entitled "I Can't Take Kennedy," that harped on the religious issue.

Registration for the November election was 4,295,000 Democrats and 2,926,000 Republicans. California followed the national pattern (ultimately a hairline 34,221,485–34,108,684 victory for Kennedy) to the extent of producing a vote so close that it was not definite until three days after the election. Late-counted absentee ballots finally yielded Nixon a California margin of 35,623 votes—3,259,722 to 3,224,099. The result, ironically, could have been swung either way by the 86,000 Californians who went to the polls but failed to mark a choice of presidential candidates on their ballots.

A "Mess at Sacramento"?

By tradition, Nixon would have become, even in defeat, the titular leader of the Republicans nationally. But the party was segmented along Eisenhower-Taft lines and was drifting, with the patriarchal figure of Eisenhower its principal landmark.

"Titular leadership doesn't mean much any more," Nixon commented candidly when, in March, 1961, he returned to California, his only base. He had obtained an "of counsel" connection with the law firm of Earl Adams, a leading contributor to the notorious "Nixon fund." Now he had to do some strategic maneuvering. Should he set his sights on the 1964 presidential race, and in the interim eschew active politics by playing the party oracle? Or, with the California gubernatorial election coming up again in 1962, was he compelled to run, to display his political virility for 1964?

For eight months Nixon temporized, inwardly oscillating between "go" and "no go," as vicissitudes of the new Kennedy administration made a 1964 presidential challenge alternately promising and unpromising.

California's Republican conservatives, not entranced with Nixon anyway, got behind the gubernatorial candidacy of Assemblyman Joseph Shell, an affable, bright young Los Angeles oilman who physically and ideologically was a streamlined version of William Knowland.

Nixon's hesitation encouraged Goodwin Knight, chafing for a political comeback, to announce his candidacy on September 11, 1961.

Nixon had always attributed a large measure of all political success to luck—"being in the right place at the right time." If any evidence was needed that he was a political gambler, it was provided by his candidacy announcement on September 27, 1961—a decision he said he had arrived at only the night before.

The decision was perhaps the most fateful in Nixon's career. Observers could count a half-dozen formidable factors militating against victory, and little in his favor. He had the "Mr. Republican" label. He had just lost a national election, and had come uncomfortably close to losing in California as well.

"Potomac myopia" obscured his assessment of two of his worst campaign liabilities: his vulnerability, like Knowland's in 1958, to allegations of carpetbagging and of seeking to use the governorship as a stepping-stone. He was more explicit than Knowland in disclaiming presidential ambitions for 1964. But his disclaimers didn't get great credence. An opinion poll in February, 1962, indicated that 4 voters out of 10 thought he had his eye on the 1964 presidential nomination.

Sixteen years' absence separated him from familiarity with state problems. His facile avowal that he intended to rectify "the mess in Sacramento" betrayed his unfamiliarity. The Brown administration had no major vulnerable points, despite misleading hints of dissatisfaction in opinion polls. Nixon could look to little substantial campaign help from the battered shell of party organization; he would be dependent on a pickup team, against an opposition that had been training for three years.

Brown, exploiting Californians' predilection for "moderation," branded Nixon as a pawn in a new foray against California by "Stone Age ultra-conservatives." He exempted Nixon personally from that category: "I would place his philosophy no further back than the 19th century," Brown quipped.

A severe case of hepatitis forced Knight, 65 years old, out of the race in January, 1962, averting a repetition of the disastrous 1958 Republican split.

Nixon followed the established practice of extolling primary competition as the wholesome means of giving the voter a choice, and then ignoring his immediate adversary and directing all his fire at his prospective November opponent, Governor Brown. In the primary in June, Shell got one-third of the vote—a significant bench-mark of hard-core conservative-Republican strength.

From there on, Nixon's campaign against "the mess in Sacramento" resembled the campaign Knowland had pursued against Brown four years before; the more he talked, it transpired, the more votes he was losing.

There were bands—conspicuously avoiding "I Love the Sunshine of Your Smile," the theme song associated with unpleasant previous campaigns. There were the prancing, well-scrubbed "Nixonette" nymphets, made of peaches, cream, sponge rubber, and Republican ideology. But Nixon's program had little that seemed spectacular. An official campaign brochure said his "program for California" was to "expand job opportunities, cut crime, attract new industry, cut the cost of government, streamline welfare programs, improve education, reorganize government, encourage agricultural development. . . ."

In an attempt to galvanize his campaign, Nixon once more pulled out his old theme of the Red Menace. The word Communist had scarcely been heard in California for years. But Nixon solemnly declaimed that Governor Brown was "not capable of dealing with the Communist threat within our borders." His documentation of the "threat" was vague, consisting mainly of the assertion that Brown's record showed "not a single item of anti-subversive legislation in four years."

Carey McWilliams, admittedly no Nixon fan, remarked in *The Nation:* "As in 1952, the faceless, amoral Nixon is still on the make, still 'fighting Communism,' still full of tricks, haunted as always by the lack of self-knowledge. . . ."

Even his 1952 Republican convention activities concerning Earl Warren came back to haunt him. Warren, now on the Supreme Court, maintained utter detachment from the California skirmishing. But there crept into the contest an ironic note of revenge. In January, 1962, Earl Warren, Jr., a 32-year-old Sacramento lawyer, changed his registration from Republican to Democrat, and was announced with fanfare as a state vice-chairman of the Brown campaign. Asked at a press conference about the 1952 contretemps, Warren voiced for the first time what could be presumed to be his father's views: He said, "Mr. Nixon, through back-door tactics, pulled the rug out, for political gain for himself," and in so doing "wronged my father and the whole state."

The campaign even had its counterpart of the 1952 "Nixon fund" *cause célèbre.* This time it was the matter of a $205,000 loan made by Howard Hughes in 1956 to the Nixon family, mainly to prop up Nixon's brother Donald's failing restaurant business. The unusual transaction had first come to light in the final days of the 1960 campaign, too close to the election to receive much attention. Now it became a matter of discussion that extended to the floor of the state legislature. The loan, effected through a series of intermediaries to screen its source, had been liquidated by transferring to Hughes the title to a small plot of land owned by the Nixons in Whittier. The candidate denied having known about the loan. But among other unexplained points was the fact that a key document in the transaction had been notarized by his mother, Mrs. Hannah Nixon, in the Senate Office Building in Washington, where it seems unlikely that she would have been without Nixon's knowledge. Asked repeatedly about the matter in the campaign, Nixon finally simply refused to discuss it. There were curious details that remained unexplained five years later, as Nixon was launching his second try for the presidential nomination.

Meanwhile Brown was waging an ebullient but cautious campaign, running on his record of accomplishments in fields ranging from education to water supply; emphasizing bipartisanship; holding fast to the "nice guy" position and luring Nixon, as he had Knowland, into disruptive brickbat-throwing postures.

In November, Nixon was defeated, drawing 2,740,000 to Brown's 3,037,000.

A myth has persisted, from remarks of Nixon himself and some of his aides, that his defeat was due primarily to the Republican right wing having deserted him in the election. This is refuted by the voting figures. Gauged by comparative party registration—4,290,000 Democrats to 3,002,000 Republicans—with the 78 per cent voter turnout Nixon got virtually all the Republican vote, plus about 400,000 Democratic votes. He halved Brown's victory margin over Knowland in 1958, but this was not enough.

Senator Thomas Kuchel, the bipartisan liberal Republican running for re-election on the same ticket, drew over 800,000 Democratic votes, to beat State Senator Richard Richards by more than 700,000 votes. The only other statewide Republican winner was Secretary of State Frank Jordan.

Contradictions in the Ballroom

Seldom has a public figure ever displayed himself as Nixon did at the Beverly Hilton news conference the morning after the election. Correspondents inured to extraordinary happenings sat in open-mouthed astonishment. Although much of the subdued tirade that streamed from Nixon's lips was condemnation of the press for allegedly slanted reporting of his campaign, this was no surprise; no one had expected much cordiality on this score. What unnerved the reporters was an uncomfortable feeling of being involuntary viewers of an appalling act of self-revelation, a convulsive venting of long-dammed bitterness toward many people.

Although Nixon appeared to be lucid—his words were unslurred, his syntax orderly—his 15-minute monologue was a patchwork of schizoid contradictions, alternating praise with caustic derogation of the press, his campaign organization, and his opponent.

His comments suggested that he had an utterly twisted conception of the press' role in a democratic society, particularly in political reporting. He wavered between contradictory intimations that publishers as a group were corrupt, that reporters were prostitutes, and yet that somehow the reporters had cleverly double-crossed their employers by biased coverage of his campaign—which, he added contradictorily, was their prerogative.

"I believe Governor Brown has a heart," he said caustically, "even though he believes I do not. I believe he is a good American, even though he feels I am not. . . . [The people] have chosen his leadership, and I can only hope that that leadership will now become more decisive. . . .

"As I leave you," he concluded bitterly, "I want you to know—just think how much you're going to be missing. You won't have Nixon to kick around any more, because, gentlemen, this is my last press conference. . . ."

[In consideration of Nixon's complaint that the press never printed all he said, the complete text of his remarks will be found in the Appendix.]

Governor Brown, at his temporary residence near by, said a few minutes later that Nixon's performance was "something he'll regret all his life."

The New York *Times'* James Reston, commenting on the "tragic story" of Nixon's farewell, said: "What was most obvious about Nixon particularly to the press . . . was his preoccupation with the machinery of politics. Everything seemed to be contrived, even the appearance of naturalness. . . . This was the root of his trouble with the reporters: not that they were refusing to report what he said, but that they were insisting on reporting all the rest of the picture—not only words but the techniques, not only the public posture but the private posture. . . . He thought the reporters should merely be a transmission belt for what he said, not why he said it. . . ."

Although some realities of California politics seemed to have reached him belatedly, Nixon needed no further reminder of the capricious forces that had projected him into politics in the first place. He knew that he was through in California politics, that if he remained he might well become a man with one vote, like Knowland.

In June, 1963, he moved to New York. His prospects with New York as a political base were problematical, but he was choosing the lesser of two evils—the other being the state where the end had come as suddenly as the beginning.

Chapter Fourteen

The Baby and the Tap-Dancer

☒ EARLY ON THE MORNING OF JUNE 3, 1964, A telephone rang in the Los Angeles bureau of an eastern newspaper. An editor in New York was calling.

"I notice," he remarked with the occasional sarcasm of editors, "that Goldwater beat Rockefeller out there. . . ."

"That," concurred a correspondent, "seems to be the case."

"Well!" The New York voice took on a note of restrained

excitement. "Does that mean Goldwater will carry California in November if he's nominated?"

"Hell, no," said the correspondent. . . .

California had been affecting national politics for a century, ever since its very annexation fired congressional debate. But 1964 was the year California, by then the most populous state, went a step further and played a wry trick on the country. It made Senator Barry Goldwater a presidential candidate. Yet California essentially never had any intention of going for Goldwater itself.

The California events of 1964 are perhaps most readily grasped in terms of a three-ring circus. In one ring the Republicans' moderate and conservative wings fought it out over Goldwater and Rockefeller. In the second ring the Democrats staged their ungainly donnybrook over the Senate seat of the dying Clair Engle. The third ring presented the flamboyant finale, in which Pierre Salinger and George Murphy were stuffed into the giant cannon, there was a roar, and George Murphy soared triumphantly into the senatorial net, while Pierre Salinger never came out at all.

Ring 1: The Republicans

For California's conservatives, it had been a tough half-century.

It was their misfortune that their party had been dominant in the era when the Southern Pacific decided to corrupt the state. The conservatives had been paying for it ever since. First the heretical Hiram Johnson and his crackpot Progressive reformers. Then more than a generation when things had gone from bad to worse: the insolent threat of Upton Sinclair; the repugnance of Culbert Olson; the duplicity of Earl Warren; the perfidy of Goodwin Knight; and finally the disaster of William Knowland.

By 1960, arch-reactionaries had reason to feel that the Republican party had left them. They were groping for rallying points. The newly formed John Birch Society, with its aura of social respectability, became a haven for thousands of Californians.

Others, more sensitive to public criticism, stayed clear of the Birch society, even though their views might be to the right of it. Some, with more money and more impatience to set the world and the nation aright, began trafficking financially with national right-wing alarmist organizations. They embraced the innocuous, if fatuous, political evangelism of Dr. Fred Schwarz's California-based Christian Anti-Communism Crusade and the venal racist fulminations of such rabble rousers as Billy James Hargis and Gerald L. K. Smith.

In 1961, 12,000 people turned out for a Fred Schwarz meeting at the Hollywood Bowl. In a curious way, the meeting was the complete obverse of the Bowl assemblages of a generation before, during the Great Depression, when the economically deprived had come to hear gospels of goofy utopianism. Now it was the economically secure seeking confirmation of their suspicions that Moscow was to blame for the fact that no more McKinleys or Frank Merriams were coming forth to gear government to their narrow interests.

In 1962, the arch-conservative thought it was probably just as well that Nixon had been beaten. After all, he had tried to read the Birch society out of the Republican party. If he had been elected, he probably would have been just like one of Them.

Whether one considered Nixon good or bad, the 1962 election had brought many conservative disappointments. Joseph Shell, the old-guard choice for governor, had lost to Nixon in the primary. The only two avowed Birchers in Congress, Representatives Edgar Hiestand and John Rousselot, both from metropolitan Los Angeles, had been unseated—despite, in Rousselot's case, a turnout of 850 people at a $50-a-plate fund-raising dinner starring Ronald Reagan speaking on "What's at Stake." Another right-wing project that had gone down to defeat was Proposition 24, an initiative measure, that sought to impose, through a constitutional amendment, a palpably unconstitutional array of sanctions on members of "subversive organizations."

The conservatives' biggest disappointment, however, was not Nixon's defeat but the victory of his fellow Republican, Senator Thomas Kuchel, the Warren protégé whose vigorous bipartisanism in Congress had infuriated the old guard. The conservatives had nursed hopes of denying Kuchel renomination. But their entry, Loyd Wright, a former president of the American Bar Association, managed to draw only 15 per cent of the primary vote. Kuchel emerged the only major Republican winner in the November, 1962, election.

The year's big consolation prize for the conservatives was the election, as State Superintendent of Public Instruction, of Dr. Max Rafferty, a staccato-speaking suburban school principal who had won national note as a crusader against progressive education. The legally nonpartisan contest turned into a highly partisan affair. Rafferty's opponent, Dr. Ralph Richardson, attracted liberal Democratic support. Aligned behind Rafferty, in a sort of trial run of conservative Republican strength, was a right-wing cadre that became increasingly prominent in succeeding elections. Among its members were oilmen Henry Salvatori and A. C. Rubel; George Murphy, the actor-turned-film-executive; his employer at Technicolor, Patrick J. Frawley, Jr.; and D. B. Lewis, the dog-food manufacturer, who died soon afterward, leaving a million dollars to the Birch society.

The rather sudden development, in the wake of President Kennedy's assassination in November, 1963, of a Goldwater-Rockefeller contest for the Republican presidential nomination turned California into a major battleground. It was last in line on the calendar among a half-dozen states whose presidential primaries served as showcases of national-convention strength.

The tenor of the Goldwater effort in California was set when former Senator Knowland emerged from six years' obscurity on his Oakland newspaper to be titular state campaign chairman: it was the old conservatives, making another try.

By then political commentators were constantly observing

that the right wing had "taken over the Republican party in California."

This was a misleading oversimplification on two counts. The Right Wing was in no wise an organized entity with a definable ideology; and there was, as usual, no effective party structure to be taken over.

Lumped semantically in the "Right Wing"—and encompassing, presumably, anyone who did not have some plain identification as a Republican liberal or moderate—was an utterly unorganized spectrum of outlooks ranging from mild orthodox conservatives to the fascistic Minutemen (whose amateur-militia nonsense California outlawed in 1965), devoid of political influence or anything but psychiatric significance.

This spectrum divided into several obvious categories, which could be labeled as conservatives, radical conservatives, extremists, and kooks. Aside from the kooks—the Minutemen, the American Nazis, and so on—these categories overlapped in both people and activities. Thus the interests of a man like Henry Salvatori, multimillionaire geophysicist and a long-time Nixon financer, might extend from support of Goldwater to support of Dr. Fred Schwarz's Christian Anti-Communism Crusade, but stop short of the Birch society. Another man, like D. B. Lewis, the dog-food magnate, might be a Birch society enthusiast but stop short of supporting such demagogues as Billy James Hargis and Gerald L. K. Smith. And the interests of yet another man, such as Walter Knott, the American-Gothic amusement-park entrepreneur, could range from Goldwater and the Birch society to active support of Hargis.

These views might be shared by thousands of less prominent citizens. But all the people who thought this way were still only a small, diffuse portion of the electorate, and their notions had political force only when—as with the much larger "senior citizens" bloc—their special interests coincided with those of a more conventional majority. The Goldwater candidacy provided such a common ground.

As usual, the Goldwater effort in California had to be a

campaign started from scratch. The state Republican organization was legally precluded from playing favorites in the primary. The "unofficial" California Republican Assembly was Goldwater-oriented from the outset. But events like the 1958 Republican defeat and the 1962 Kuchel victory had engendered dissension that left the CRA a weak husk, with only a few thousand adherents out of nearly 3 million party members. It had become too conservative for party moderates and liberals, and too liberal for the conservatives. A large bloc of conservatives had seceded in 1963 and formed a rival organization, the United Republicans of California.

The moderates and liberals, who as recently as the 1962 Nixon-Shell primary had constituted two-thirds of the party following, now had no rallying point. They went in a half-dozen different directions in their affinities—many for Rockefeller, some for Nixon, some for Pennsylvania's Governor William Scranton, some for Michigan's Governor George Romney, and even some for Harold Stassen, the party's superannuated boy wonder.

This moderate-liberal diffusion gave the Goldwater people a substantial advantage in the basic business of going into California's 58 counties and organizing units. The Rockefeller people countered by mounting the best campaign that money would buy, engaging the Los Angeles campaign-management firm of Spencer-Roberts, and pouring millions of dollars into the gamut of propaganda devices. Goldwater operatives asserted that the Rockefeller outlay was bigger than theirs by 3 to 1; this was probably an exaggeration, but it was still indicative. The Goldwater drive was no amateur effort, either; it used the pioneer campaign-management firm of Whitaker and Baxter in San Francisco, and the firm of Baus and Ross in Los Angeles.

By the March deadline for filing entries in the June presidential primary, only Goldwater and Rockefeller had qualified. The large number of moderates and liberals who favored the other Republican hopefuls panicked so badly they could not grasp the elementary arithmetic that two minus one was one, and that anyone who really wanted to stop the Goldwater conservative juggernaut should go all-out for Rockefeller in the primary. Hypersensitive about factional feelings, the anti-Goldwaterites backed and filled until mid-May, less than a month before the primary, before coalescing into the Committee of Responsible Republicans in order to rally the Rockefeller vote.

Their bemusement probably made history. The California primary vote was critical. State primaries elsewhere had so far produced something of a standoff. Goldwater had led in Illinois, Indiana, and Texas; he had run second to Lodge but ahead of Rockefeller in New Hampshire; and he had run behind Rockefeller and Lodge in Oregon. Goldwater himself, along with numerous other observers, thought California could make or break the tide of sentiment on which he hoped to ride into the Republican convention six weeks later.

The California contest, gauged by a succession of opinion polls in its final days, was a deadlock to the end. Some observers thought it took no more than the news of the second Mrs. Rockefeller's going to the maternity hospital two days before the June 2 primary—reviving memories of the governor's side-street romance, divorce, and remarriage to tip the scales.

The vote was close: 1,120,403 for Goldwater to 1,052,053 for Rockefeller. But psychologically the winner took the whole pot. Goldwater had carried the nation's most populous state. After that, the San Francisco convention was just an informality.

Ring 2: The Democrats

For the Democrats the 1964 campaign began with the deceptive appearance of a cut-and-dried affair in California. But it ended in historic upheaval.

The Democrats still had their million-vote margin over the Republicans in registrations; they were buoyed by California's history of regularity in presidential elections (and, nationally, rejection of an incumbent President was a rarity); Democrats were in firm control of the state; one possible 1964 Republican nominee, Nixon, had already been rejected by California; and it remained for any other Republican to prove that he could cut substantially into the California Democratic vote.

California's only other important race was a Senate contest, and the incumbent, Clair Engle, had long been such a bipartisan vote-drawer that a conspicuous after-you-Gaston atmosphere prevailed among possible Republican challengers.

Then, typically, a political thunderstorm broke over the state.

The first rumble was the news, in August, 1963, that Senator Engle had undergone a brain operation in Washington. It immediately raised doubts about his ability to run again, and speculation about alternative candidates.

The essential impotence of the official party organizations in California was never demonstrated better than on January 25, 1964, when 100 members of the Democrats' state executive committee met to discuss what could be done about the Senate race. Their problem was to keep from repudiating Engle, yet to avert a vacuum if he suddenly became obviously incapacitated; and to forestall a self-defeating intraparty rat-race, yet not to transgress the code under which party organizations maintained impartiality in primaries.

The committee had only one course: it pronounced the nomination "open" to all comers—including Engle if he was able.

A major question now was what action would be taken by the Democrats' "unofficial" endorsing arm, the California Democratic Council. Its relations with the party's office-holding "professionals" had been further strained by an episode in the 1962 campaign. Assembly Speaker Jesse Unruh, as a coordinator of legislative and congressional campaign activities, had flaunted his custodianship of campaign contributions, and had affronted the "amateurs," by spending $100,000 on a corps of hired get-out-the-vote workers in Los Angeles.

The field of aspirants for the Senate nomination, besides

Engle himself, included State Controller Alan Cranston, one of the CDC's founding fathers; Representative James Roosevelt, the erstwhile candidate for governor; and Attorney General Stanley Mosk, Democratic national committeeman, who was Unruh's choice.

On February 23 the CDC endorsed Cranston. Roosevelt dropped out. Two weeks later, under pressure from Governor Brown and some other party leaders, Mosk withdrew—in the name of party harmony, but grudgingly.

The primary filing deadline was less than a month away. A flurry of reports circulated that Mosk and Unruh, determined to thwart the other factions, were casting about frantically for an anti-Cranston candidate. Mosk, on a visit to Washington two months before, had talked in a jocular vein with Pierre Salinger about the possibility of Salinger's running for Congress from his native California. They had surmised that Salinger's Virginia residence made such a race legally impossible. But Mosk, on returning to California, had researched the law and concluded—academically at that point—that whereas out-of-state residence might preclude competing for a House seat, this did not apply to the Senate. The information now became singularly useful. Telephone wires hummed between California and Washington. On March 19, one day before the primary filing deadline, Salinger gave his notice at the White House and departed, with Lyndon Johnson's blessing and a farewell gift of his $450 filing fee, for California.

The primary battle between Cranston and Salinger (Engle withdrew on April 28) accordingly was an out-and-out factional clash, with no real issues.

It ended in a vote of 1,177,000 for Salinger and 1,037,000 for Cranston—the difference between them amounting to little more than the sentimental 119,000 votes cast for the noncompeting Engle. Cranston spent $823,307 in what was probably the most expensive campaign, at that level, in the state's history. Salinger spent $489,573. Cranston's defeat was the first such reverse for a CDC endorsee for a statewide office. The trauma, in combination with the CDC's preoccupation with "globaloney," caused the "unofficial" organization that had spearheaded the Democrats' renaissance to lapse within two years into impotence.

Meanwhile, equally debilitating factional stresses were setting in on another front. Mayor Samuel Yorty of Los Angeles, the Democratic maverick who had supported Nixon in 1960 but who was aligned with Jesse Unruh in detestation of the CDC, saw an opportunity to flex his political muscle at virtually no cost. Through the easy formality of collecting 13,000 petition signatures—with shouts that Brown and his cohorts were "captives of the left-wing CDC"—Yorty entered an insurgent slate of pro-Johnson national convention delegates in the primary, in competition with the regular pro-Johnson slate headed by Governor Brown. The Yorty slate, as expected, was defeated, but it rolled up 798,000 votes to Brown's 1,693,000. That, too, was a development that would have repercussions two years hence.

Ring 3: The Tap-Dancer

When George Murphy materialized from the limbo of late-evening television in December, 1963, to announce his candidacy for the Senate, opinion was almost unanimous that he didn't have a chance. If Clair Engle wasn't elected, some other Democrat would be.

But Murphy had seen enough of California politics to know that defeat is as uncertain as victory. He had been quietly active in California Republican affairs for years, even serving a brief interim state chairmanship, and as a theatrical expert he had stage-managed several Republican national conventions.

His smartest initial move was to keep tactfully at arm's length from the contentious Goldwater campaign. This turned his own candidacy into a fine storm-cellar for Republicans of many hues who didn't want to sit out the campaign. Richard

Nixon's right-hand man, Robert H. Finch, became Murphy's campaign manager. Murphy coasted through the Republican primary without substantial opposition.

Murphy had played movie "nice guys" for years, and now he pre-empted the "nice guy" tactical role. By contrast, Salinger, with his cigar and his Washington expertise, seemed like a walking smoke-filled room. Although before going east he had worked more in California politics than Murphy had, his eleventh-hour entry made him a laboratory case in carpetbagging, and Murphy made a big issue of it. Governor Brown's appointing Salinger to the interim Senate seat after Clair Engle died in July did not give him the hoped-for impetus. A large number of Democrats were so disaffected by their own party's factional mayhem that they would have voted for any Republican.

Finally, Salinger made the Knowlandish mistake of tying his campaign to the volatile open-housing initiative issue on the November ballot. In 1963 California had banned racial discrimination in residential transactions by a measure called the Rumford Act. The real estate industry and property owners' organizations mounted a massive initiative campaign to nullify the law through a constitutional amendment guaranteeing citizens "absolute discretion" in conveying property. Governor Brown and liberal Democrats mounted an equally intense campaign to defend the law and defeat the initiative, which became Proposition 14 on the ballot. Murphy shrewdly refused to get involved in the controversy, declaring that it was outside the scope of the Senate contest.

On Election Day, Murphy attracted about 700,000 Democratic votes, beating Salinger by 3,628,000 to 3,411,000. The anti-open-housing measure Salinger had opposed was favored by almost two voters out of every three—4,526,000 to 2,395,000—even though it was subsequently held unconstitutional by the California supreme court.

California's presidential vote, in contrast, followed party lines almost precisely. The estimated Democratic turnout on

Election Day was about 4,168,000; Johnson got 4,171,000. The estimated Republican turnout was about 2,800,000; Goldwater got 2,879,000.

Despite all the Republican primary clamor that had identified Goldwater closely with California in the public mind, it turned out that pro-Goldwater sentiment was stronger in 20 other states, from North Carolina to North Dakota, than in California.

In the potpourri of election results could be discerned the California inclination toward moderation. Johnson was more moderate than Goldwater; and Murphy seemed more moderate than Salinger. Also, there had been demonstrated once again the power of the carpetbagging issue, and the hazard of a candidate's getting involved in a ballot-proposition argument.

Conservatives found ground for jubilation in the Murphy victory, but there was a larger meaning to it than that: it showed that the Republicans, despite their minority status, were not impotent if they stuck together to exploit opposition mistakes.

The right wing had made a major effort in 1964 to sail candidates for Congress and the state legislature in on the tide of Goldwater sentiment. Three Birchers who had won nominations for Congress were defeated. Only one avowed Bircher won: John G. Schmitz, a junior-college teacher, who won the state senate seat for Orange county and gained the distinction of being the first Bircher in the legislature. Most of the Birch effort had been centered on winning seats on the Republican county central committees. John Rousselot, the Birch society's western director, claimed that its members had captured between 30 and 40 seats on the 270-member Los Angeles county committee. But these victories had, in the ensuing two years, no visible effects whatever—inasmuch as the reforms of a half-century before had made dead ends of such committees. Like Pierre Salinger, the Birchers still had some things to learn about California politics.

Chapter Fifteen

"Three Cheers For—!": The Image-Makers

☒ A SACRAMENTO BARBER WAS TELLING A YOUNG capital newspaper reporter his troubles. It was 1930 and the barbers of California wanted a regulatory board established, under the state's business-and-professions code, covering the tonsorial field. But they had gotten nowhere in their overtures to legislators.

The reporter thought he knew a solution. For a fee of

$4,000, he undertook to get the right wires pulled and buttons pushed, all quite legitimately, to get the barbers their board.

Foreseeing certain obstacles if he approached the key legislators directly, he instead went to their constituencies, Carey McWilliams recounts, and stirred up such a froth of sentiment for the creation of a barbers' board that the lawmakers quickly complied. His success suggested the great possibilities of getting things done in politics not through familiar lobbying techniques but by "lobbying the people."

This obscure episode was the germination of what today is the newest and most controversial phenomenon of politics, in both California and the nation.

The young reporter was named Clem Whitaker. The mission for the barbers led him to establish a new industry: the business of political-campaign management, whose arcane practitioners of late have acquired the suspicion-tinctured appellation of "image-makers."

All the world loves a conspiracy. From the plots of Shakespeare to the exploits of James Bond, intrigue commands popular fascination.

There's a special sort of masochistic appeal when it's real life, and the public can conceive of itself as the victim of a conspiracy, particularly when the issue is academic and the injury not palpable.

Journalists have long been familiar with a popular notion that newspapers have great hoards of suppressed information. "What's the *real* story?" people say—when swarms of reporters have been scrambling to produce the real story and get it on the market before their competitors. In recent years there has been intense interest in the idea of governmental "news management," the thought that the public is being conspiratorially kept in the dark—even though, as some newsmen are always pointing out, it is almost impossible for a fact of commanding public interest to be suppressed very long in a free, competitive society. The widespread fascination with the notion of a second Kennedy assassin is another case of the conspiracy syndrome.

In the last few years, the public's discovery of the image-makers has provided a new way for people to torture themselves with dark speculations.

With political candidates being advised, groomed, coached, shepherded, and showcased by brigades of professional experts, is it not possible that dreadful frauds might be perpetrated on the country? Drew Pearson, the Washington columnist, reflected the popular concern when he wrote, in the wake of the 1966 campaign: "Electing a governor or a Senator has now become a question of selling a candidate with the same Madison Avenue techniques as you sell underarm deodorants. The secret of political success is not in letting the public know what the candidate stands for, but in hiring the right public relations firm. And that PR firm may decide that the easiest road to victory is to hide what a candidate stands for, not advertise it. . . ."

And the New York *Times* joined in, saying: "If their work were limited to technical services it would make little difference what their political beliefs were, or even whether they favored their respective clients. But while they may not be quite the 'kingmakers' they are reputed to be, they are clearly more than mechanics. [They are in] the business of projecting images for profit—any images that will pay."

The liberal-Republican Ripon Society, scrutinizing particularly California, saw in the activities of the political stage-managers more than just a question of misrepresentation. "In radically changing the 'image' of a candidate," a Ripon report said, "they are beginning to assume responsibility for the candidate's program. Approaching the point where they will be able to 'sell' a prospect a 'campaign package' for Congress or the Assembly or whatever, they will be dictating candidate selection, with the party only able to protest weakly and attempt to pick up the pieces afterwards."

Several questions arise about these alarums, upon which California's experience as the spawning-ground of image-makers provides some illumination:

Do they represent a radical new departure in principle?

How did they come about?

How do they operate?

What, if anything, should and can be done about them?

A look at the record suggests that what has lately acquired the name of image-making is simply the culmination of a logical evolution in political campaigning.

Clem Whitaker's transformation into a professional campaign director was a direct result of California's unusual politics. In 1933, not long after Whitaker's work for the barbers, a battle developed over distribution of electric power from the vast new Federal Central Valley water project in California's agricultural heartland. The Pacific Gas and Electric Company mounted a referendum campaign to repeal the state act authorizing the project. Irrigation interests hired Whitaker to mastermind the opposition to the referendum. His $40,000 campaign carried the day.

In the course of the effort, Whitaker had occasion to collaborate with a comely young lady named Leone Baxter, who was manager of the Redding chamber of commerce. Out of this developed both a matrimonial and a business alliance. Over the next three decades the San-Francisco-based firm of Whitaker and Baxter handled some 70 California campaigns, involving both candidates and ballot issues, and won nearly all of them. They would handle as many as six initiative measures in one campaign.

They flourished because they filled a need. The important electoral device of the initiative was becoming a far bigger affair than the simple citizen-petition operation the Progressive reformers had envisioned. Many of the issues were multi-million-dollar matters. Consequently, expenditures by contending forces were running into hundreds of thousands of dollars. It was sensible to have such outlays handled with professional skill.

Campaigning for office, in a state where candidates could count on little help from their party organizations, likewise called for professional assistance.

In 1934 Whitaker and Baxter were the nerve center of the California League Against Sinclairism. In 1942, when Earl Warren first ran for governor, W-B were enlisted to warm up his rather plain, austere "image." They coached him on more frequent use of his capacious smile, and emphasized his warmth as a family man—making the three Warren daughters national figures.

Later, W-B handled campaigns for Knowland, Nixon, and Kuchel. The firm's preoccupation with Republicans simply reflected the party's predominance at the time. W-B often handled opposing viewpoints at different times, considering themselves essentially specialists in political dynamics.

On the basis of their work for the California Medical Association opposing Warren's health-insurance program, W-B in 1949 were retained at $100,000 a year to guide the American Medical Association's campaign in the Federal medicare fight.

"Clem Whitaker," wrote Carey McWilliams in 1951, "knows more about politics than any other living Californian. Beyond any doubt these talented hucksters have had more direct influence on California's legislation in the last 15 years—and I speak of influence, not of power—than any combination of politicians or special-interest groups, including the entire trade-union movement. Campaigns won by Whitaker and Baxter decided the key issues of 15 years of California politics."

W-B's operations were divided among four subsidiaries: Campaigns, Inc.; a public relations branch; an advertising agency; and a newsfeature syndicate. Whitaker died in 1961. The firm is being carried on by Clem Whitaker, Jr. Leone Baxter runs a separate organization, Whitaker-Baxter International, with overseas operations.

The key to W-B's success was the recognition that, especially in California's loose partisan milieu, voters are motivated by many factors. The object is to evoke as many of these interests as possible.

"A Democrat," Whitaker said, "is also a consumer and a taxpayer; he may be a farmer, a truck driver, or a college professor; a Catholic or a Mason; and a veteran." His formula was to "hit" every voter seven times during a campaign, each time appealing to a different interest.

Whitaker formulated 50 rules for campaigning, and they

included the basic precepts being followed today: "Politics is merchandising men and measures." . . . "Keep it simple." . . . "People's attention is hard to get: you must put on a fight or a show." . . . "More Americans like corn than caviar." . . . "You can't beat something with nothing. You have to offer an alternative."

People see a political candidate as just someone who appears out of nowhere and steps on the platform to solicit their support. But the immense amount of technics behind such an appearance is formidable. It includes fund raising and budgeting, research, strategy formulation, organizing, logistics, speech writing, advertising, and publicity.

All these elements have figured, at least implicitly, in campaigns as far back as politics go. But in the modern era they have grown in scale far beyond the capacity of a candidate and his immediate advisers to handle.

A campaign for the state legislature in California today costs up to $50,000, a Congressional campaign up to $100,000, and a Senate campaign the better part of $1 million. In the 1966 gubernatorial contest, upward of $4 million was authoritatively estimated to have been spent by, or on behalf of, each of the candidates.

A candidate's full time and energy today are taken up just in physically making the appearances necessary to get his story before the voters. The other things have to be done by hired specialists.

By the 1950's, dozens of campaign-counseling enterprises had developed. Some of them were essentially one-man advisory operations, like Murray Chotiner's role in the Nixon campaigns, starting in 1946. Others offered comprehensive services, from strategy formulation to publicity. In Los Angeles, the firm of Herbert Baus and William Ross became a counterpart of Whitaker and Baxter, and handled the successful 1964 Goldwater California primary campaign.

Nationally there were indications of a similar evolution. In

1952 the role of "Madison Avenue" in the Eisenhower-Stevenson campaign drew national attention.

The most flamboyant of the new California practitioners was Los Angeles' Hal Evry, who jarred people with his hyperbolic, iconoclastic treatment of political traditions. Although he operated with a battery of data-processing machines and standard methods, Evry claimed that the best tactic was to keep a candidate as quiet as possible and reduce any campaign arguments to the utmost simplicity—preferably making them so simple as to be devoid of meaning. He said he thought a man could be elected attorney general simply on the slogan, "End the Parking Meter Racket!" He insisted that the best campaign theme was simply reiteration of the slogan, "Three Cheers for Joe Smith!" and he claimed to have won local elections just on this basis.

In his stress on simplicity, Evry was simply applying one of the cardinal maxims of Whitaker and Baxter. In his partiality to the simple exhortation, "Three Cheers for ——!" Evry was saying in effect that the basic election problem in this tumultuous era is to register a candidate's identity; any campaign refinements come after that.

The most strikingly successful management organization is Spencer-Roberts & Associates of Los Angeles, which consists of two youngish men named Stuart Spencer and Bill Roberts. Their most spectacular accomplishment was taking a man they had, in 1964, included in a list of right-wing "extremists," and selling him to the California electorate as a moderate: Ronald Reagan.

They saw no deceit in the transformation. "In 1964, we weren't concerned with putting Reagan's best foot forward," they said. "In 1966, that was our job."

Roberts was a television dealer, Spencer a suburban city recreation director when they met as activists in Republican politics in the era of the Knowland disaster. Dismayed by the haphazard, amateurish conduct of many candidates' campaigns, they set up in business in the back room of a travel agency in

1960 to see if there wasn't "a more scientific way to get our men elected."

Their first clients were Representative Alphonzo Bell, a wealthy moderate, and—concurrently—John Rousselot, who later became spokesman for the John Birch Society. In 1962, they handled Senator Thomas Kuchel's successful repulse of the right-wingers. The coup that first brought them attention came in the nonelection year of 1963, when they directed two special congressional contests at opposite ends of the state, winning victories for Don Clausen in northern California and Del Clawson in suburban Los Angeles, in districts that had been Democratic. Their strategy essentially was to stage well-financed campaigns to get their candidates' identities established, and then import "flying squads" to get out the vote on Election Day.

In 1964, Spencer and Roberts ran Governor Nelson Rockefeller's California presidential primary campaign. He lost, but not by much, and their performance caused them to be tapped for the 1966 Reagan campaign.

Spencer and Roberts typify the advance of campaign management a major step beyond Clem Whitaker's psychological wizardry. They were born into the age of computers, which can take basic census data about a district's population, ethnic extractions, and age and income levels, and combine it all with registration and voting records and opinion-survey results to give a precise mathematical "profile" of the district's political inclination.

Campaigning has become so elaborate and complex that half the battle is in knowing where to focus vote-getting efforts. To send a simple postcard to a party's complete registration in California costs upward of $50,000. Multistation television costs thousands of dollars a minute. Hence statewide appeals can be indulged in only sparingly. Most of the time it's a problem of selecting segments of the electorate as targets.

The same factors accentuate the importance of integrated management of a campaign, since strategy, logistics, and propaganda are so interdependent.

"We decide where our candidate goes and how he uses his time," Roberts says. "We say when and how he should spend his dollars. We decide to whom mailings should be made. We put precinct workers in position and tell them what to say. We control the timing—when you move on different issues."

Like most campaign-management people, Spencer and Roberts have no elaborate establishment. Their offices are a modest suite in a prosaic side-street business building. Their permanent organization consists of themselves, two assistants, and a secretary. In a campaign, the payroll may swell to 150.

What they have to offer is mainly in their heads, plus volumes and volumes of computer-analyzed electoral data. (They have helped to set up an affiliated computer-organization, Datamatics, Inc., run by Vincent Barraba, a marketing expert.)

A Spencer-Roberts fee runs between 10 and 20 per cent of the outlay for a campaign. In the Reagan campaign it was reported to be $150,000. Spencer and Roberts have stuck to Republican candidates because that was their original orientation, and they feel that switching parties raises ethical questions.

Although they might profit from cultivating a reputation as magicians, they scoff at the idea that anyone can give a candidate a false front.

"We're not image-makers, as our critics like to call us," Roberts says. "We don't find what kind of candidate people want and revamp our man to fit the mold. Up to a point, we don't care what a candidate believes, as long as it doesn't make him unelectable."

"That kingmaker stuff is a lot of bull," Stuart Spencer adds. "In politics you don't change a guy's image and put words in his mouth, people see right through him. A guy has X number of qualities. You emphasize some and not others, that's all."

California's experience indicates that the alarums about the menace of professional campaign-management involve some false assumptions. One mistaken notion is that all this represents anything new in principle. Essentially, nothing is being done now that wasn't done 30 or even 100 years ago. It is merely being done on a larger scale, more methodically, and with new contemporary tools of communication and information processing.

There is also an imputation of something covert about campaign management. Yet there are few pursuits in which decisions have to be translated so quickly into action for the public to observe.

Another fallacy is the implicit assumption that image-making is a one-sided operation, with a candidate operating in effect in a vacuum. This of course is not true—a candidate's opponent has his campaign managers, too. And each side is as much concerned with exposing the opposition's vulnerable points as in magnifying its own good points. This is the basic answer to critics' implications that a safe-cracker might be dressed up with the right policies and speeches and presented to the electorate as an upstanding citizen.

If there is any misrepresentation in the putting of a candidate before the electorate, that deception is after all a responsibility of the candidate himself. If he is the sort of person who would countenance such deception, he would hardly be honest even if he were running without professional guidance.

The picture of the candidate as a hypnotized puppet at the mercy of the image-makers is erroneous. Every campaign brings instances of candidates and professional handlers disagreeing about policies or procedures: sometimes the candidate dismisses the managers; sometimes the agent drops the client.

Another thing generally overlooked is the fact that the image-makers do not have an unbroken record of victories. In most contests the image-making resources on both sides are fairly evenly matched. When one image-maker's efforts prevail, an opposing image-maker's presentations have been rejected by the electorate.

Those who argue that cleverer handlers may be within reach of one candidate rather than the other are only pointing to the problems of differing financial resources—problems long antedating the profession of campaign management.

The criticism that image-makers commit the heinous offense of discovering what voters want and tailoring a candidate's appeals to fit is an argument that meets itself coming around the corner. Installing officials who agree with voters' views is the object of elections. A candidate who diametrically misrepresented where he stood on fundamental questions would not last long in politics, and no instances of such misrepresentation come to mind which are attributable to contemporary image-making. It seems probable that professional managers' measurements of public opinion orient candidates' policies better than does the old-time seat-of-the-pants method.

The fear that image-making in general could become the means for wholesale deception of voters seems to presuppose a naïveté on the part of the electorate that history refutes.

Perhaps the ultimate answer to the alarm-criers about image-making is the utter impossibility of doing anything about it. The idea is beyond belief that any code of ground rules could be propounded for the extraordinarily complex processes of political management, or that anybody could be set up as a censor or monitor over such operations.

Limiting campaign expenditures is the proposal currently in vogue as a panacea for many election problems. But if a way ever is found to limit expenditures, it will make the optimum use of the limited funds all the more important. And professional managers will be more in demand than ever.

One California practitioner in the field of professional campaigning deserves special attention, because he is unique.

That is Richard Tuck, who is in his forties but whose curly-haired boyishness enables him to pass for everything from college student to railroad yardmaster—which are only two of many disguises he has adopted.

Tuck is often an unacknowledged attaché of state or national Democratic campaign organizations in the field of psychological warfare. The range of his activities is infinite.

They have included the purloining of opposition documents, the forging of credentials, the overnight publication of pseudo-newspapers with subtly invidious contents, and the rapid marshaling of demonstrations ranging from a handful of pickets to a large-scale formal assemblage. In the 1966 California gubernatorial campaign, he convoked on short notice a statewide gathering of intellectuals to steal the thunder from a simultaneous hostile convention of the New Left.

In the 1960 presidential campaign, after the first Kennedy-Nixon debate, it was Tuck who got an old lady (a Democrat wearing an insincere Nixon button) to rush up to Richard Nixon at an airport with the demoralizing assurance: "He beat you last night, but don't worry—you'll do better next time."

In 1964 Tuck's handiwork made front pages across the country when he smuggled a comely female spy aboard the Goldwater campaign train to distribute subversive literature.

A University of California graduate, Tuck got his first training in undercover activities as a World War II frogman in the Marines. His first bit of political legerdemain was clinching the election of a state senator by publicizing, contrary to political dogma, the fact that the man drove a Rolls-Royce. The success of this reverse-English launched him on a career of exploiting the classic weapon of surprise.

Tuck's almost untoppable surprise concoction, many political reporters felt, was a large banner in Chinese characters that was carried aloft behind Richard Nixon throughout a campaign visit to Los Angeles' Chinatown in the 1962 gubernatorial campaign. After countless photographs had been taken, Nixon discovered belatedly that the Chinese characters spelled out: "What about the Hughes loan?"

In 1966 Tuck made his one egregious mistake. He ran for office himself, for one of the new state senate seats from Los Angeles—and was beaten in a five-candidate primary.

His comment pinpointed the essential fallibility of the most Machiavellian backstage manipulators in current politics.

"The people have spoken—" he said, *"darn 'em!"*

Chapter
Sixteen

1966: "Nice Guy" Finishes First

☒ ". . . OR SHOULD MOSES HAVE TOLD THE children of Israel to live in slavery under the Pharaohs? Should Christ have refused the Cross? Should the patriots at Concord Bridge have thrown down their guns and refused to fire the shot heard 'round the world? . . ."

The words, reminiscent in flavor of William Jennings Bryan's impassioned peroration about the "Cross of Gold," reverberated from millions of television sets across the nation in 1964 as the climax of a half-hour taped pitch in support of the presidential cause of Senator Barry Goldwater.

The cause lost, but the oration won. It produced a host of new fans for the speaker, who already had wide renown as an actor in some 40 motion pictures and as *compère* of television's *Death Valley Days:* Ronald Reagan.

Even Reagan was surprised by the response (said to have included $500,000 in campaign contributions), inasmuch as the oration was only a slight modification of "The Speech"—the lecture on behalf of conservative government that he had been delivering for eight years as a free-enterprise lecturer for the General Electric Company.

But Reagan was of no mind to quibble about this windfall of popularity. Nor were an important bloc of California Republicans, political zombies for more than six years, who had been wondering whom on earth they might run in 1966, in at least a token effort to derail the Democratic juggernaut piloted by Governor Edmund "Pat" Brown.

Characteristically, with California's feeble party apparatus, the Republican cupboard was almost bare of seasoned political timber able to present an effective challenge. The one person in sight who had a good chance of corralling the bipartisan vote necessary to dislodge Brown was Senator Thomas Kuchel, but his liberal voting in Congress had made him anathema to the conservatives; his candidacy seemed certain to precipitate a party blood-bath. And he was disinclined to give up his influential position as Senate minority whip.

Aside from Kuchel, the best that party ranks contained were such figures as San Francisco's former mayor, George Christopher, shopworn after his 1962 defeat as Nixon's running-mate; and Caspar Weinberger and Laughlin Waters, San Francisco and Los Angeles lawyers who, despite having been Republican state chairmen, were unknown to most of the electorate. Weinberger resisted the temptation to run. Waters campaigned briefly and dropped out. Christopher declared himself a candidate, but it was very problematical whether, if nominated, he could garner a winning portion of November votes.

Reagan at first blush seemed the most implausible of candidates. California two years before had sent George Murphy, identified primarily as an actor, to the United States Senate. But no state had ever installed as its governor an actor without a day's experience in public office.

Yet in Reagan's case there were extenuating factors—factors that eventually proved decisive. To begin with, he had a veneer of identification with politics and public affairs; and he had that very valuable asset in California, a bipartisan background.

Reagan had had urges toward both theatrics and politics ever since boyhood. He was born in the little downstate Illinois town of Tampico on February 6, 1911. His father was an unaffluent shoe salesman and shoe merchant of Irish extraction, with a weakness for alcohol. Reagan spent a Tom Sawyerish boyhood as the family moved from one little Illinois town to another. His mother, he recalls in his autobiography, was "the dean of dramatic recitals for the countryside. It was her sole relaxation from her family and charitable duties; she executed it with the zeal of a frustrated actress. She recited classic speeches in tragic tones, wept as she flung herself into the more poignant, if less talented, passages of such melodramas as *East Lynne,* and poured out poetry by the yard."

The big event of Reagan's youth was his going off to Eureka College, a picture-postcard nineteenth-century institution with only 250 students in a hamlet near Peoria. He worked his way through college by washing dishes and lifeguarding; he played on the football team; and he starred in campus dramatics. His first taste of quasi-politics was as a leader of a Depression-days student rebellion against a proposed drastic cutback in the college's curriculum. It fell to him to present a mass-meeting motion for a student class-attendance boycott (which ultimately succeeded in averting the retrenchment).

"They came to their feet with a roar," he has recalled.

"Even the faculty members present voted by acclamation. It was heady wine. Hell, with two more lines, I could have had them riding 'through every Middlesex village and farm'—without horses, yet."

After graduation Reagan worked as a radio sports announcer in the Midwest, his forte being breathless play-by-play simulations of big-league baseball games from typed wire reports. Radio work took him, in 1937, to Hollywood, a successful screen test, and a $200-a-week job as a contract actor. Soon he moved into a vacancy as the contract-actor representative on the board of the Screen Actors Guild. This led eventually to the presidency of the union—in which, ingratiating, articulate, and organization-minded, he served six one-year terms.

In this post he gained experience in administration, labor negotiations, and public affairs as an industry spokesman during the hectic McCarthy-era days of Communist infiltration in Hollywood and ensuing government investigations.

After fighting World War II at a desk in the Air Force's Hollywood film-making branch, Reagan returned to postwar civilian life as, he has said, a "bleeding-heart liberal," joining with alacrity such leftish movements as the American Veterans Committee and the Hollywood Independent Citizens Committee for the Arts, Sciences and Professions. Disenchantment came soon, he has related, when he discovered that in his orbit liberal sentiments were welcome only as long as he didn't append any derogation of Communism.

"From being an active (though unconscious) partisan in what now and then turned out to be Communist causes," he said in his autobiography, "I little by little became disillusioned, or perhaps, in my case, I should say awakened."

He severed his left-wing connections. But, a hereditary Democrat, as late as 1950 he was active in Helen Gahagan Douglas' senatorial campaign against Richard Nixon. Reagan changed his affiliation to Republican after being a Democrat-for-Nixon in the 1960 presidential campaign. In 1962, he was chairman of the unsuccessful Republican primary campaign of Loyd Wright, a right-wing Los Angeles lawyer, against Senator Thomas Kuchel.

Reagan had now swung as far to the conservative side as he had once been liberal. The shift had a certain correlation with his personal fortunes. Divorced by Jane Wyman on grounds of incompatibility, in 1952 he had married Nancy Davis, a neophyte film actress and the daughter of Dr. Loyal Davis, a Chicago neurosurgeon of pronounced political conservatism. Reagan's unspectacular but lucrative acting career had gone into a slump.

"I'd been making handsome money ever since World War II," he said, "but that handsome money lost a lot of its beauty and substance going through the 91 per cent bracket of the income tax. The tragic fact of life in this evil day of progressive taxation is that, once behind, it is well-nigh impossible to earn your way out."

Finally his agents arranged an unusual deal under which Reagan would host and act on the *General Electric Theater* television program, while devoting part of his time every year to visiting GE's 135 plants across the country. His mission was to address personnel as part of the notably conservative corporation's "community relations" program, with the dual purpose of promoting the television show and extolling free enterprise, while deploring the assorted burdens imposed on American business by "big government."

Reagan, known in the studios as a "quick study" (a facile memorizer) became a walking encyclopedia of arresting economic facts and figures of the sort relished by the arch-conservative Chamber of Commerce of the United States and the National Association of Manufacturers—the mounting numbers of Federal bureaucrats, the soaring rates of taxes, the extent and anomalies of Federal farm subsidies.

On the Hollywood dinner-party circuit, some of his more intellectual acquaintances tabbed him as having a "*Reader's*

Digest mind," because of his propensity for regaling parlor audiences with such superficialities as how far the national debt would reach if it were in dollar bills laid end-to-end.

But such titbits, crocheted together with an actor's feel for the dramatic, and overlaid with fervent if abstract appeals to patriotism, provided the nucleus for The Speech of 1964, which suggested to some that Ronald Reagan was not only an actor but a latent politician.

It is a myth of American politics that our electoral system puts into office the ablest people in terms of academic occupational qualifications. The system, by definition, puts into office the most electable people—the most agile performers in an obstacle race whose hazards range from the physical rigors of a campaign to instantaneous coping with policy enigmas. These hazards correlate in a vague way with the range of contingencies a man may have to deal with in public office.

The big initial hurdle in such a race, in the era of population explosion and an astronomical web of public distractions, is for a political aspirant simply to establish his identity, so that people will even consider voting for him. In California, with the vote resting with 8 million people scattered among 12 million other people over an expanse of 158,000 square miles, the job of establishing a public identity is tremendous. It involves an investment, in time and effort, equivalent to many millions of dollars. The process must start years before a major election contest; there is not time in a campaign, regardless of outlay of money, to establish a previously unknown personality.

From this standpoint, Reagan offered a built-in asset that was invaluable in terms of cold cash and campaign effort: ready-made recognition that was in the main highly favorable. For every voter who had observed him orating for Goldwater and had been repelled by his ideology, there probably were three voters who knew him only as the "nice guy" of movie and television fiction, and who could be persuaded that his real-life personality was equally acceptable.

This asset was recognized by a small coterie of conservative

Republican activists led by A. C. Rubel, the retired oil executive who had been a 1962 Rafferty supporter and a 1964 Goldwater delegate.

Seeking professional guidance on launching a Reagan candidacy, this junta turned to the experts who had given them formidable opposition in 1964: the campaign management firm of Stuart Spencer and William Roberts, the impresarios of Governor Nelson Rockefeller's narrowly unsuccessful California presidential primary campaign against Barry Goldwater.

On June 26, 1965, what purported to be only an exploratory letter went out to 7,500 leading Republicans throughout the state. The letter came from 41 "Friends of Ronald Reagan" —predominantly Goldwaterites, with the window-dressing of two 1964 Rockefeller-slate members. Ostensibly the "Friends" were just sounding out potential support. Actually, the die had been cast; this was the opening gun of the Reagan campaign, under way a year in advance of the 1966 primary.

Neglect of Fact One

The Brown administration had been good, in some ways remarkable, in dealing with problems of a higher order than confronted most states. In eight years, California had acquired 5 million more people—a 33 per cent increase. State university and college enrollments had doubled, but no qualified applicant had been turned away, thanks to campus expansion under a master plan for higher education that had evoked international admiration. All the economic indices had risen. In the 1958–66 period, California, with one-tenth of the nation's population, had produced one-sixth of the new employment. A $2 billion statewide water-redistribution project, stymied by sectional politics since Warren's day, had been activated.

A subtle testimonial that Brown had kept faith with the tradition of California's best governors was the participation of Chief Justice Warren, along with former Governor Knight, in a "nonpartisan" Sacramento banquet Brown staged at the height of the gubernatorial campaign, on August 21, 1966, nominally to honor a retiring department head who had worked in all three administrations. Warren did not make such appearances lightly.

But the Democrats' downfall, notwithstanding their apparent strength, had been envisioned as far back as 1964 by one of the party's leading figures, Assembly Speaker Jesse Unruh. He warned party activists on numerous occasions that the future was threatened by factionalism (in which Unruh was far from a neutral) and by legislative drift "too far out ahead of the people."

The hazards he cited went unremedied. The 1965 legislature lapsed into a fruitless imbroglio over tax reform. Factional skirmishing between Brown-oriented and Unruh-oriented elements intensified. Rioting on the University of California's Berkeley campus, and the great Watts riot of August, 1965, created an atmosphere of tension and instability in the state.

As Brown swung into the 1966 primary campaign, this accumulation of frictions worked against him.

The help Reagan got from Spencer-Roberts was not so one-sided a matter as many inferred. Brown had an even more experienced group of political managers, although they were not formally organized as a consulting firm. They included Frederick Dutton, the former assistant secretary of state in Washington, who had managed his 1958 campaign; Don Bradley, long the executive director of the state Democratic committee and California's most knowledgeable political technician; and Hale Champion, State Finance Director. There was also Harry Lerner, a top-drawer San Francisco campaign consultant. In addition, the Baus-Ross firm, a counterpart of Spencer-Roberts, was retained for the special mission of attracting the liberal-Republican vote.

Brown and his handlers assumed that a history of eight years of competent administration spoke for itself.

"I'm entitled to win on my record," the governor kept saying.

They neglected Fact One of California politics: Since the last campaign in 1962, the electorate had grown by a million people, many of them newcomers unfamiliar with the Brown regime. To them, and to many other pragmatically minded voters, Brown and Reagan started off on an even footing.

Brown's handlers quarrelled about strategy. But the one that materialized was:

Get rid of Christopher, the more threatening competition for the "moderate" vote, in the primary. Then Reagan can be disposed of as a right-winger and an actor with no qualifications to be governor.

In devious ways, such as exhuming an old business scandal in which Christopher had been involved, Democrats worked to help Reagan beat Christopher.

But the Brown effort encountered mounting troubles. Private opinion-surveys revealed an alarming phenomenon: The "blue-collar" working people, a Democratic mainstay in the past, had prospered so much in the last few years that they had turned conservative, and now they were as concerned about high taxes and "big government" as many Republicans. Another issue cutting across party lines was "open housing." Voters had repudiated the open housing law in 1964, but the constitutionality of their action had been challenged and the state supreme court had finally handed down its decision invalidating the action. This aggravated the irritations of 1964 against Brown as an advocate of open housing.

The usual absence of any unified party control of the campaign was illustrated in a divisive race that developed for the lieutenant-governor nomination. This contest involved the incumbent, Glenn Anderson; Thomas Braden, an Oceanside publisher close to the Kennedy clan; and Lloyd Hand, a last-minute "carpetbag" entry from the ranks of the Johnson administration.

The nominal voice of party rank-and-filers, the California Democratic Council, which eight years before had been an instrument of victory, now suddenly consummated its decline as a constructive force. Its president, Simon Casady, launched into a personal crusade against the Vietnam war involvement. Brown was impelled to intervene. The ensuing organizational squabble about Casady's replacement made the CDC a party liability—and an easy target for anti-Brown jibes about "left-wing domination."

Nor was Brown getting the help he needed from the anti-CDC "professionals."

Some little-noticed handwriting went up on the wall when Jesse Unruh, after announcing that he was backing Brown to the hilt, fell curiously silent, and presently embarked on a foreign tour that kept him out of the state until the eve of the election.

Poised to exploit Brown's troubles was the party maverick, Los Angeles' Mayor Samuel Yorty. One of California's most experienced politicians, with a Congressional and legislative career going back 30 years, Yorty was looking upward again. Challenging Brown from the safety of his mayoral job was an easy way to pick up momentum, win or lose. Yorty's announcement of his candidacy for the nomination, only a month before the March filing deadline, was discounted by the Brown people as a minor harassment. Brown, in the approved California fashion, ignored Yorty and directed his attack at his presumable November opponent, Reagan.

On Saturday, June 4, three days before the primary, Brown, with such Hollywood personalities as Barry Sullivan and Susan Oliver window-dressing his entourage, made an 800-mile airplane swing ranging from Santa Maria, in mid-California, to El Centro, on the southern border. At Santa Maria, where Democrats predominate, it was a festive Elks Rodeo Day. More than 25,000 people lined the sidewalks of the main street for a mile to watch the governor's parade. Bands and horsemen drew bursts of applause. The governor's car, despite the amplified pep-talk of the parade director, passed in eerie silence. "They must be Republicans—they aren't saying anything," a girl driver remarked. The governor's campaign manager, lanky Don Bradley, customarily had a lugubrious poker face, unchanged by the wildest political developments. Now his jaw dropped.

Doctors in the House

The Reagan campaign blossomed under the ministrations of two sorts of doctors: experts in voter dynamics . . . and a medical doctor.

Dr. Gaylord Parkinson, a youthful, immaculate-looking San Diego obstetrician, has no trouble remembering his most difficult accouchement. It was the two-year process over which he presided that induced the birth of unity in a party that had all but extinguished itself through internal strife.

"This is not time for recriminations," he crisply told party leaders as he took over the Republican state chairmanship late in 1964. "We've got work to do. We're going to make this a party of consensus."

Toward this end, he promulgated "Parkinson's Eleventh Commandment." It said: "Thou shall not speak ill of any other Republican." It was the ultimate extension of the California practice, cultivated in the Republicans' previous lean era, of minimizing primary competition to avert rancor that would bring critical voter defections. When, as the 1966 campaign warmed up, George Christopher, Reagan's primary opponent, waxed waspish about the actor, Parkinson publicly rebuked him. Parkinson's injunction, in effect, was: "Get your campaign impetus by directing your attacks at the Democratic opposition, so we won't be a shambles when go to the voters in November." Reagan discerned the strategic wisdom of this, and more than once when he was asked provocative questions about his opponent he replied: "If I answered that, I'd be violating the Eleventh Commandment."

This application of artificial respiration to resuscitate party harmony deprived voters of a discussion of the differing views held by rival Republican entries. But it encouraged the "consensus" that, by sheer arithmetic, the minority Republicans needed as a pre-condition to making effective inroads on the November vote of Democrats.

The other doctors of the Reagan campaign, Spencer and Roberts, had the task of presenting a Reagan whom Republicans could unite on, and whom, subsequently, moderate Democrats could bring themselves to support.

"We had to overcome three things," Bill Roberts explained later, "—Reagan's inexperience, the actor bit, and his lack of knowledge of state government.

"We decided not to compete with Brown on a knowledge level on specific issues. Brown had been in public office for more than 20 years, and been governor for eight years. Surely he was more knowledgeable. So we admitted Reagan was not a professional politician. In effect we said: 'He may not know much about these issues, but he's got good ideas and good intentions.' "

Three years earlier the New York *Times*' chief Washington correspondent, Tom Wicker, had limned a hypothetical "candidate of tomorrow" in the nation's changing political climate. He described him as ". . . the television-oriented candidate . . . to some degree detached from reliance on the party organization, who appeals beyond the bounds of party. This candidate's appeal tends to be generalized on issues, free of strident party appeals, heavily centered on his own reputation for being more than a courthouse hack or machine product. . . . [he is] dependent on public-relations techniques. . . ." Reagan fitted these specifications with uncanny precision.

True to the Wicker prescription, Reagan pursued a campaign of bland generalities, leaning heavily on such nebulous concepts as "morality." Paradoxically, the tangibles in his campaign were a carbon copy of things Nixon had propounded unsuccessfully in 1962. Reagan talked about "the Brown machine," "welfare costs," "fiscal chaos." He lifted verbatim a number of Nixon themes: on California being "first in crime, first in high taxes, first in bungling bureaucracy"; on the Federal government's lamentable exclusion of cheap Mexican farm labor; and on the need for "local control of schools." He struck a responsive chord with his basic contention that contemporary government is really a simple matter that requires mainly the application of common sense.

Brown and the Democrats played into his hands.

"They opened their campaign," Bill Roberts analyzed later, "on the 'extremist' issue. That was a mistake. It was an over-the-hill issue people were tired of. I would never have attacked Reagan. He had the image of a decent person of integrity. They should have killed him with kindness. I would have said: 'He's a decent, fine person and no doubt has a future in politics—but maybe he should start at a lower level.' "

George Christopher helped Reagan by running a singularly weak primary campaign. In the June 7 primary election, Reagan corralled two out of every three Republican votes. Brown, although he won comfortably, was hit in the face by a defection to Sam Yorty of nearly a million Democrats—who presumably were fair game for Reagan in November.

Sin in River City

Many national observers, watching Reagan's fortunes soar, construed this as a triumph of California's widely noted right wing. The fact is that the militant right was not numerous enough to swing any such coup; and once Reagan had been endorsed by Republican moderates the right-wing faction became preoccupied with two other causes. One was a bemused attempt to regulate pornography through a ballot initiative, Proposition 16, promoted by a group calling itself the "California League For Enlisting Action Now" ("CLEAN").

Their campaign was one of those oddities that crop up recurrently in the ungainly efforts of the psychically immature to reconcile their neurotic Puritan-Calvinist ethic with the mores of the twentieth century. Usually some catalyst precipitates these onsets of the book-burning syndrome, someone who cries: "There's SIN in River City!" In this case it was a San Diego opportunist named William K. Shearer (later to emerge as the spokesman for Alabama's George Wallace), whose ventures as a professional propagandist had taken him as far afield as writing for the Mississippi-based, white-supremacist Citizens Council.

For reasons that perhaps only some psychiatrist knew, Shearer's alarums about s-m-u-t struck a responsive chord in Patrick J. Frawley, Jr., a wealthy, determined crusader for Schick razor blades, against alcoholism, for "Americanism," and against anything as menacing to national security as a printed reference to the mechanics by which, presumably, he was conceived. Other sponsors included Loyd Wright; Walter Knott, the patriotic amusement-park operator; Joe Crail, the millionaire head of the Coast Federal Savings and Loan Association; and Fritz Burns, a real estate developer whose wife was a prominent member of the Birch society.

Proposition 16 would have redefined pornography, in disregard of the United States Supreme Court's exemption of works tinged with "redeeming social importance." It would have put regulation in the hands of local moral vigilantes, with petit juries sitting in judgment. The proposition was vigorously opposed by the state attorney general and the state's leading district attorneys, as well as by civil liberties groups and some major church organizations.

The CLEAN people's big electioneering effort was a color tabloid inserted as advertising in millions of Sunday newspapers just before the election. In 11 pages of Victorian froth about "rape, perversion . . . venereal disease," and "protecting our wives and daughters," the document conspicuously omitted any delineation of the proposed law.

But through a chain of references to "Pavlov's conditioned responses," "brain-washing," and "Korean prison camps," it hinted at the Birchite theme that pornography was the result of a Communist plot to undermine morality. The 12th page bore an advertisement for Frawley's Schick-Eversharp company, which put $185,000 into the CLEAN campaign.

Reagan mildly endorsed the proposal as something that perhaps should be put to a legal test, but he avoided tying his campaign to it. The proposition was defeated, 3,271,000 to 2,533,000.

The other right-wing drive, to unseat four of the seven state supreme court justices because they had invalidated the 1964 anti-open-housing measure and had upheld legislative reapportionment, also came to naught. The judges, up for periodic reconfirmation by the voters, got strong support.

In the panic that seized the Democratic forces after the primary, Brown made the strategic mistake of abandoning the defensive "nice guy" position on the pedestal of incumbency, and clambering down to scuffle in the grass with Reagan about "issues"—a futile procedure because the disparity in the two men's positions produced only confusing dialogue.

There were assertions that Reagan exploited "white backlash"—public resentment against the fractious turn taken by the racial-equality movement. Reagan often did refer to "crime in the streets," an expression that had nationally become a euphemism for Negro militance. And he seemed to imply that Brown was to blame for the Watts rioting. But any support Reagan extracted from racial tensions appeared to be derived largely from a national wave of feeling, evidenced both in opinion polls and election results generally, that the civil rights movement was one of a number of things that had gone "too far too fast." Unless one out of 20 of all Californians—and one out of six voters—could be classified as bigots, "white backlash" was not a critical factor in Reagan's eventual victory.

Factionalism erupted again to embarrass Brown. With the August biennial state party meeting approaching, a fight developed over who was to become state chairman. Mrs. Carmen Warschaw, the Unruh-faction vice-chairman, who normally would succeed to the office, was challenged by Assemblyman

Charles Warren of Los Angeles, candidate of the CDC and other anti-Unruh forces. Brown tried to play neutral. Mrs. Warschaw, a member of the wealthy Harvey aluminum family, was beaten by five votes. With the fury of a woman scorned, she publicly accused Brown of virtual treachery, and intimated that she would vote for Reagan. Her walkout was of particular psychological significance: it lent an aura of respectability to Democratic defection, the swing that the Reagan people had to precipitate to win.

It is an axiom that California voters prefer "moderate" candidates. But the meaning of "moderate" can vary from election to election, depending on the particular ideological contrast of rival candidates and on the electorate's not always predictable conception of where the "center" lies. Brown appeared "moderate" in 1962 by comparison with Richard Nixon's middle-of-the-road Republicanism. Four years later, many observers expected Brownian "moderation" to prevail again over the more conservative Republican identification of Ronald Reagan. But in the context of 1966, voters were persuaded that Brown's ideological inclinations were more "extreme" than the "extremism" imputed to Reagan.

Election day, November 8, 1966, brought a landslide for Reagan and most of his ticket. When the ballots were counted Brown had been swamped by a vote of 3,742,000 to 2,749,000. All the other major Democratic candidates went down to defeat with him, except Attorney General Thomas Lynch.

Using almost the same words that the Progressives had used to hail their victory in 1910, that Warren had used to categorize the defeat of Sinclair in 1934, and that Warren and his successors in office had applied to their own victories, Reagan at 10:32 P.M. on election night said:

"Let us remember that we didn't achieve any narrow partisan victory. . . . Many friends from the other party and the independents had a part in it too. . . . Partisanship ends as of today. . . ."

The Capricious Million

Ronald Reagan's election could be attributed to Democrats rather than Republicans. It had been expected that he would get the Republican vote. But if little more than half the Democrats who voted for him had voted for Brown, Brown would have won the election.

The results were all that was needed to complete the documentation of the most important immediate fact of California politics:

The Democrats' nominal advantage of more than a million in registrations over the Republicans is illusory.

Approximately a million Democrats are Democrats-in-name-only. They will vote Democratic sometimes. But they are just as likely to vote Republican—in the same election. They are the ticket-splitters. And, composing about 16 per cent of actual election-day turnouts, they hold in their unpredictable hands far more than the margin of votes by which candidates generally win and lose elections.

Whether the Capricious Million are a fairly fixed group, of individuals, or a revolving portion of the electorate, of particular mental bent, remains to be determined. But they have been mathematically evident in every election since at least 1958.

In 1958, the Capricious Million swung Democratic. Brown got all of the Democratic turnout and beat Knowland by more than 1 million votes. Moving down the ticket, the Capricious Million strayed more and more, until, in the vote for secretary of state, a majority had swung to the Republican side: the Democratic candidate, Henry Lopez, in losing to Frank M. Jordan, ran some 600,000 *under* the Democratic turnout.

It was the Capricious Million that crossed up Richard Nixon in 1962. Most of them voted for Senator Thomas Kuchel, giving him about 750,000 votes over the Republican turnout.

But in the gubernatorial race they split between Brown and Nixon; and, considering the smaller Republican registration, half a loaf for Nixon was not enough.

In 1964, the same bloc swung against Pierre Salinger and gave George Murphy the senatorship. Salinger's deficiency in Democratic votes corresponded closely to Murphy's excess over the Republican vote.

In 1966, to zero in on the phenomenon precisely, the Republican turnout on Election Day was about 2,808,000. This can be measured from the party's total registration, minus the non-voters, who under California law are stricken from the rolls after every state election. The Democratic turnout was 3,629,000—some 800,000 more than the Republicans.

Thus for this election the Democrats' registration advantage of 1,370,000 was reduced by 500,000 non-voters. Reagan ran 934,000 over the Republican turnout. Brown ran 880,000 under the Democratic turnout. (For simplicity, the votes of the 187,000 unaffiliated voters are consolidated here with the major-party vote.)

Robert Finch, in the lieutenant governor contest, polled 1,026,000 more votes than the Republican turnout; Lieutenant Governor Glenn Anderson, the weakest Democratic candidate, ran 1,051,000 under the Democratic turnout. Moving down the roster of candidates, the Capricious Million shifted slowly back to a Democratic vote, until, in the attorney general contest, the Democratic incumbent, Thomas Lynch, corralled about 250,000 of his party's ambivalent mavericks and beat the Republican entry, Spencer Williams, by nearly 500,000.

(The aggregate votes in the different contests do not match because of a progressive drop-off in voting; some 234,000 persons who voted for governor did not vote for secretary of state.)

Overall, the election results indicated that, as of 1966, from a practical standpoint the Republicans were the majority party. The only measure of hard-core Democratic strength was the minimal vote of 2,578,000 for Lieutenant Governor Anderson. Since no Republican candidate polled less than the party turnout, the Republican hard-core can only be gauged from the party turnout, which was 2,808,000.

The Capricious Million undoubtedly include some habitual ticket-splitters who are registered Republicans, as well as the 250,000 perennial registrees outside the major parties. But the pattern of voting figures from election to election indicates that the Million are mostly nominal Democrats.

The principal reason for their concentration under the Democratic label is believed to be that much of the heavier migration to California in recent years has been from "one-party" states where people habitually registered Democratic even if they were conservative, and a Republican vote meant a lost vote. California gave these people their first chance to really vote Republican.

But an equally important factor probably is the looseness of party ties that applies to all California voters—the tendency to vote "the man, not the party."

In any case, the import of the Capricious Million is that it is fallacious to extrapolate from national-election behavior and try to classify California in state affairs as either a Republican or a Democratic state.

California can only be classified as bipartisan. It belongs to whoever, regardless of party, can convince the Capricious Million.

Chapter Seventeen
The Two Reagans

☒ "WELL, GEORGE, HERE WE ARE ON THE LATE SHOW AGAIN. . . ."

It was just after midnight, in the opening minutes of Monday, January 2, 1967.

In the drafty rotunda of the baroque state capitol at Sacramento, 32 television cameras focused on the cluster of 150 specially invited guests.

Associate Justice Marshall McComb of the state supreme court administered the oath. Then Ronald Reagan, covering his nervousness with a quip, turned to his old Hollywood friend, Senator George Murphy, and made his wry reference to television's frequent revivals of their old movies.

New Year's Day had fallen on a Sunday, so Monday was a quasi-holiday, with public preoccupations that would have conflicted with an elaborate daytime ceremony. And Reagan was eager to take over immediately after the legal expiration of Governor Edmund Brown's term at midnight. Actually the ceremony was superfluous. Unwittingly Reagan had taken the oath of office a week earlier, in signing before a deputy secretary of state a declaration that he thought was simply the standard state employees' loyalty form.

But, one way or another, the administration of California's 33rd governor, and perhaps the state's most interesting experiment in government, had begun.

It would be convenient for a political analyst, writing after the first year of the Reagan administration, to be able to classify it as either a revolutionary success or an unmitigated disaster. But state government is not that sensitive, in the short run, to a change in leadership. A $5-billion-a-year enterprise, operated by 167,000 personnel on behalf of 20 million people, has a momentum of its own. So what unfolded was, in essence, a 12-month demonstration of two facts: on the one hand, that the realities of the times are not to be dispelled by voter endorsement of a simplistic approach to government; and on the other hand, that a state which has weathered more than a century of strenuous vicissitudes is not easily unhinged.

In theory, the Republicans had had eight years in which to study what was wrong with the state, what they would do on regaining office, and who would be the best appointees for the work. That is the way it might have been in another state.

But in California two facts made any such methodical

transition dream-stuff. One was that the Republican party was too weak and uncoordinated to have done any such systematic preparation. The second fact was that the Reagan who landed in Sacramento was less a Republican party product than the result of a transitory bipartisan voter consensus.

So the 53 days between the 1966 election and Reagan's accession were taken up with a frantic quest for key personnel to man the new administration, and hasty familiarization with fundamentals of the state's government. Reagan, for instance, professed to have discovered with astonishment that the state had been spending a million dollars a day more than it had been taking in. This was not so outlandish as he made it sound. It amounted to a year's deficit of $365 million, or a cash-flow maladjustment of less than 10 per cent of the state budget, which in part was a matter of bookkeeping intricacies. In any case, it had been a matter of public record.

Under the circumstances, it was hardly surprising that the Reagan inaugural address was an undistinguished grab-bag of notions and proposals, fitting only vaguely into his own theme of a "Creative Society" that would establish a new intimacy between citizens and government and revivify private initiative.

He spoke of a broad program of legislation against crime, and particularly against "smut and pornography." He mentioned "removing politics from the appointment of judges"—a bow to long-standing pressure from the state bar to enlarge its already sizable role in judicial nominations. Reagan reiterated in politic terms his campaign promises to rid welfare rolls of a presumably large quotient of parasites, and to obtain revision of the Rumford Act, which outlawed racial discrimination in real estate transactions.

Somewhat cryptically—since there had been no great public clamor on the subject—he advocated new laws for balloting secrecy in union elections, an enlarged state labor mediation service, and increases in benefits such as workmen's compensation. Somewhat cryptically also, he recommended broadening Social Security coverage and eliminating the 160-acre ownership limitation on Federally irrigated lands—both Federal matters a governor could do little about.

He reserved maximum emphasis for what was to emerge quickly as the dominant motivation of his administration—governmental economy and tax reductions. "The cost of California government is too high," he said. "It adversely affects our business climate. We are going to squeeze and cut and trim until we reduce the cost of government."

Democratic State Assembly Speaker Jesse Unruh, next to the governor the most imposing political figure in the state, when asked his opinion of the inaugural message, commented with wry equivocation: "It was forward-looking."

Images and Men

The Reagan that materialized at Sacramento was a dual personality. On one side was Reagan the dapper, poised actor, playing "Mr. Smith Goes to Washington," short on background but long on convictions and "common sense," facile in sensing his audience and articulating elementary sentiments in an appealing, even lofty, way with connotations of statesmanship. Obversely, there was Reagan the apprentice politician, with a knack for wheeling and dealing, above average in administrative sense, unsophisticated in areas ranging from public finance to jurisprudence, and prone to lurch into blunders—but with an acquired politician's charm and agility in extricating himself.

It was the first of these two images that Reagan projected to the world at large. It was an unpredictable mixture of the two that became familiar in California.

Visitors to the governor's office in the early months of 1967 sometimes got the eerie feeling that they had walked onto a Hollywood set. The appurtenances looked appropriate: rich, dark paneling, gleaming colonial furniture, family pictures on the table behind the desk. And the governor himself, glossily groomed, tailored with the slight over-sharpness of Hollywood's mid-1950's, was sitting obliquely at his desk as if for a camera-angle. But whereas governor's desks usually are piled with documents representing the day's business, Reagan's office might be conspicuously devoid of as much as a single sheet of paper. The stage-like atmosphere would be broken only when an assistant popped in with a document to get the governor's signature or a quick yes-or-no concurrence.

Reagan had a made-to-order mentor in the complexities of state government, in the person of Lieutenant Governor Robert Finch, who although he had never held office before was exceptionally knowledgeable in public affairs. But Finch was burdened with several intrinsic heresies. He was a former Nixon aide; he leaned more toward the liberal Republican side than the conservative; and in the election he had marred the illusion that Reagan had some kind of magic allure, by polling 92,000 more votes than Reagan.

Reagan turned away from Finch, conversing with him sometimes no oftener than at a weekly luncheon. Instead, Reagan installed as his right-hand man, in the position of executive secretary, Philip Battaglia. A 32-year-old Los Angeles lawyer, moon-faced, soft-spoken, fast-moving, and capable, Battaglia had been Reagan's state campaign chairman. When Battaglia left the administration suddenly after eight months, his place was taken by a solemn, efficient scion of a wealthy ranching family, William P. Clark, Jr., also a lawyer.

The other figure who quickly moved to the forefront as a top-ranking aide was Franklyn (Lyn) Nofziger, a portly, sardonic newspaperman, on leave from the Copley papers' Washington bureau, who had been campaign press secretary. Now given the title of "communications secretary," Nofziger functioned actually as a policy and strategy adviser on both state and national matters.

Reagan also leaned heavily on an unofficial, absentee "kitchen cabinet" of a dozen business and professional men in San Francisco and Los Angeles who had been movers in Republican affairs. They included Henry Salvatori, the wealthy Los Angeles oilman; Leland Kaiser, San Francisco financier; Holmes Tuttle, a crusty, conservative Los Angeles automobile dealer; and Taft Schreiber, an executive of MCA, the big entertainment enterprise, who had been Reagan's agent. Reagan maintained contact with these men and a few others by telephone and in quiet meetings, from week to week, at private clubs in San Francisco and Los Angeles.

"My administration makes no bones about being business-oriented," Reagan said. He further exemplified this orientation in his major appointments. Laments arose from leaders of organized labor when the post of state labor commissioner, traditionally filled from labor's ranks, went to William C. Hern, a bakery executive, and the directorship of the department of industrial relations went to another management man, Albert C. Beeson, executive of a food-processing equipment corporation.

"Squeeze and Cut and Trim"

Reagan's repeated references to a "nonpartisan" approach to government seemed to mean that partisanism was not a factor as long as any individuals in question were conservative; but the available conservatives seemed to be almost uniformly Republican. A more partisan tenor in administration had hardly been evident since Culbert Olson's ill-starred efforts, from 1938 to 1942, to revert to an old-style Democratic party line. Reagan's appointees were almost all Republicans; his "kitchen cabinet" comprised rock-ribbed Republicans. And, in the atmosphere of a forthcoming national election, Reagan was impelled repeatedly to identify himself in public utterances as a devout Republican, in terms that limned Democrats as the benighted enemy.

This outlook tended to polarize party alignment in the legislature to Reagan's disadvantage. The bipartisan wave that had swept him into office had not extended to the lower political levels. The legislature still had a narrow Democratic margin in both chambers: 42–38 in the Assembly, 21–19 in the Senate. What this meant strategically, when Reagan hopefully began unlimbering some "Creative Society" measures, was a standoff between him and the legislature. The Democrats had enough votes to pass or block measures contrary to Reagan's desires, but they did not have the two-thirds majority necessary to override any vetoes he chose to exercise.

Also, a psychological-warfare stalemate immediately developed between Reagan and the legislature's leader, Assembly Speaker Unruh, a steely politician who had bucked Governor Brown and ordinarily would have had at a governor of the opposing party. But Unruh discerned that Reagan's public popularity was such that a conventional assault on him would have made Unruh a "heavy." Conversely, however, Reagan's advisers realized that much of his appeal lay in his amateur image, and that a clash with Unruh would tend to put Reagan in the more vulnerable uniform of a professional. Accordingly, virtually all of Reagan's legislative ideas had to be sidetracked in the ensuing six months of parliamentary shadow-boxing over the imperative task of producing a balanced state budget for the fiscal year starting in July.

Informed, as he took office, that Ohio's Governor James Rhodes had instituted an impressive economy program, Reagan sent an aide east to find out about it. He learned that Rhodes had imposed a 10 per cent cutback in departmental budgets, eliminated 5,000 state employees, recruited teams of businessmen to make efficiency surveys of government, and stretched payrolls by urging state employees to work on Lincoln's and Washington's birthdays.

Quickly Reagan ordered a 10 per cent across-the-board cutback in state departments, projected the elimination of some 4,000 state employees, recruited a businessmen's task force for efficiency studies, and exhorted state employees to work on the

February holidays. Most refused. But a freshet of other economy moves followed, ranging from cancellation of a projected $4 million building in Sacramento to abolition of the official highway maps that are a fixture of many states. "Anybody who wants a map can get it at a gas station," Reagan said.

But he found, as countless previous economy-bent officials had, that upward of 70 per cent of the state budget was in commitments locked in by constitutional provisions or statutes, and beyond his control. Ultimately, all Reagan was able to "squeeze and cut and trim" was $127 million—less than 3 per cent of the total budget. He discovered meanwhile that the previous year's $4.6 billion budget had been balanced only through a one-time "windfall" of receipts resulting from a shift to "accrual" or anticipated-revenue bookkeeping, and that inexorably mounting state expenses called for still larger revenues. Reagan finally had to ask for over $900 million in new and increased taxes to balance the biggest state budget in national history, $5.09 billion.

Among a succession of controversies touched off by administration moves, the most acrimonious and protracted was Reagan's battle with the University of California over finances. Casting about for state expenditures within his veto power, Reagan's eye fell on the university's budget. The state appropriation had been $245 million for 1966–67, and the 90,000-student institution had drafted an increase to $278 million for the following year, under an expansion program geared to its century-old policy of admitting all qualified students.

Reagan evoked a storm of protest from the university's nine campuses, and from educational circles across the nation, with a proposal that the appropriation be cut back to $196 million and that the university's future funding be supplemented by an unprecedented tuition fee. Months of haggling pushed the $196 million figure back up to $231 million, which the university's regents agreed to supplement with $20 million in reserve funds to avert a cutback in university operations. The tuition proposal was rejected.

Another *cause célèbre* developed over the governor's residence. For decades California governors had been complaining about the inadequacies of the governor's mansion, a gingerbready Victorian relic built privately in 1879, and at one time the boyhood home of Lincoln Steffens. The oft-refurbished firetrap at 16th and H Streets in downtown Sacramento had become hemmed in by gas stations and motels and roaring truck traffic. A previous legislature had authorized the expenditure of $750,000 for a new mansion, but there had been disagreement about where it should be.

Eight weeks after they had moved in, the Reagans pronounced the mansion unworkable, particularly from the standpoint of their two young children, Patricia and Ronald. They moved to an elegant $150,000 rented home on the outskirts of Sacramento. Reagan designated Leland Kaiser, the San Francisco financier of his "kitchen cabinet," to head a committee to raise $500,000 in contributions to build a new governor's residence by public subscription rather than with state funds. The project drew criticism from many quarters—including former governors Knight and Brown—that disapproved in principle of a state facility being privately financed. The plaints of impropriety mounted when Kaiser sent a fund-solicitation letter to the complete roster of registered lobbyists, who as a group demurred at contributing. By the end of the year, it was reported that the fund drive had attracted only $150,000.

"Mr. Average"

When the legislature recessed in August, Reagan's aides were put to work compiling a brochure of the administration's "accomplishments." They had to scrape. Beyond the balanced budget ("meeting the fiscal crisis"), there were only three areas of tangible accomplishment that could be cited—some minor measures concerning crime and traffic safety, and token "property tax relief" in the form of a $145 million education subvention to counties. An enactment requiring local law-enforcement agencies to "report full information regarding misdemeanors or violations of obscenity laws to the Bureau of Crime Statistics," and eight other equally unspectacular measures, were officially described as "a sweeping crime prevention and control program." The prime agenda outlined in Reagan's inaugural address remained largely unaccomplished.

"Reaganism," said *Fortune* magazine's A. James Reichley in July, "is almost completely negative in character. It promises to keep things from happening: not to free the world from Communism or to alter the course of history but to keep the forces of government, whether an increase in the property tax or an open-housing law, away from the patio steps."

More pungently, San Francisco's widely read longshoreman-philosopher, Eric Hoffer, boomed out in a nationwide television interview with Eric Sevareid: "Reagan's a B-picture hero. He has a mortal hatred against A-pictures. He wants to turn California into a B-picture to be run on a B-picture budget."

But such voices were in a great statistical minority. Reagan's administrative vicissitudes seemed to have little effect on public opinion. After he had been in office nearly nine months a statewide opinion poll indicated that 53 per cent of voters approved of his administration—exactly the same proportion registered in a similar poll six months before.

"He is a sort of Mr. Average, expressing in everyday language the everyday fears, prejudices and instincts of everyday people going about their everyday lives," said the New York *Times'* Tom Wicker, citing other observers' analysis of the Reagan mystique. "Reagan's deepest appeal, in this view, is to those Americans disturbed about a variety of issues arousing deep-seated racial fears and antagonisms—open housing, for instance, welfare costs, crime in the streets, public schools, rioting and demonstrations."

Gains, and a Gap

Concurrent developments brightened the Republicans' legislative prospects, but they also dimmed the supposed magic of the actor-in-politics motif that Reagan's election had highlighted.

The Republicans won quasi-control of the state senate when Democratic Senator Eugene McAteer of San Francisco died and, in a special election on August 12, 1967, to replace him, the leading Democratic candidate, Assemblyman John Burton, was defeated by Judge Milton Marks, a Republican. This left the division of seats in the senate at 20–20, with tie votes subject to being broken by the presiding officer, Lieutenant Governor Finch.

But Californians' presumed predilection for projecting theatrical luminaries into politics manifested its limit when Shirley Temple Black, the former movie child-star, now the 39-year-old wife of a utilities heir, blossomed out as the most prominent Republican candidate in a special Congressional election in San Mateo county, a rock-ribbed-Republican suburb of San Francisco. Although she campaigned energetically—and was shepherded by the pioneer image-maker firm, Whitaker and Baxter—the electorate of 150,000 seemed unimpressed by her newfound interest in public affairs. In a two-party elimination primary November 14, involving seven candidates, Mrs. Black was topped by another Republican, Paul N. McCloskey, Jr., a lawyer and a Korean war hero. He drew some 50,000 votes to her 33,000, and a month later won the seat in the run-off election.

The most discomfiting contretemps of Reagan's first year drew nationwide attention. A succession of unexpected resignations from his executive staff stirred widespread speculation about policy differences. But this gave way to rumors that some of the departures had resulted from the discovery of homosexual activities among some of Reagan's aides. The rumors were traced to word dropped privately by communications secretary Lyn Nofziger to at least a half-dozen newsmen, both in Sacramento and during the National Governors Conference cruise to the Virgin Islands in October.

On October 31 Drew Pearson, the syndicated Washington columnist, reported that, starting some ten months before, Reagan investigators had obtained evidence regarding an eight-man homosexual ring. Pearson said two of the eight were members of the governor's staff who belatedly had been dismissed. Asked about the report at his Sacramento news conference the same day, Governor Reagan heatedly called Pearson a liar and said in effect that he knew nothing about any such misconduct. Dramatically he called upon his chief security officer, Arthur Van Court—the reported investigator of the scandal—and Nofziger to corroborate his disavowal, which they did. His statements produced a bald "credibility gap" between his position and that of his communications secretary, as attested by some of the nation's leading political reporters. It was surmised that Reagan had adopted a vulnerable position on a matter in which there obviously was some truth, and that Nofziger had sought to rectify matters and deflate the scandal as an issue by deliberately "leaking" the truth.

An opinion poll taken in November, after Reagan had declared the homosexual subject "closed," indicated that 61 per cent of Californians thought there was some truth in the allegations; that 36 per cent thought the incident would damage Reagan's reputation; and that 45 per cent thought it would make no difference.

The "Non-Candidate"

If victory in the gubernatorial election found Reagan less than fully prepared to take over the reins of state government, he left little doubt that he had given thought to possibilities beyond Sacramento.

Presidential murmurings had hovered around his name even before the 1964 election, and after the 1966 election they swelled to a subdued chorus. When the inevitable presidential question came up at his first post-election press conference, he had a ready answer. As governor he would automatically head California's powerful 86-vote delegation to the Republican national convention. "There could be circumstances," he added, that would move him, as delegation leader, to be also a "favorite son" candidate. However, he went on, this would be a purely nominal candidacy, to provide a rallying point for a unified delegation, and to avert turning California's June, 1968, presidential primary into the divisive donnybrook among outside aspirants that the 1964 Goldwater-Rockefeller primary fight had been.

"Circumstances" to justify the favorite-son role already existed, in the prospective rival candidacies of such figures as former Vice-President Nixon and Michigan's Governor George Romney. On February 28, Reagan made his intention explicit.

In cold fact, Reagan was confronted with a dilemma. Whatever his ambitions, he was stepping into the 1968 presidential picture too late to take the standard route of competing in state primaries and beating the bushes nationally for delegates. And any overt bid for the nomination would have seemed so presumptuous as to be self-defeating. Yet, if only out of consideration of his party's interests, no one in his position could forgive himself if he shunned the 1968 presidential competition and it developed later that he might have had some chance.

The indicated solution to the dilemma was a strategy of keeping-a-foot-in-the-door, or waiting-for-the-lightning-to-strike: Keep disclaiming presidential ambitions, but meanwhile keep the "non-candidate" on display as much as possible, subtly advertising his availability and palatability.

A good pretext for doing this lay in the hundreds of communications pouring into Reagan's office every week, inviting him to speak all over the country. By centering his appearances on Republican fund-raising dinners, Reagan could always purport to be simply doing his duty by the party. Professed non-candidacy and the mission of party weal provided a smooth and inoffensive entree even into strategic areas where more overt aspirants, such as Nixon and Romney, were scrabbling to line up support.

Even the inability to campaign openly in key state presidential primaries was only a qualified handicap: three key primary states—Wisconsin, Nebraska, and Oregon—now had laws calling for all nationally prominent presidential possibilities to be listed on the ballot, unless they expressly declared themselves non-candidates. Reagan had a convenient excuse for *not* making any such formal disavowal: to do so would be legally inconsistent with his favorite-son candidacy in California, however nominal that was supposed to be. On the ballots in those three states alone, as a passive candidate Reagan conceivably might make enough inroads on the front-runners to give significant impetus to a Reagan groundswell that could crest at the Republican convention.

A groundswell already was gathering nicely. As far back as 1964, someone had started a "Reagan for President" movement in Owosso, Michigan. Now such movements were germinating in state after state, although Reagan insisted that he was doing everything he could to discourage them. In a sense these organized efforts were a liability because they could not, under the circumstances, be coordinated. But Reagan was hard put to conceal his gratification at such manifestations.

Asked how, despite his "non-candidacy," he would react to a presidential "draft," he was impelled to acknowledge candidly: "If the Republican party comes beating at my door, I wouldn't say 'Get lost, fellows.' But," he added, in his arch hero's-best-friend manner of movie days, "that isn't going to happen. . . ."

The tentativeness of this waiver was underscored when, asked later how he felt about a possible vice-presidential nomination, he stated flatly that it was something he had no interest in whatever.

On the Road

Even before his inauguration, Reagan had proved the star attraction at a Republican governors' meeting in Colorado Springs in December, 1966. By March, 1967, he had made three trips back to Washington for various reasons, getting constructive headline exposure each time, and on one foray eclipsing Governor Romney in a joint appearance before 2,000 Republicans at a $500-a-plate dinner.

His stock took a big jump in May when, appearing on the CBS television program, *Town Meeting of the World,* with New York's glamorous Senator Robert Kennedy, he confronted a left-leaning, anti-American group of European students over an international television hookup. About 15 million persons in the United States watched the program, and the consensus of political observers and laymen alike was that Reagan had decidedly bested Kennedy in the keenness of his responses to the students' heckling questions.

During 1967, the dynamics of the Republican presidential race tended to push Reagan to the fore. George Romney, whose earnestness exceeded his agility in political dialogue, kept talking himself into holes. Nixon, despite a meticulously laid-out campaign to corral convention delegates, continued to display the disheartening look of the shopworn loser. Republicans yearning for a candidate with acumen and verve were talking more and more about New York's Governor Rockefeller. He was maintaining studied aloofness, but the presumption was that he could be had. Reagan had shown himself in California to be that rare article, a personality on whom both liberals and conservatives in the party could unite. By July, such nationally respected commentators as the New York *Times*' James Reston were ruminating in print about the possibility of a Rockefeller-Reagan ticket.

This was the setting as Reagan, his onerous legislative

interlude in California finally ended, swung into some intensive cross-country stumping. Various staff members had been quietly sent to reconnoiter key states and confer with local party leaders. Nominally these expeditions were simply to sift speaking invitations—but that was a chore that could have been done by mail or phone. The seriousness of Reagan's touring was indicated when one of his top administration assistants, Thomas Reed, was detached to go on the Republican state committee payroll as a full-time advance man for Reagan's speaking appearances.

In a span of six weeks, from late September to mid-November, Reagan made three trips, delivering a dozen speeches in ten states—most of them states of special significance in the 1968 picture, such as Illinois, Wisconsin, Texas, and South Carolina. The sounding-board for most of his appearances was $100-a-plate Republican fund-raising dinners. His audiences aggregated about 50,000. He was the magnet for about a million dollars in contributions.

To underscore the theme of "non-candidacy," Reagan traveled by chartered executive jet with just two or three aides, omitting the arrangements for a press entourage customarily made even by undeclared candidates.

"The Dragons Were Familiar"

On the paramount issue of Vietnam war policy, which had proved such a pitfall to some other figures in the presidential competition, Reagan displayed his political adroitness. He avoided the trap of prescribing any specific course of action, which inevitably would draw rebuttal from some quarter. He was for winning the war—"a cause your sons are sent to fight and die for is a cause worth winning"—and the Johnson administration wasn't doing it right. But how it should be done, he said, was not something a governor should prescribe; that was properly up to the military.

Reagan's reception across the country ranged from the enthusiastic to the ecstatic. At a $100 Republican dinner in Columbia, South Carolina—where the Republican organization had been leaning toward Nixon—Reagan's familiar strictures about "crime in the streets," undeserving welfare recipients, and Federal centralism evoked gusts of jubilant rebel yells.

"Reagan's visit to Columbia was a pure revival of the Goldwater road-show," commented Washington columnist Charles Bartlett. "The faces had changed but the dragons were familiar. . . . Reagan still wears the exuberance and assurance that invariably bedeck first-time winners in politics. 'How many more chances do you think we'll get if we don't do it this time?' he roared at his audience. And few left the auditorium with any doubt that he is looking for support for his own candidacy."

Reagan's standard speech, crafted like a theatrical script with finely honed laugh lines and applause points, had four parts. These were calculated to convey in turn that Reagan was the warm, entertaining fellow of screen roles, now turned unassuming but earnest statesman; that he was a dedicated foe of undue governmental power and extravagance; and that he had implanted a remarkable common-sense citizen's approach to government in California, with particular attention to economy. Capping all this was an unabashed flag-waving finish bespeaking Republican unity and equating the party's future with the welfare not only of the nation but all the world.

"I'm glad to see you all at this Republican love-in," he would begin. "You know, if we don't win the next election, $100 is likely to become the *regular* price of a dinner. . . . You know, the Democrats had a $1,000 dinner in Washington the other night. I don't see how they can run those dinners at such a profit—and run the country at such a loss. . . .

"I'm part of government now—a funny thing happened to me on my way to Death Valley," he would continue, alluding to his last television series. "Out in California we have a form of on-the-job training. When I first got to Sacramento,

I felt like an Egyptian tank-driver, reading a set of Russian instructions. . . .

"But I'm just as fearful as I ever was about government's capacity for growth and government's appetite for power. . . . Since 1960, the civilian bureaucracy of the Federal government has grown two and a half times as fast as the increase in population. The payroll increased seven and a half times, and total government spending has increased eight and a half times. The government is spending $450 million a year on public relations alone—to tell us how well off we are. . . .

"When I got to Sacramento, I found that normal, everyday business practices were unknown. . . . We put a freeze on replacing state employees, and now have 2½ per cent fewer. We saved $41,000 on the purchase of high-speed tires for the California Highway Patrol . . . cut the budget for out-of-state travel by 78 per cent. . . . We've reduced the office space for state employees from 9 million square feet to 7 million. . . ."

Some of the heartiest applause usually was evoked by his declarations that "It's the function of government to protect society from the lawbreaker, not the other way around," and "Welfare is a colossal and almost complete failure. The time has come to stop being our brother's keeper, and start being his brother—and I think he'll keep himself."

After about 40 minutes would come the rousing finale:

"I think it's become the destiny of our party to raise a banner to which the people of all parties can repair—a banner that rejects the sickly pastels of expediency, the cynical shades of those who would buy the people's vote with the people's money. There's a crying need for statesmanship in this land today. Mankind is going to live for a thousand years with the decisions we make in the coming election. . . ."

During a year in office, Reagan spent more than a month making appearances outside California—about half the time in his speech-making swings as a "non-candidate."

Even before his most intensive burst of stumping was completed, Reagan's emergence as a possible nominee had moved Governor Rockefeller to remark that Reagan "could make it very difficult" for Nixon to clinch the nomination before the Republican national convention in Miami in August. "Which of the two is stronger, I don't know," Rockefeller said. "But I think it's a very tough thing for Nixon."

And pollster Louis Harris, after a national survey, reported:

"Governor Reagan has made a major political impact on American public opinion in a remarkably short period of time. He is now known to 86 per cent of the electorate, and, by 4 to 1, the public thinks he is doing a good job as governor. . . .

"The hallmark of Reagan's appeal is personal. Sixty-two per cent of the public look on him as 'very attractive, charming and sincere.' Fifty-eight per cent believe he represents 'a new approach to politics.' "

Chapter
Eighteen

1968: The Future and Its Faces

☒ IN THE RHETORIC OF POLITICS, EVERY ELECTION is a "crossroads," every year a "year of decision." Yet 1968 dawned as a year that really seemed to justify such hyperbole. A pattern of political circumstances, baroque even by California standards, suggested that the coming period would be one of the most pivotal in decades.

It was not just a question of whether 1968 would turn out

to be a Democratic year or a Republican year. It was a question of the direction in which events would bend the whole course of state politics; of what might happen to men who for years had been pinnacles on the political landscape.

Organizationally, both parties were in such disarray they seemed to be facing the ultimate alternatives: reconstruction or oblivion. Upon the resolution of this question, in each case, there possibly hinged perpetuation of the pattern of California politics that had emerged from the reformist dust-cloud of the Hiram Johnson regime 50 years before.

Also hanging in the balance were the careers of numerous figures besides Ronald Reagan. Among them were the minority floor leader of the United States Senate, Thomas Kuchel; the speaker of the California assembly, Jesse Unruh; the mayor of Los Angeles, Samuel Yorty; and California's lieutenant governor, Robert Finch.

"To really keep up with what is happening among the many factions of the party in my native state, you almost need a 'morning line' like the horse players use to figure the odds on the races. But even if there were a daily political 'morning line,' the horse players would have the best of it: horses don't change as much." Thus spake, in 1967, California's wryly humorous Representative Thomas Rees. He was a Democrat, referring to his own party. But his words applied almost equally well to both parties.

Harmony, Republican Style

Ronald Reagan's election, the product of a transitory consensus of Republican and Democratic voters, in itself had done little to promote harmony in either party.

On the Republican side, the party's official organization consisted, in the time-honored mode, of a letterhead and some obscure offices; of a nebulous roster of officials and state committee members, precluded by law from having much to do with working politics in the critical pre-primary stage; and of a series of periodic hortatory pronouncements by the state chairman.

Such rank-and-file organization as there was—representing only a tiny fraction of the party's 3 million registration—was split into three blocs. There was the California Republican Assembly, the original "grass roots" organization, now deteriorated into a strident right-wing splinter claiming 12,000 adherents. There was the United Republicans of California, an ultra-right spin-off from the CRA, claiming 9,000 members. Party moderates' only rallying point was the California Republican League, which claimed a minuscule 4,000 in membership.

The instability and latent antagonisms of such groups as these which had clustered behind Reagan in 1966, posed a discomfiting threat to his power base. The focus of this hazard was Senator Kuchel's expected bid for re-election in 1968.

The wrath that Earl Warren's bipartisanism had engendered among conservatives of his own party had been matched only once since Warren's time—the target being Warren's protégé, Kuchel.

Stocky and long-jawed, Kuchel had an earnest, bespectacled mien, and a comical sense buried deeply enough for political safety. He came from a pioneer German family, transplanted from San Francisco to newspaper publishing in Orange county, the conservative stronghold. After getting a law degree and serving two terms in the state assembly, Kuchel was elected to the state senate in 1940. That same year he became Republican state chairman. Shortly after Kuchel returned from Navy duty in World War II, Governor Warren appointed him to the vacant state controllership. Elected to two full terms as controller, he was appointed by Warren in 1952 to the U.S. Senate seat vacated by Richard Nixon in his move to the Vice-Presidency.

Conservative when he first went to the Senate, Kuchel soon discerned, as the Republicans' long grip on state politics weakened, the serviceability of Warren's studied appeal to both parties. Soon he was getting paradoxically comparable ratings for his Senate voting record from the liberal Americans For Democratic Action and the ultra-conservative Americans For Constitutional Action.

But the right wing in California thought he should never be anything but conservative. Vexation mounted as Kuchel became one of the nation's most outspoken critics of the Birch society and right-wing "fright peddlers." He was branded a renegade for non-support of Nixon in 1962, Goldwater and Murphy in 1964 (when Kuchel headed the Rockefeller primary campaign in California), and Reagan in 1966.

Ever since 1962, when the simultaneous election victories of Kuchel and Dr. Max Rafferty, for state superintendent of public instruction, had aroused such contrasting emotions among the conservatives, they had been champing for an opportunity to "dump Kuchel." Their leading prospect turned out to be Rafferty.

Some analysts have suggested that the outstanding characteristic of the radical right is a desire for simplistic answers in an age of complex questions. Rafferty, a sort of Westbrook Pegler in a mortarboard, had a remarkable talent for articulating the frustrations of such people so forcefully as to leave the impression that the troubles had been exorcised. After a flight of rhetoric like:

> In the last three years we have found out for ourselves that our morals are rotten, our world position degenerating so abysmally that a race of lash-driven atheistic peasants can challenge us successfully in our own chosen field of science, and our rate of juvenile murder, torture, rape and perversion is so much the highest in the world that it has become an object of shuddering horror to the rest of the human race. . . .

almost anyone could sit back comfortably with a well-he-told-them-off feeling, relieved of doing anything himself. Unless, that is, he searched Rafferty's statement for substantial meaning. (What is the gauge of "rotten morals"? What proof is there that the Russians are ahead of us in "science"? How does the United States "perversion rate" compare with that in Britain or Bolivia? Who are some of the people gripped by "shuddering horror"?)

Rafferty, who grew up in California, had as a suburban school administrator projected himself into the national limelight with a series of well-turned polemics against "progressive education," published under the title of "Suffer, Little Children." His essential definition of "progressive education" was the widespread restructuring of teaching in terms of life rather than classic texts. "The quest for the Golden Fleece has been crowded out by the visit of Tom and Susan to the zoo," he said. "Jackie pursues his insipid goal of a ride on the district garbage truck while the deathless ride of Paul Revere goes unwept."

Rafferty in 1962 indicated his determination, if elected, to shift California's whole vast educational system from this wayward path. Actually, the state superintendent is an administrative officer who executes policies set by the appointed state board of education. Rafferty spent much of his first four years jousting spectacularly with liberals on the board, while California education continued pretty much on its accustomed course. But he projected a reassuring image of dauntless warfare against the bad guys.

Running for re-election in June, 1966, against three obscure contenders in a nonpartisan contest, Rafferty rolled up an impressive vote of confidence that exceeded the combined vote of Reagan and Brown in their simultaneous primary contests.

With Reagan's victory in 1966, and with the Senate contest impending, Rafferty began shifting his strictures from progressive education to Kuchel and national and international problems. He called the Johnson administration "a sorry set of political pirates," and his aspersions on Kuchel (". . . . talking and acting like a left-wing Democrat . . .") finally brought a public rebuke from Republican state chairman James Halley, who reminded him of the 11th Commandment about not knocking fellow Republicans.

Both conservative and moderate party leaders begans sensing the unwisdom of an intraparty fight over Kuchel: it could produce frictions that would not only jeopardize the Senate seat but would spoil the unity Reagan hoped to have as California played its potentially critical part in the presidential race.

Kuchel was about as distasteful to Reagan as to many other Republicans. But the governor was realistic enough to see that there were times when one had to make short-term sacrifices for the sake of long-term gains. Starting only a month after the election, he held a series of peace-pipe sessions with Kuchel in California and Washington. Word went out from Reagan's moneyed supporters that they were disinclined to finance a Rafferty *putsch* against Kuchel. Reagan, as the star speaker at the California Republican Assembly's 1967 convention, in unmistakable terms that stopped just short of naming Kuchel, exhorted the organization to eschew a divisive course. The CRA spurned the advice and, amid anti-Kuchel speeches containing such words as "treason," resolved to support some other Senate candidate who would more "effectively further the aims and goals of the party." The United Republicans took a similar tack, lionizing Rafferty in person at their convention. It remained for the moderate California Republican League to welcome Senator Kuchel to its convention and endorse him.

Despite the misgivings of many party members about Rafferty's aspirations, his undeclared candidacy gathered momentum and organization. In December, 1967, he indicated that his effort to corral a million-dollar campaign fund was progressing satisfactorily.

The prospective Republican cleavage over the Senate nomination was about the only bright spot on the Democrats' horizon.

The Democrats: "Nobody's Talking To Each Other"

No political party looks graceful in defeat. But with the Democrats, after November, 1966, it was like a crumbling building whose initial subsidence is followed by a suspenseful succession of additional groans and crunches—and whose remains are then assaulted by gratuitous visitations of flood, fire, and hurricane.

> Former Governor Pat Brown [said Representative Rees in a stock-taking letter to constituents six months after the election] heads one faction and right now the national committeeman and committeewoman are on his side. At the helm of another faction is Los Angeles Mayor Sam Yorty, our well-known maverick, who supported Nixon in 1960, ran against Brown in the gubernatorial primary last year, and then sandbagged the governor in the final election. Then there is Assembly Speaker Jesse Unruh, who, for the moment, is the most powerful Democratic office-holder on the scene. Jesse does not get along with the ex-governor, and actively dislikes the national committeeman [Eugene Wyman]. He gets along with Yorty, but it is doubtful that both of them could ever share the same spotlight gracefully. We also have an Attorney General [Thomas Lynch], the only Democrat to win statewide in the last election—a charming individual who says he can get along with everyone. This claim causes hard-bitten pros in the state to collapse into convulsions. Now all this might change next week or next month, but today this is the "morning line."

He charitably omitted some of the more depressing aspects of the situation. The defeated Governor Brown had dropped into the obscurity of private law practice. While going through some motions of titular leadership, he was having trouble getting others in the party to listen. Even President Johnson was moved to joke about the Democratic squabbling in California. At a party dinner in Los Angeles in June, he quipped that a motion picture of California's party chieftains in a smoke-filled room could dispense with a sound track, "because nobody's talking to each other anyway."

"What ever happened to the Democratic party in California?" Bob Houser, Long Beach's astute political editor, asked rhetorically in one of his columns. "It was just a little more than three years ago that the Democratic state central committee was wangling along with a $16,000 a month budget, plenty of staff, several offices throughout the state, and a program. Today, nothing. The state committee is in financial trouble. The Los Angeles County central committee, which once had a staff of ten, has virtually gone out of business. . . ."

The Democrats' state chairman, Assemblyman Charles Warren, described the party as "broke," with a $20,000 deficit. Brown himself reported unpaid campaign debts of another $62,500.

"Cheer up," party members were telling each other. "Things could be worse." And, in demonstration of the fact, they quickly got worse.

As harried leaders were pondering how they could weld the squabbling factions into a viable pro-Johnson slate of convention delegates for the June, 1968, primary, the California Democratic Council, now only a skeletal remnant of the party's once-powerful rank-and-file organization, once more rocked the boat as it had in the 1966 campaign. The body called for the entry of an anti-Johnson slate of delegates—easily organized under the law—in the Democratic primary.

Other partisans, similarly disaffected over the Johnson administration's Vietnam war policies, joined the "Dissenting Democrats" movement led by Robert Vaughn, a television actor.

Then two third-party movements burgeoned. Each had the potentiality of diverting party-line votes in the election. One was the Peace and Freedom party, the latest crystallization of New Left opposition to the war in Vietnam. The other was the American Independent party campaign of Alabama's recent governor, George Wallace, a Democratic apostle of "states' rights" and segregation. It was not much consolation to Democrats that the Wallace venture seemed as likely to siphon off Republican votes as Democratic ones.

By September, the auspices for the Johnson cause were depressing. A statewide opinion poll indicated that a "peace delegation" slate in the 1968 Democratic primary, even without a specific presidential candidate, might pull virtually as big a vote as would a Johnson delegation. Another survey indicated that, as a choice for President, Johnson at that point was topped in popularity by Governor Rockefeller (who was still disclaiming any intention of running), 50 per cent to 38 per cent.

After months of touchy backstage overtures, the Democratic factions achieved a degree of accommodation. In December, California Attorney General Lynch announced that, with White House sanction, he would lead the "organization" slate of delegates tacitly dedicated to President Johnson in the Democratic presidential primary competition. The negotiating had revolved around the seemingly insoluble problem of reconciling the interests of factional leaders. One reason a degree of harmony had been achieved, it transpired, was that by then both Unruh and Yorty were wary of involving themselves too conspicuously in what might be a losing cause.

"The fact is," observed Richard Bergholz of the Los Angeles *Times,* "that one Democratic office-holder after another is already planning a 1968 campaign adequately stocked with ten-foot poles—the better to avoid a Johnson 'rub-off' effect."

Big Daddy

For Assembly Speaker Jesse Unruh, the long-time "strong man" of California politics, 1968 would contain a series of critical imponderables. One was the problem of simply getting re-elected to the assembly. A second was the problem of getting enough Democrats elected to the assembly—in a year that might bring a national Republican sweep—so that he would not be deposed from his powerful speakership to a role no better than that of minority leader.

A third imponderable, completely beyond Unruh's control, was what would happen to Governor Ronald Reagan. If events swept Reagan, one way or another, into national politics, advancing Lieutenant Governor Robert Finch into the governorship, it would be a new ball game at Sacramento, with an array of further imponderables for 1969, 1970, and beyond.

It was a typical anomaly of California politics that, whereas Ronald Reagan's authority had stemmed from 3,742,-913 votes, Unruh's comparable influence, during 1967, had as its immediate source only 37,387 votes cast for him in his Los Angeles suburban constituency of Inglewood, the area of the Los Angeles International Airport and the Hollywood Park race track.

How is so much influence built on a base of only one assembly district? The answer lies partly in the unusual dynamics of California government and partly in the unusual dynamics of Jesse Marvin Unruh.

Forty-five years old as he began maneuvering for the 1968 competition, Unruh was truly a phenomenon of American politics. The youngest of five children of an impoverished, illiterate Kansas sharecropper, Unruh in a remarkably short span of years had climbed to the eminence of being probably the nation's foremost state legislator, a potential governor of California, and perhaps a candidate for even higher estate—subject of course to the ever-unpredictable vagaries of California politics.

Unruh's family moved to Texas when he was young. As a youth he learned sheet-metal work, and he put in a year at Wayland Baptist College before joining the Navy in World War II and serving in the Aleutians. After leaving the service he went to the University of Southern California, and there he got his first taste of politics.

"I joined a veterans' organization on the campus, just to

know someone," he recalls. "The fraternities and sororities controlled student politics. All they cared about was whether everyone had a white shirt in the cheering section. We fought for a seat in the student senate, and I ran for it. That's how politics started for me."

He could hardly wait for graduation in 1948 to run for the state assembly. He lost out in two elections, meanwhile supporting himself working for a freight-forwarding concern. In 1954 he was elected.

Unruh sized up the dynamics of the legislature quickly—a bunch of part-time, semi-professional politicians (then paid only $6,000 a year), conspicuously lacking in party cohesion or other coordination. Power was there for the taking, through sedulous Tammany-style development of a network of alliances and obligations. The key spot, he discerned, was the assembly speakership, whose power over committee memberships and the progress of bills vastly enlarged the possibilities for skillful logrolling. In the absence of substantial party organizations, campaign contributions, for one thing, tended to funnel through the speaker, to be parceled out as he chose.

"Money," Unruh has remarked candidly and often, "is the mother's milk of politics."

Six years of wheeling and dealing as chairman of the assembly finance and insurance committee, and the ways and means committee, gave him the caucus strength to win the speakership on his 39th birthday in 1961.

By that time Unruh had already set his sights higher. Then weighing a massive 285 pounds, and popularly nicknamed "Big Daddy" both for his size and his tough, paternalistic exercise of influence, he was the most conspicuous Californian to clamber aboard the 1960 bandwagon of Senator John F. Kennedy. He headed Kennedy's campaign in southern California, and led the Kennedy bloc in California's ambivalent 1960 Democratic convention delegation. His obvious design was to become, if nothing more, the main California link with the Kennedy administration.

When the assassination in Dallas atomized this dream, Unruh continued methodically enhancing his credentials as more than a provincial legislator. By now well-read, urbane, and coolly articulate and impressive—with an intrinsically handsome if jowly visage—he disdained politicians' clichés to talk, at every gilt-edged speech-making opportunity, about the technology of government. In 1962 he wangled a Chubb Fellowship lecture visit to Yale University, and in 1963 he made a speaking tour of universities in the Far East under the auspices of the State Department. He was elected the 1966 head of the National Conference of State Legislative Leaders.

Unruh's big weakness, from the standpoint of advancement, was that his operations centered in the world of political professionals. He was contemptuous of the troublesome, idealistic, resolution-passing of such rank-and-file party activists as the California Democratic Council. And the animosity was reciprocated.

"I have very little to do with the mechanism of the party any more," he remarked in 1967. "I did that. You get very little out of it, but a lot of scars in the in-fighting. I used to believe in bloc-building. I don't any more. Not in California, anyway. I think it's really a matter of who you are for and how you project. If you can do that right, the factions in political parties will have to get on with you because you are the most electable."

Conscious that his "electability" was threatened by his lack of rapport with ordinary voters, Unruh began revamping his image. He renounced cigars—the badge of the cartoon politician—dieted down to a svelte 200 pounds, tempered the autocratic tone of his maneuverings at Sacramento, and looked for ways to shore up his political position against the Democratic reverse he saw threatening for 1966.

But events had boxed him in. There was no ready avenue for broadening his political base beyond his small constituency in Inglewood. He had to scramble to win re-election in 1966. Although he was secure once again in the speakership, the slim Democratic majority, and Governor Reagan's public popularity, precluded any notable Unruh triumphs in the 1967 session.

The 1968 session, with Reagan rapidly shedding his mantle of the appealing amateur, might be another story. Alluding undoubtedly to Unruh among others, Alan Cranston, recently the leader of the Democrats' anti-Unruh "volunteer" wing, commented:

"There are ambitious men, eager to seize just the right moment and the right issue for an all-out attack on Reagan. More than one hopes to lead the first general assault, and thus establish himself as a front-runner for the governorship in 1970."

Swingin' Sam

Tacitly concurring with Unruh in recoiling from the national Democratic tribulations of 1968 was the party's foremost maverick in California, a monument to the state's curious political convolutions, Samuel William Yorty.

Yorty was a unique exception to the axiom that defeat in California politics means oblivion. Beaten three times in tries for the United States Senate, he repeatedly rebounded. He accomplished the miracle through shrewd perception of the political realities of the moment, consummate nerve, and a gift of gab—and by maintaining, in effect, his own political party. It was the Sam Yorty party, quick to change policies to suit the political winds, and deft in catering to the disaffected of both major parties simultaneously. In other words, he was an archetype of California pragmatism, of whom Hiram Johnson might not have been proud but with whom he could hardly have helped feeling empathy.

Yorty landed in Los Angeles from Nebraska during the raucous Sinclair era. His first dabble on the fringe of politics was as local secretary of the Technocracy movement. When he went to the state assembly in 1936, he was considered a "flaming liberal." In his second term, he swung just as far to the right, and was a creator of the legislature's controversial committee on "un-American activities."

In 1940, Yorty made his first pass at the United States Senate; but Hiram Johnson, cross-filed, beat him for the Democratic nomination. In 1950, when Richard Nixon defeated Helen Gahagan Douglas for the Senate, Yorty was the man who fell heir to her House of Representatives seat. He served two terms. Defeated by Thomas Kuchel for the remainder of Nixon's Senate term in 1954, Yorty tried again in 1956, but he was denied endorsement by the California Democratic Council. This was the genesis of a shrill and abiding Yorty animosity toward the CDC; of Yorty's growing rapport with that other CDC foe, Jesse Unruh; and of his methodical cultivation of the large bloc of conservative Democrats-in-name-only.

Temporarily back in private life practicing law, Yorty drew attention in 1960 by defecting from the Democratic fold to support Nixon. He issued a manifesto, "I Can't Take Kennedy," which Governor Brown called an unscrupulous attack on Kennedy's Catholicism.

In his seemingly impulsive moves, Yorty was as calculating as a billiard player. His 1960 maneuver gave him the bipartisan coloration he needed when, the following year, he staged an underdog campaign for mayor, relying heavily on television, and toppled the Republican establishment's nominally nonpartisan wheelhorse, Norris Poulson.

By the same token, Yorty's 1964 leadership of an insurgent pro-Johnson convention delegation that challenged the Brown-led regular slate, was a warm-up for 1966, when he helped split the Democratic party by challenging Brown for the gubernatorial nomination. The 900,000 anti-Brown votes that Yorty attracted matched almost precisely the bonus of Democratic votes that put Reagan across five months later. From the primary on, Yorty was blatantly pro-Reagan.

In 1967, he struck terror in orthodox Democratic ranks with a dual threat: that he might once again organize an insurgent pro-Johnson convention delegation, and that he might compete for the Senate nomination and crowd out some more dependable party choice.

"To all of California's Democratic congressmen, to virtually all of the existing party leaders, perhaps to the White House," Richard Bergholz reported, "Yorty is just plain bad news. They have marked him as a renegade and they fear massive party defections if Yorty should win the nomination."

Sighs of relief followed Yorty's indication, late in 1967, that he had decided against making any fight over the delegation. His position on the Senate race remained more fluid. He stirred speculation by suggesting in October, that Unruh would be a good candidate, whom he would be willing to support—a possibility Unruh himself had not broached.

Apart from Unruh, the Democrats had no imposing candidate to go against Kuchel. Among a half-dozen possibles—whose possibilities had not gone much beyond the conversational stage—the most prominent was Alan Cranston, the recent state controller. He had run stronger than any defeated candidate on the 1966 Democratic slate, and he had evinced definite interest in the Senate contest.

Cranston, a tall, bald, scholarly-looking man, was a onetime foreign correspondent and a former president of the United World Federalists who had gone into business in San Francisco. He had been a founder and first president of the California Democratic Council in the palmier days when it was building toward the party's 1958 sweep.

Cranston's 1964 defeat, by Pierre Salinger, for the Senate nomination only enhanced his appeal with party liberals. But his liberal identification threatened to be a liability in a showdown, before historically "moderation"-minded voters, with Kuchel's versatile liberal-conservatism.

Opinion polls late in 1967 showed that among Republican voters Kuchel was a 50–32 favorite in percentage ratings over his fellow Republican Max Rafferty, and that he was comparably strong against possible Democratic contenders. A bipartisan survey of voters gave Kuchel a 51–26 advantage over Cranston, 54–29 over Yorty, and a less decisive 40–27 rating against Unruh.

But it still seemed possible that a crypto-Democrat like Yorty could capitalize on the dissension among Republicans. Kuchel's undeclared campaign for re-election, which got under way late in the year, was directed by the same managers who had handled Reagan: Spencer and Roberts. The opening gun was the inevitable "Friends of Tom Kuchel" dinner on November 9. Among some 120 persons listed as sponsors, there were not more than two or three who had figured visibly in the campaign of Senator Kuchel's fellow Republican, Ronald Reagan.

The Man in the Iron Mask

Jesse Unruh's poignant personal interest in what happened to Ronald Reagan, in 1968 and beyond, was exceeded by that of only one other person: Lieutenant Governor Robert Hutchinson Finch.

Overlooked in the fanfare of Reagan's accession was the fact that the election had also placed in Sacramento the man who beyond any question was the California Republicans' most knowledgeable and promising professional on the state level—the man who had brought off the feat of topping Reagan's vote by more than 92,000.

Finch, who was only 40, might have been the gubernatorial candidate himself. But, he explained to friends, he felt too closely identified with Richard Nixon so soon after Nixon's defeat of 1962 and the ascendancy of Goldwater conservatives in party affairs in 1964. Finch, a lawyer and a party activist since his college days in Los Angeles, had run unsuccessfully for Congress twice, had been Nixon's executive assistant in Washington, and had managed Nixon's nearly successful 1960 presidential campaign. Finch was plainly stamped as a middle-of-the-roader with liberal leanings, but he had established some rapport with party conservatives through his management of George Murphy's 1964 Senate campaign.

Finch made his strategic decision early and announced his candidacy for lieutenant governor before there was any certainty about who the entries for the top spot might be. As things turned out, considering the disaffection expressed by the electorate with the Brown administration, Finch might have won the governorship. But as it was he had hedged his bets adroitly. For the first time he had broken through the obscurity of managerial roles to win a major public office. The California lieutenant governor's job is considerably more than a Wintergreenship. In addition to presiding over the state senate, the lieutenant governor is an ex officio member of the state lands commission and other important agencies. He is acting governor, on average, nearly one-third of the time, while the governor is out of state.

Although there was a studied effort by the Reagan contingent at Sacramento to keep Finch in the background during the initial months of the new administration (a New York *Times* dispatch referred to Finch as "The Man in the Iron Mask"), it seemed certain that he would not remain in the background indefinitely.

Like Unruh, Finch was biding his time. The future might bring a significant showdown between Unruh and Reagan in 1968 or 1970. By the same token, developments might pit Unruh against Finch . . . or even Finch against Reagan.

If this seems like an excessive cat's-cradle of contingencies, recall the words of Jesse Unruh, which have gathered corroboration with each passing year: "In California politics, I've learned never to be surprised at anything."

Chapter Nineteen

California and the Nation: A Laugh, or a Lesson?

Throughout much of the nation California politics is viewed as a political carnival. . . . But the overriding conclusion about the political experience of California in this century is not the erratic character of its politics, but how closely it has paralleled the national experience.

—Robert L. Woodbury

☒ OUR QUEST FOR THE ORIGINS OF CALIFORNIA'S unusual politics has brought us to an inscrutable tomorrow. As one of the state's most experienced political observers warned us at the outset, little "symmetry" can be observed in the evolution.

Instead, there is an ever-changing interplay of forces—primarily, the frontier urge for experimentation, on one hand, and the innate desire for security on the other.

The result: independent voting and its myriad anomalies, tempered by an underlying affinity for moderation . . . independent voting . . . weak party organization . . . an odd, tribrid sort of "nonpartisanism": true nonpartisanism on the local level, degrees of bipartisanism at the state level, conventional partisanism on the national level.

Out of it all comes a calvacade of distinctive phenomena: the handicap of the party label . . . the peril of party splits . . . chronic discontinuity in party activity . . . voter preoccupation with personalities rather than issues and ideology . . . the corresponding power of the "nice guy" image, and the prominence of the image-makers . . . the hazards of "carpetbagging," "stepping-stoning," and "Potomac myopia" . . . the volatile vagaries of "direct legislation." . . .

Yet emerging from all these curiosa in the end is an exceptionally serviceable government, superior in many respects to the products of conventional politics.

Why?

Probably because government is a matter less of forms and procedures than of intent. Some banana republics have constitutions modeled after the United States constitution, yet they are afflicted with tyranny, corruption, and instability, because of immaturity of intent.

If the intent is right, one must conclude, things will get straightened out—even if it takes some awkward improvisation, some spectacular pragmatism.

The Untenable Situation

It's perhaps reassuring that the California system is the despair particularly of two quite disparate groups: the scholars and the professional politicians.

The scholars deplore it because it doesn't fit into an orderly blueprint of an efficient way to bring the democratic consensus to bear.

The politicians bemoan it because its quirks are forever thwarting the aim of every politician: the concentration of power.

In their classic text on California government, Dean McHenry and Winston Crouch say:

> Denied the emblem of party . . . the voter has been forced to grope through the excessively long ballot without proper aid. . . . Confronted with a task that staggers the most alert citizen, the average man must pick up his civic data on a hand-to-mouth basis. . . .
>
> Although possessing many of the trappings of democracy . . . California falls short of truly responsible politics.
>
> In every state and nation of any size, political parties have been found essential to the proper functioning of democratic politics in big government. Therefore California should explore every avenue of strengthening parties. Reform began with the abolition of cross-filing. Party bodies should be given sufficient power to activate themselves and freedom to adopt their own organizational forms. Party committees or pre-primary conventions might well be empowered to indicate preferred candidates on the primary ballot. . . .
>
> The existing situation is unsatisfactory and untenable. Either parties ought to be given conditions under which they can live and provide the expected services, or they ought to be eliminated. . . .

The politicians' feelings are strikingly similar.

Jesse Unruh inveighs against the vacuum: "California municipal and county elections with rare exceptions are horrible examples of the effects of nonpartisanship. Few know the candidate as an individual, and his philosophy cannot be estimated by reference to party affiliation."

Republican Representative Alphonzo Bell: "The two-party system is being jeopardized. . . . The spoils of politics are more often than not going to the self-styled independent. I cannot join the present-day eulogizing of the political independent."

After the Democrats' 1966 defeat, state Democratic chairman Charles Warren echoed the academicians: "Those who take pride in nonpartisanship are actually working against the two-party system. If partisanship isn't important, as some have alleged, then I say the two-party system is no longer important."

Lieutenant Governor Robert Finch has limned restoration of partisan politics at the local level as an essential base for revitalizing parties. Governor Edmund Brown, urging changes, remarked: "Most of our laws are a half century old, written in the Hiram Johnson administration, to correct abuses which no longer exist."

The Ripon Society, a national liberal-Republican group, after making an intensive study of California, in 1967 urged the repeal of basic Johnsonian reforms. Restore partisanship at the local level, the society recommended; give the rank-and-file "equitable" representation on party state committees; let the committees engage in pre-primary intraparty politicking; curb use of the initiative, referendum, and recall.

But there are few indications that any such changes will materialize in the immediate future.

Nobody seems to like the existing system except the people.

Labels Unwanted

The public couldn't seem to care less whether the scholars and the politicians are happy about how things are.

Not having known, for two generations, the presumed advantages of conventional partyism, people don't feel they're missing anything in dispensing with it in favor of flexibility and pragmatism—and they aren't even aware that they are tacitly making a choice.

What the people know is that in an age when the miasma of bureaucracy, red tape, and computerization (the calculations on the bank statement are perfect, but they sent you somebody else's statement) grows more oppressive, it seems a relief not to have yet another entity, the political party, interposing itself in any effective way between them and their government.

The public's implicit attitude is that the scholars and the politicians had their day in court, with their blueprints and their diaphanous "party responsibility," and what came out was eastern machine politics and the Southern Pacific "Octopus."

Nearly every session of the California legislature produces a bill to restore partisanism to local and county elections. Usually the bills are studiously ignored. In 1961 one such proposal got as far as being approved by a state assembly committee. The bill did not advocate outright repeal of the prevailing system, but it would have permitted candidates' party affiliations to be listed on the ballot.

The resulting furor was as if someone had proposed dynamiting the Golden Gate bridge. A statewide cry of protest was typified by the Los Angeles *Examiner:*

> This deceptively innocuous proposal blandly ignores the notorious corruption in local government which is inescapable when the label of partisanship becomes an issue with voters.
>
> It is precisely this system which for generations has vitiated great cities like New York, Chicago and Boston, each with its own version of the partisan favoritism and graft made notorious by Tammany Hall. . . .

In Los Angeles, the county board of supervisors and the city council both voted unanimously in condemnation of the proposal, one supervisor suggesting that it could not have been of California origin but "appears to be an attempt by Eastern interests to invade the local California political scene."

Most Californians couldn't tell you exactly what Tammany Hall is (it is the New York county Democratic organization headquarters), but they have the name on the tips of their tongues as the epitome of corruption. It is possible that Tammany (whence came some of California's early political figures) just by its name has done more for the politics of California than for the politics of New York.

A 1963 opinion poll indicated that Californians, by a margin of nearly 3 to 1, were opposed to any alteration in municipal and county nonpartisanism.

Their zest for ticket-splitting seems unslackened. In 1962, they simultaneously elected Brown, the Democrat, and Kuchel, the Republican; in 1964, they voted for Johnson but against Salinger. In 1966 a majority of Californians cut across the party line to return Democratic Attorney General Thomas Lynch to office; and Robert Finch's 92,000-vote edge over Ronald Reagan indicated that many voters had split their tickets between governor and lieutenant governor.

A big obstacle to tidy party polarization in California is that the parties have no distinct images calculated to attract voters, and little scope for projecting such images. Altering party structures to make them more meaningful would have to be a bootstrap operation, one bucking the legal obstructions to party activities.

The decline, by 1967, of both parties' putative mass-membership organizations, the California Republican Assembly and the California Democratic Council, into radical splinter groups had in effect turned the clock back more than a generation, to the era when discontent with legal restrictions on official party organizations had engendered these "unofficial" volunteer groups as channels of rank-and-file expression.

Presumably partisans eager to express themselves collectively will devise a vehicle. But, as of 1967, party fragmentation made a revival of "volunteer" movements problematical for the immediate future. Party leaders spoke of trying to develop rank-and-file organization under the wing of official party structures. But to do that called for a change in the laws, which couldn't be brought about very well until a lot of rank-and-file opinion was already mobilized.

A sudden shift in public attitudes on the matter seemed unlikely. The population influx that has been such a factor in

California's loose-jointed politics is due to continue unabated for at least another generation; the only foreseeable stabilizing influence will be a gradual increase in the present minority of new residents who are home-grown rather than immigrants.

The Democrats' state chairman, Assemblyman Charles Warren, conceded that the 1966 election results indicated a pronounced public sentiment of: "To hell with the party—any party." So much so, he said, that if a less pointedly conservative figure than Reagan had been elected, there would be reason to despair of ever resuscitating the Democratic party.

And Alan Cranston, another staunch partisan, said: "The people of California have a new attitude toward government. . . . I believe more voters will be more critical of their government in the future—and they won't much care about the party label. These newly aware citizens will have little interest in and no patience with traditional party politics. They will be thinking in terms of the administration and the opposition."

California, the Laughed-At Leader

California is used to being laughed at.

Californians have gotten to the point where they even get some amusement out of the derision themselves.

So many times they have seen their innovations mocked by the rest of the country, only to see the rest of the country soon avidly embracing the same innovations.

Swimming pools, drive-in banks, backyard barbecues, hot-rods, Capri pants, "ranch-style" homes, Mexican food, the surfing craze. . .

For years now California's politics have been singled out as freakish and atypical. But could this be another instance in which California is no more than a jump ahead of the nation?

Some may recoil at the suggestion. No one would wish on his best voting friend such esoterica as cross-filing, unpredictable eleventh-hour candidacies and firing-squad demises, and such anomalies as a Democratic governor who used to be a Republican being defeated by a Republican who used to be a Democrat.

But these are superficialities that only California has to live with. The essence of California politics, the source of these oddities, is nonpartisanism in its various guises.

And as for nonpartisan, anti-organization, anti-machine politics, it seems demonstrable that California once again is simply in the vanguard of national developments.

> . . . The absence for a number of years past of genuine political issues dividing the two parties, which has worked ill in taking moral and intellectual life out of the parties, and making their contests mere scrambles for office, has at last worked well in disposing intelligent citizens to sit more loose to party ties, and to consider, since it is really on men rather than on measures that they are required to vote, what the personal merits of candidates are.

That was James Bryce, writing so perceptively more than 80 years ago—about the United States.

The trend he perceived may have taken longer than he anticipated to become prevalent. In the nation, as in California, there has been a sentimental attachment to obsolete forms and nomenclature. But the reorientation now is plainly at hand.

The most persuasive evidence of this, perhaps, is New York, so long the citadel of gut-bucket party politics. Even there the old order has been demonstrating its bankruptcy.

For all its orthodox emphasis on "party responsibility," discipline, and continuity, for all its well-oiled machinery, the New York State Democratic party in 1967 found itself worse off than its diffuse California counterpart. New York's Democrats had a superiority of nearly 900,000 in registration—yet they had not won a governorship since 1954.

The outgrowing of old forms cut both ways. "Even in so Democratic a city as New York," the New York *Times*' James Reston commented in 1965, "John Lindsay saved the Republican party by repudiating it, and won the mayoral election by appealing above party to all moderates and progressives, while the Democrats lost by appealing on narrow partisan grounds."

"The Democratic party of New York, which once controlled both the city and the state," a disheartened partisan lamented in the *Times* in 1966, "now controls neither."

In March, 1967, J. Raymond Jones, the man occupying the historically influential position of leader of Tammany Hall, abdicated because, according to the *Times,* there was "little power or patronage left in his once-powerful post."

Shortly after that, New York—as California had done a half-century before—abandoned state party conventions (beloved by machine politicians for their malleability) as the vehicle for nominating candidates. In place of conventions, New York adopted a modified primary system, under which party state committees could tentatively propose candidates but were subject to being overridden by voters in ensuing statewide voting.

The Jolly Green Independent

That bête noire of party politicians, the independent voter, has become the Jolly Green Giant. A Democratic electoral majority in California, growing since 1932, did not prevent four successive Republican gubernatorial victories, beginning in 1942. A preponderance of nominal Democrats in the nation did not prevent the defeat of Adlai Stevenson in 1952 and 1956. All those contests were swung by the independents.

> The growing fact in American politics [wrote Reston in November, 1966] is that no party except in a few states in the Old Confederacy can any longer take the voters for granted, or go too far in any one direction. There is undoubtedly in the country now a growing instinct for moderation, balance and competition between the two parties, alongside noisy minority movements of the extreme right and left. . . .

> Both parties are increasingly moderate, progressive, tolerant and self-contradictory in most states, and the old assumptions about them are less and less reliable. . . . These tendencies are not new in American politics. The two national parties are merely occasional clearing houses for the 100 G.O.P. and Democratic parties in the 50 states, and as party allegiance has declined, independent, mind-changing, party-crossing, ticket-splitting habits have become stronger. . . . The decline of partisanship and of central party control has never been more apparent than in the last few months.

Late in 1966, George Gallup, the pollster, reported that since 1940 the number of people considering themselves Republicans had dropped from 38 per cent of the electorate to 29 per cent, while those considering themselves Democrats had risen from 42 per cent only to 44 per cent. The differential comprised those who classified themselves as "independents"; their share had risen steadily from 20 per cent in 1942 to 27 per cent in 1966—making independents nearly as numerous as Republicans. By the time of a resurvey nine months later, the trend had reached an epochal point: the proportion of independents had risen to 31 per cent, while Republicans had dropped to 27 per cent, making the Republicans in effect only a "third party."

In April, 1967, Republican national chairman Ray Bliss extended a hand of welcome to Democrats to run as Republican candidates.

"We're the minority party," he said. "Only 29 per cent of American citizens declare themselves as Republicans, whereas between 40 and 50 per cent consider themselves Democrats. We are going to have to attract votes from the Democrats. We will welcome any new converts to our cause." His remarks were occasioned by the example of Philadelphia's Democratic district attorney, Arlen Specter, running for mayor on the Republican ticket.

It sounded like Hiram Johnson's California Progressives,

arranging things so they could draw strength from opposing parties.

"I do not know," says Walter Lippmann, "whether I can make myself believe that a party system which has come down to us from an age that is passed can be made to work in the gigantic urban complexes of our modern times. . . .

"We must prepare ourselves for political inventions which are as radical as the technological revolution in which we are living. The Founding Fathers did not foresee the party system as it has developed and what they knew about its early beginnings they disliked intensely. . . . The time may be coming when men will look back with amazement and distaste upon the crudity, the coarseness, the fakery and the phoniness of our partisan political behavior."

Heresy. With a California flavor.

"Something to Think About"

"What," James Reston asked me, "does California have to give to the nation?"

Well, I said, for one thing it offers the example of a large number of people who have scrapped the party system in its orthodox American form, and have got along fairly well nevertheless.

It has demonstrated that with the most ramshackle, illogical arrangements for party politics, citizens still can keep closely in step with national political trends, and state government can be kept honest and progressive, when "the people" have the means of correcting aberrations.

(In 1967, Dr. John O. Wilson, a Yale economist working under the auspices of the Midwest Research Institute, undertook a scientific comparison of the relative merits of the 50 states in terms of social values. As criteria, he used nine "national goals" arrived at by a nonpartisan presidential commission appointed in 1960. The goals ranged from dignity of the individual to the vitality of agriculture. California ended up in first place among all the states, as providing "the highest composite level of quality of life in the nation.")

California didn't invent political propaganda or political management. But it pointed the way the nation was going in applying the massive new machinery of communications and electronics to "merchandising" candidates. It produced a spectacular example of the detached "television-oriented" candidate that Tom Wicker envisaged in 1963.

California has acknowledged, with characteristic pragmatism, that government today is operated essentially by hired professional bureaucrats, and that its figurehead may not have to be a technologist in government any more than the president of General Motors has to know how to adjust a spark plug.

This seemed to be the message in Californians' seemingly capricious elevation of an actor to the governorship. Such experimentation may work or it may not. If it falls on its face, the inference is, voters feel they can rectify it before much damage is done—even as they replaced Culbert Olson with Earl Warren. Who can say, they imply, that the mistakes they make are any worse than those arrived at by other procedures?

"What else does California have to offer the people of this country?" Reston asked.

"Chiefly," I said, "a little thing called shelter. According to Federal and state projections, California and its system may encompass, for better or for worse, as many as one American in every seven by 1980. By the year 2,000 it may have as many as one person in every *five*. . . ."

"That," said Reston, "is something to think about."

It is.

Appendix One
California's Population Growth

1848	14,000	*1910*	2,406,000
1852	223,000	*1920*	3,554,000
1860	379,000	*1930*	5,711,000
1870	560,000	*1940*	6,950,000
1880	864,000	*1950*	10,586,000
1890	1,213,000	*1960*	15,717,000
1900	1,490,000	*1968*	19,535,000

All figures are rounded out by the omission of numbers under 1,000.

The figures for 1860–1960 are from the U.S. Census and the State Department of Finance, as presented in the *California Statistical Abstract.*

The 1848 figure is the generally accepted estimate of Hubert Howe Bancroft, the great nineteenth-century California historian.

The 1852 figure was produced by a special state census, conducted to rectify what was considered a sketchy and inaccurate 1850 Federal census.

The 1968 figure was the official mid-year (1967) estimate of the State Department of Finance.

Appendix Two

The Governors of California

	Party	Elected	Inaugurated
1. Peter H. Burnett	D	Nov. 13, 1849	Dec. 20, 1849
2. John McDougal	D	*	Jan. 9, 1851
3. John Bigler	D	Sept. 3, 1851	Jan. 8, 1852
		Sept. 7, 1853	Jan. 7, 1854
4. J. Neeley Johnson	A	Sept. 5, 1855	Jan. 9, 1856
5. John B. Weller	D	Sept. 2, 1857	Jan. 8, 1858
6. Milton S. Latham	D	Sept. 7, 1859	Jan. 9, 1860
7. John G. Downey	D	*	Jan. 14, 1860

	Party	*Elected*	*Inaugurated*
8. Leland Stanford	R	Sept. 14, 1861	Jan. 10, 1862
9. Frederick F. Low	U	Sept. 2, 1863	Dec. 10, 1863
10. Henry H. Haight	D	Sept. 4, 1867	Dec. 5, 1867
11. Newton Booth	R	Sept. 6, 1871	Dec. 8, 1871
12. Romualdo Pacheco	R	*	Feb. 27, 1875
13. William Irwin	D	Sept. 1, 1875	Dec. 9, 1875
14. George C. Perkins	R	Sept. 3, 1879	Jan. 8, 1880**
15. George Stoneman	D	Nov. 7, 1882	Jan. 10, 1883
16. Washington Bartlett	D	Nov. 2, 1886	Jan. 8, 1887
17. Robert W. Waterman	R	*	Sept. 13, 1887
18. Henry H. Markham	R	Nov. 4, 1890	Jan. 8, 1891
19. James H. Budd	D	Nov. 6, 1894	Jan. 11, 1895
20. Henry T. Gage	R	Nov. 8, 1898	Jan. 4, 1899
21. George C. Pardee	R	Nov. 4, 1902	Jan. 6, 1903
22. James N. Gillett	R	Nov. 6, 1906	Jan. 8, 1907
23. Hiram W. Johnson	R	Nov. 8, 1910	Jan. 3, 1911
		Nov. 3, 1914	Jan. 8, 1915
24. William D. Stephens	R	*	Mar. 15, 1917
		Nov. 5, 1918	Jan. 7, 1919
25. Friend W. Richardson	R	Nov. 7, 1922	Jan. 9, 1923
26. Clement C. Young	R	Nov. 2, 1926	Jan. 4, 1927
27. James Rolph, Jr.	R	Nov. 4, 1930	Jan. 6, 1931
28. Frank F. Merriam	R	*	June 7, 1934
		Nov. 6, 1934	Jan. 8, 1935
29. Culbert L. Olson	D	Nov. 8, 1938	Jan. 2, 1939
30. Earl Warren	R	Nov. 3, 1942	Jan. 4, 1943
		Nov. 5, 1946	Jan. 6, 1947
		Nov. 7, 1950	Jan. 8, 1951
31. Goodwin J. Knight	R	*	Oct. 5, 1953
		Nov. 2, 1954	Jan. 3, 1955
32. Edmund G. Brown	D	Nov. 4, 1958	Jan. 5, 1959
		Nov. 6, 1962	Jan. 7, 1963
33. Ronald Reagan	R	Nov. 8, 1966	Jan. 2, 1967

*Succeeded from lieutenant-governorship.

**Elected to three-year term under constitutional revision of term dating.

Parties: A—American (related to national "Know-Nothing" party)
U—Union (Civil War coalition of anti-slavery Democrats and Republicans)
D—Democratic
R—Republican

Appendix
Three
Richard Nixon's Post-Election Press Conference Remarks,
November 7, 1962

Good morning, gentlemen. Now that Mr. Klein has made his statement, and now that all the members of the press are so delighted that I have lost, I'd like to make a statement of my own.

I appreciate the press coverage in this campaign. I think each of you covered it the way you saw it. You had to write it in the way according to your belief on how it would go. I don't believe publishers should tell reporters to write one way or another. I want them all to be free. I don't believe the F.C.C. [Federal Communications Commission] or anybody else should silence . . . [*indistinct*]

I have no complaints about the press coverage. I think each of you was writing it as you believed it.

I congratulate Governor Brown, as Herb Klein has already indicated, for his victory. He has, I think, the greatest honor and the greatest responsibility of any governor in the United States.

And if he has this honor and this responsibility, I think that he will now have certainly a position of tremendous interest for America and as well as for the people of California.

I wish him well. I wish him well not only from the personal standpoint, because there were never on my part any personal considerations.

I believe Governor Brown has a heart, even though he believes I do not.

I believe he is a good American, even though he feels I am not.

And therefore, I wish him well because he is the governor of the first state. He won and I want this state to be led with courage. I want it to be led decisively and I want it to be led, certainly, with the assurance that the man who lost the campaign never during the course of the campaign raised a personal consideration against his opponent—never allowed any words indicating that his opponent was motivated by lack of heart or lack of patriotism to pass his lips.

I am proud of the fact that I defended my opponent's patriotism.

You gentlemen didn't report it, but I am proud that I did that. I am proud also that I defended the fact that he was a man of good motives, a man that I disagreed with very strongly, but a man of good motives.

I want that—I for once, gentlemen—I would appreciate if you would write what I say, in that respect. I think it's very important that you write it—in the lead—in the lead.

Now, I don't mean by that, incidentally, all of you. There's one reporter here who has religiously, when he was covering me—and incidentally, this is no reflection on the others, because some of you, you know, weren't bothered. One reporter, Carl Greenberg—he's the only reporter on the [Los Angeles] *Times* that fits this thing, who wrote every word that I said. He wrote it fairly. He wrote it objectively.

I don't mean that others didn't have a right to do it differently.

But Carl, despite whatever feelings he had, felt that he had an obligation to report the facts as he saw them.

I am saying these things about the press because I understand that that was one of the things you were particularly interested in. There'll be no questions at this point on that score. I'll be glad to answer other questions.

Now, above everything else I want to express my appreciation to our volunteer workers.

It was a magnificent group. Five hundred thousand dollars was spent, according to *Newsweek* magazine, to get out the vote on Election Day. They had a right to do that if they could get the money. We didn't have that kind of money. But, believe me, we had wonderful spirit.

And our 100,000 volunteer workers, I was proud of. I think they did a magnificent job. I only wish they could have gotten out a few more votes in the key precincts, but because they didn't Mr. Brown has won and I have lost the election.

I'd like to say a word nationally. I know that some of you are interested in that. I have not been able to appraise the results for the Congress because not enough of them are in.

. . . I understand we picked up five in the House. We can't tell, because California isn't in on that yet.

Well, the most significant result of this election was what happened in four major states: Rockefeller's victory in New York, Scranton's victory in Pennsylvania, Rhodes's victory in Ohio, Romney's victory in Michigan—means that in 1964 the Republican party will be revitalized.

Now, it will be revitalized, of course, provided the Republicans in California also can under new leadership—not mine—because I have fought the fight and now it's up to others to take this responsibility of leadership, and I don't say this with any bitterness, because I just feel that that's the way it should be.

But the Republican party under new leadership in California needs a new birth of spirit, a new birth of unity, because we must carry California in '64, if we are to carry the nation.

But when you look at New York and Pennsylvania, Ohio and Michigan and the solid Republican Midwest, 1964 is a horse race.

I say this with no indication that I don't think that President Kennedy has immense popularity at the moment— popularity which came out as a result of his handling of the Cuban situation.

But, on the other hand, now the problems arise: what will happen in Cuba? Can we allow this cancer of Communism to stay there? Is there a deal with regard to NATO? Is there going to be with regard to NATO and the Warsaw pact? Are we going to continue any kind of an agreement in Cuba, which means that Khrushchev got what we said we would never agree to before he made his threat with regard to his missiles and that is, in effect, ringing down an Iron Curtain around Cuba?

These are the things that Mr. Kennedy, of course, will have to face up to, and I just hope—and I'm confident that if he has his own way he will face up to them, if he can only get those who opposed atomic tests, who want him to admit Red China to the U.N., all of the woolly heads around him—if he can just keep them away from him and stand strong and firm with that good Irish fight of his, America will be in good shape in foreign policy.

Domestically—I'm answering these questions because I know that some of you will ask them—Domestically, the economy needs to get going again. The Cuban thing, of course, has had a tendency to obscure that. A lot of defense contracts have come into California and other areas. I'm not complaining about it. That's the way the political game is played.

But I do feel that it is important that the economy get going again and I trust that through tax reform or some other device, relying on individual enterprise and individual opportunity, that the economy will get going again.

To me, more important than anything else, America has got to move now. It's got to move forward economically, with productivity. It's got to move forward—I'll say it in the presence of my good friend from Britain here—Ed Tetlow [of the London *Telegraph*]—it's got to move forward relying on individual enterprise and individual opportunity.

One last thing: What are my plans? Well, my plans are to go home. I'm going to get acquainted with my family again. And my plans, incidentally, are, from a political standpoint, of course, to take a holiday. It will be a long holiday. I don't say this with any sadness. I couldn't feel, frankly, more—well, frankly, proud of my staff for the campaign they helped me to put on. We campaigned against great odds. We fought a good fight. We didn't win. And I take the responsibility for any mistakes. As far as they're concerned, they're magnificent people, and I hope whoever next runs in California will look at my staff and take some of these people—use them—because they are—they're great political properties, shall we say, putting it in the—in a very materialistic way.

One last thing: People say, What about the past? What about losing in '60 and losing in '64 [*sic*]? I remember somebody on my last television program said, "Mr. Nixon, isn't it a comedown, having run for President, and almost made it, to run for governor?" And the answer is I'm proud to have run for governor. Now, I would have liked to have won. But, not having won, the main thing was that I battled—battled for the things I believed in.

I did not win. I have no hard feelings against anybody, against my opponent, and least of all the people of California. We got our message through as well as we could. The Cuban thing did not enable us to get it through in the two critical weeks that we wanted to, but nevertheless we got it through, and it is the people's choice.

They have chosen Mr. Brown. They have chosen his leadership, and I can only hope that that leadership will now become more decisive, that it will move California ahead and, so that America can move ahead—economically, morally and spiritually—so that we can have character and self-reliance in this country. This is what we need. This is what we need to move forward.

One last thing. At the outset, I said a couple of things with regard to the press that I noticed some of you looked a little irritated about. And my philosophy with regard to the press has really never gotten through. And I want to get it through.

This cannot be said for any other American political figure today, I guess. Never in my 16 years of campaigning have I complained to a publisher, to an editor, about the coverage of a reporter. I believe a reporter has got a right to write it as he feels it. I believe if a reporter believes that one man ought to win rather than the other, whether it's on television or radio or the like, he ought to say so. I will say to the reporter sometimes that I think well, look, I wish you'd give my opponent the same going over that you give me.

And as I leave the press, all I can say is this: For 16 years, ever since the Hiss case, you've had a lot of fun—a lot of fun—that you've had an opportunity to attack me and I think I've given as good as I've taken. It was carried right up to the last day.

I made a talk on television, a talk in which I made a flub—one of the few that I make, not because I'm so good on television but because I've done it a long time. I made a flub in which I said I was running for Governor of the United States. The Los Angeles *Times* dutifully reported that.

Mr. Brown the last day made a flub—a flub, incidentally, to the great credit of television that was reported—I don't say this bitterly —in which he said, "I hope everybody wins. You vote the straight Democratic ticket, including Senator Kuchel." I was glad to hear him say it, because I was for Kuchel all the way. The Los Angeles *Times* did not report it.

I think that it's time that our great newspapers have at least the same objectivity, the same fullness of coverage, that television has. And I can only say thank God for television and radio for keeping the newspapers a little more honest.

Now, some newspapers don't fall in the category to which I have spoken, but I can only say that the great metropolitan newspapers in this field, they have a right to take every position they want on the editorial page, but on the news page they also have a right to have reporters cover men who have strong feelings whether they're for or against a candidate. But the responsibility also is to put a few Greenbergs on, on the candidate they happen to be against, whether they're against him on the editorial page or just philosophically deep down, a fellow who at least will report what the man says.

That's all anybody can ask. But apart from that I just want to say this:

Among the great papers in this country that the people say that I should be concerned about—the Louisville *Courier,* the New York *Post,* the Milwaukee *Journal,* the Fresno and the Sacramento *Bee*—I couldn't be—disagree with that more. I want newspapers. If they're against a candidate I want them to say it.

I believe they should say it. I don't mind reporters saying it. I would hope that in the future, as a result of this campaign, that perhaps they would try at least simply to see that what both candidates say is reported, that if they have questions to ask of one candidate they ask the same questions of the other candidate.

The last play. I leave you gentlemen now and you will now write it. You will interpret it. That's your right. But as I leave you I want you to know—just think how much you're going to be missing.

You won't have Nixon to kick around any more, because, gentlemen, this is my last press conference and it will be one in which I have welcomed the opportunity to test wits with you. I have sometimes disagreed with you.

But, unlike some people, I've never canceled a subscription to a paper and also I never will.

I believe in reading what my opponents say and I hope that what I have said today will at least make television, radio, the press first recognize the great responsibility they have to report all the news and, second, recognize that they have a right and a responsibility, if they're against a candidate, give him the shaft, but also recognize if they give him the shaft put one lonely reporter on the campaign who will report what the candidate says now and then.

Chapter
Notes

AN EXPLANATORY NOTE:

No special references are given for material from obvious sources of public record, or material that is specifically attributed in the text. Some basic public documents on the subject are the annual *California Statistical Abstract,* published by the State Department of Finance, Sacramento; Winfield J. Davis's *History of Political Conventions in California, 1849–1892,* published by the State Library in 1893 (and now, alas, as scarce as the Gutenberg Bible); and the *Legislative Sourcebook, 1849–1965,* edited by Assemblyman Don A. Allen, Sr., and published by the State Assembly.

Opinion polls not otherwise attributed were conducted by the Mervin Field organization of San Francisco; and by the Don

Muchmore organization of Los Angeles under arrangement with the Los Angeles *Times.*

Some works cited frequently, and listed only briefly below, are James Bryce's *The American Commonwealth* (abridged Capricorn paperback edition, Putnam, 1959); *California Government and Politics,* by Winston W. Crouch, Dean E. McHenry, John C. Bollens, and Stanley Scott (second edition, Prentice-Hall, Englewood Cliffs, N.J., 1960); *The Governors of California,* by H. Brett Melendy and Benjamin F. Gilbert (Talisman Press, Georgetown, Calif., 1965); Carey McWilliams' *Southern California Country* (Duell, Sloan & Pearce, 1946) and *California, The Great Exception* (A. A. Wyn, 1949); George E. Mowry's *The California Progressives* (paperback edition, Quadrangle Books, Chicago, 1963); *California Votes,* by Eugene C. Lee (University of California Institute of Governmental Studies, Berkeley, 1963); Dean R. Cresap's *Party Politics in the Golden State* (Haynes Foundation, Los Angeles, 1954); and *The California Legislature,* by Joseph Allan Beek (State Printing Office, Sacramento, 1960).

Frontier magazine, formerly published in Los Angeles, was absorbed in 1967 by *The Nation* magazine, New York.

CHAPTER 1

P. 3. Salinger, Pierre. *With Kennedy,* Copyright © 1966 by Pierre Salinger. Reprinted by permission of Doubleday & Company, Inc.

P. 4. Bryce, James. *The American Commonwealth.* See explanatory note.

P. 4. White, Theodore H., *The Gentlemen From California,* in *Collier's,* Feb. 3, 1956.

P. 12. Phillips, Herbert. In *California, The Dynamic State* (anthology), McNally & Loftin, Santa Barbara, California, 1966.

CHAPTER 2

Comprehensive histories of California are surprisingly few, but one leading writer in the field was Robert Glass Cleland. His *A History of California* (Macmillan, 1923) and *California in Our Times, 1900–1940* (Alfred A. Knopf, 1947) are cited often in this book.

P. 19. Reinhardt, Richard. *California: the Swinging Voters,* in *Look,* June 28, 1966. Copyright 1966 by Cowles Communications, Inc.

P. 21. Seabury, Paul. *The Antic Politics of California,* in *Harper's Magazine,* May 27, 1965.

CHAPTER 3

P. 27. Lewis, Oscar. *The Big Four,* Knopf, 1941. A major work on the Southern Pacific Railroad.

P. 32. Swanberg, W. A. *Citizen Hearst,* Scribner, 1963.

P. 33. Stone, Irving. *Men to Match My Mountains,* Doubleday, 1956.

P. 33. Storke, Thomas. *California Editor,* Westernlore Press, Los Angeles, 1958.

P. 33. Steffens, Lincoln. *The Autobiography of Lincoln Steffens,* Harcourt, Brace, 1931.

P. 33. Van Devander, Charles. *The Big Bosses,* Howell, Soskins, 1944.

P. 34. Steffens.

P. 35. Cleland.

P. 35. Swanberg.

P. 36. Holbrook, Stewart. *The Age of the Moguls.* Doubleday, 1953.

P. 36. Bryce.

P. 37. Cresap, Dean R. See explanatory note.

P. 37. Lewis.

P. 37. Swanberg.

P. 38. Mowry, George. See explanatory note.

CHAPTER 4

P. 42. People's Independent Party. Davis, See explanatory note.

P. 43. White, William Allen. *The Old Order Changeth,* in *The Progressive Movement* (anthology), edited by Richard Hofstadter. Prentice-Hall, 1963.

P. 43. Schlesinger, Arthur M., Sr. *Political and Social Growth of the United States, 1852–1933,* Macmillan, 1934.

P. 44. Steffens.

P. 44. Lewis.

CHAPTER 5

P. 52. Beek, Joseph Allan. See explanatory note.

P. 57. Cresap.

P. 58. Findley, James C. *Cross-Filing and the Progressive Movement in California Politics,* in *Western Political Quarterly,* September, 1959.

P. 59. Reed, Thomas H. *The Cross-Filing Fraud,* in *Frontier,* April, 1952.

CHAPTER 6

Elections reports in *Legislative Sourcebook*. See explanatory note.

P. 64. Weinberger, Jack. Letter to the New York *Times,* September 4, 1956.

P. 65. Mowry. Steffens.

P. 66. Beek.

P. 67. Findley.

P. 70. Hyer, Richard. *California, The First Hundred Years,* in *Our Sovereign State,* edited by Robert S. Allen, Vanguard Press, 1949.

P. 72. Dana, Julian. *A. P. Giannini, Giant in the West,* Prentice-Hall, 1947.

CHAPTER 7

The New York *Times* during 1934 published a series of excellent reports by Turner Catledge on the Sinclair campaign.

P. 79. Sinclair, Upton. *The Autobiography of Upton Sinclair,* W. H. Allen, London, 1963.

P. 81. McWilliams, Carey. *Southern California Country*. See explanatory note.

P. 84. Van Devander.

P. 85. Van Devander.

P. 87. McWilliams.

P. 89. Burke, Robert E. *Olson's New Deal For California,* University of California Press, Berkeley, 1953.

CHAPTER 8

Two excellent biographies of Earl Warren were published in 1967: Leo Katcher's *Earl Warren* (McGraw-Hill); and John D. Weaver's *Warren—The Man, The Court, The Era* (Little, Brown), which was excerpted in *Holiday,* April–June, 1966. Irving Stone wrote a campaign biography, *Earl Warren* (Prentice-Hall), in 1948.

P. 96. Los Angeles *Times,* May 11, 1941.

P. 99. Burke.

P. 103. Stone.

P. 106. Weaver.

P. 106. Moley, Raymond. *Independence of Governor Warren,* in *Newsweek,* June 17, 1946. Copyright, *Newsweek,* Inc., June, 1946.

CHAPTER 9

P. 112. Crouch and McHenry. See Explanatory Note.

CHAPTER 10

P. 126. Thomas, Hugh S. Reported in *State Government News,* July, 1966, Council of State Governments, Chicago.

P. 128. Carney, Francis P. *The Rise of the Democratic Clubs in California,* Eagleton Institute, 1959.

P. 128. Blanchard, Robert. Los Angeles *Times,* June 15, 1961.

P. 129. Beek.

P. 132. Lockard, Duane. In *State Legislatures in American Politics,* edited by Alexander Heard, Prentice-Hall, 1967.

P. 132. From an "unofficial inquiry": Richard Bergholz. Los Angeles *Mirror,* January 31–February 3, 1961.

P. 133. Los Angeles *Times,* September 15, 1965.

P. 134. Heard, Alexander. See Lockard above.

P. 137. Armbrister, Trevor. *The Octopus in the State House,* in the *Saturday Evening Post,* February 12, 1966. California lobbying reports are compiled by the State Legislative Analyst, Sacramento.

CHAPTER 11

P. 142. Phillips, Herbert, in the Sacramento *Bee,* September 16, 1954.

P. 148. Alsop, Stewart. *The Great California Drama,* in the *Saturday Evening Post,* October 18, 1958.

CHAPTER 12

P. 156. Anderson, Totton J. *California: Enigma of National Politics,* in *Western Politics,* edited by Frank H. Jonas, University of Utah Press, Salt Lake City, 1961.

P. 159. San Francisco *Chronicle.* Quoted in *Frontier,* December, 1958.

CHAPTER 13

P. 168. Mazo, Earl. *Richard Nixon: A Personal and Political Portrait,* Harper, 1959.

P. 171. White, Theodore H. *The Making of the President, 1960,* Atheneum, 1961.

P. 175. McWilliams, Carey, in *The Nation,* June 2, 1962.

P. 178. Reston, James, in the New York *Times,* November 9, 1962.

CHAPTER 15

P. 192. McWilliams, Carey. *Government By Whitaker and Baxter,* in The *Nation,* April 14, 1951.

P. 193. Pearson, Drew, in the Los Angeles *Times,* November 14, 1966.

P. 193. The New York *Times,* July 19, 1966.

P. 195. McWilliams (above).

CHAPTER 16

P. 205. Reagan, Ronald, with Richard Hubler. *Where's the Rest of Me?,* Duell, Sloan & Pearce (Best Books paperback edition), 1965.

P. 214. Wicker, Tom, in the New York *Times Magazine,* June 9, 1963.

CHAPTER 17

P. 231. Wicker, Tom, in the New York *Times,* December 10, 1967.

CHAPTER 18

P. 248. Houser, Bob, Long Beach (Calif.) *Independent Press-Telegram,* October 23, 1967.

P. 249. Bergholz, Richard, Los Angeles *Times,* August 29, 1967.

P. 250 Unruh, Jesse. Quoted by Richard R. Mathison in *California's Political Muscle Man.* Los Angeles *Times* (West Magazine), June 21, 1967.

P. 253. Yorty, Samuel. The principal compendium of information on Yorty is Ed Ainsworth's *Maverick Mayor —A Biography of Sam Yorty of Los Angeles,* Doubleday, 1966.

P. 255. Bergholz, Richard, Los Angeles *Times,* February 14, 1967.

CHAPTER 19

P. 258. Woodbury, Robert L. *What's So Crazy About California Politics?,* in California Institute of Technology's *Engineering and Science,* April, 1967.

P. 260. Crouch and McHenry.

P. 262. Los Angeles *Examiner,* March 12, 1961.

P. 265. Bryce.

P. 265. Reston, James, in the New York *Times,* November 6 and 13, 1966.

P. 266. Reston, James, in the New York *Times,* November 7, 1965.

P. 268. Lippmann, Walter, in the Los Angeles *Times,* December 7, 1966.

Index

Because the Democratic and Republican parties and such institutions as the California legislature are mentioned throughout the text, no individual references for them are listed.